GRANT TAIT is a qualified chartered accountant with an MBA from INSEAD in France. His career included more than 25 years managing teams in Europe in multinational corporations whose headquarters were in USA, Italy, Switzerland and Japan. Throughout his career, he met and worked with managers that never make decisions.

Grant writes on LinkedIn and on his blog about these no-decision managers: www.nodecisionmanager.co.uk. He has also written humorous articles about life in these multinationals, anonymously or as Grant Petrie to protect his employment. They were published in various professional magazines such as *Management Today*, *Personnel Journal* and *Management Accounting*. He now lives in France.

HOW TO BECOME A
NO-DECISION MANAGER

Become an enlightened subordinate of
a no-decision boss

Manage a team of no-decision managers

Grant Tait

SilverWood

Published in 2021 by SilverWood Books

SilverWood Books Ltd
14 Small Street, Bristol, BS1 1DE, United Kingdom
www.silverwoodbooks.co.uk

Copyright © Grant Tait 2021

The right of Grant Tait to be identified as the author of this work has been
asserted in accordance with the Copyright, Designs
and Patents Act 1988 Sections 77 and 78.

All rights reserved. No part of this publication may be reproduced,
stored in a retrieval system, or transmitted in any form or by any means,
electronic, mechanical, photocopying, recording or otherwise,
without prior permission of the copyright holder.

ISBN 978-1-80042-013-7 (paperback)
ISBN 978-1-80042-014-4 (ebook)

British Library Cataloguing in Publication Data
A CIP catalogue record for this book is available from
the British Library

Page design and typesetting by SilverWood Books

To Liz and James

Contents

Epigraph	21
Preface	23
1 Introduction	27
Summary of the book	28
Methodology	28
Studying no-decision managers	30
Objective	30
Sample size and representation	30
Method of observation	31
Means–end task	31
Analysis of data	32
Hypotheses	33
Limitations	33
Findings	34
Studying the subordinates of no-decision managers	34
Objective	34
Sample size and representation	35
Method of observation	35
Analysis of data	35

	Hypotheses	35
	Limitations	36
	Findings	36
	Discussion	36
Studying the bosses of no-decision managers		37
	Objective	37
	Sample size and representation	37
	Method of observation	37
	Limitations	37
	Hypotheses	37
	Findings	38

Other research — 38
    Research on 'decision fatigue' — 38
    Research on mentally ill patients — 39

Conventions used in this book — 41
    No-decision manager — 41
    Structure of chapters — 42
    Case studies — 43
    To 'make a decision' or to 'take a decision' — 43
    Impartial and unbiased — 44

References to people who find it difficult to decide — 45
    Literary references — 45
    Political references — 47
    Business and managerial references — 48

2 The World of the No-Decision Manager — 51

Information no-decision managers — 51

What is a no-decision manager?	51
The no-decision manager's definition of a decision	51
The no-decision manager's definition of a manager	53
Where do no-decision managers work?	54
Never the top job	55
Impact of no-decision managers on people in organisations	55
How can no-decision managers work with this inability?	59
Mintzberg's managerial roles for no-decision managers	60
Kotter on managers vs. leaders with no-decision managers	62
'How to' advice for no-decision managers	64
Become a member of the Shelter	64
Memorise the definition, learn the rules and roles	66
New no-decision managerial roles	68
Modification of managerial roles	69
Origins of no-decision managers	71
Instinct-based behaviours	72
Permanent procrastination	72
Imposing incremental information	76
Practising the instinct-based behaviours	76
Summary – steps 1–9 to become a no-decision manager	77

3 Understanding the Simple Tactics of Decision Avoidance   80

'How to' advice for no-decision managers	80
Read, understand, reflect, experiment and remember	80
Simple tactics of decision avoidance	81
Active avoidance	81
Active avoidance tactic 1: Judicious absence	82

Active avoidance tactic 2: Ignoring	85
Active avoidance tactic 3: Physical barriers	87
Active avoidance tactic 4: Artificial agreement	88
Active avoidance tactic 5: Meaningless meetings	90
Delay decisions	92
Delay decision 1: Incremental information improved	93
Delay decision 2: Announce an action	99
Delay decision 3: Task force	102
Delay decision 4: Consultant	103
Business decision vs. delay decision	105
Summary – steps 10–11 to become a no-decision manager	106

4 Understanding the Complex Tactics of Decision Avoidance 107

'How to' advice for no-decision managers	107
Deviation of delegation	107
Deviation of delegation 1: Deviated downward delegation	108
Deviation of delegation 2: Deviated upward delegation	110
Deviation of delegation 3: Deviated diagonal delegation	117
Deviation of delegation 4: Deviated sideways delegation	120
Implement the decisions of others	122
Tactic to avoid other pending decisions	123
Implement decisions precisely	125
Advantages of implementing but not taking decisions	126
Outrageous behaviour	128
1 A tactic to delay decisions	129
2 A simple message to subordinates to stop insisting	129
3 A complicated message to subordinates asking them to work positively	129

Outrageous behaviour 1: Inept information	131
Outrageous behaviour 2: Blatant change of opinion	133
Outrageous behaviour 3: Outright lie	135
The No-decision-making System	139
Summary – steps 12–18 to become a no-decision manager	139

5 How to Become a Great No-Decision Manager — 142

'How to' advice for no-decision managers	142
Three core skills	142
Core skill 1: Great analysis	143
Core skill 2: Great knowledge	147
Core skill 3: Great understanding	147
Other character traits required by no-decision managers	152
1 Clear but changing opinions	152
2 Friendly, but does not care	154
3 Selective shamelessness	155
Co-operation with other types of manager	156
1 Procrastination manager	156
2 Indecisive manager	157
3 Liar manager	157
4 Incompetent manager	160
5 Normal manager	161
Summary – steps 19–23 to become a no-decision manager	164

6 How No-Decision Managers Survive — 166

'How to' advice for no-decision managers	166
Separated specialised informal networks	167

Five core activities of informal networks	169
Normal managers and the five activities	173
Influential people network	173
Headquarters network	174
Colleague network	174
Employee network	175
Human Resources network	175
Technology network	175
Competition and industry network	177
Blandish the bosses	177
Your boss	177
Your boss's boss	181
Handling of hierarchy	183
Relationship rectangle	186
Rumsfeld resolution	188
Organisations that no-decision managers should avoid	190
No-decision managers in great companies	191
No-decision managers in organisations with decentralised decision-making	192
Bosses that no-decision managers should avoid	193
No-decision boss	193
Micro-manager boss	195
Information on no-decision managers	196
Decision dilemma	196
No-decision managers do not always survive	198
Summary – steps 24–31 to become a no-decision manager	199

7 How to Become an Enlightened Subordinate — 201

'How to' advice for subordinates — 201
- Initial reactions to a no-decision boss — 201
- Frustration — 203
  - Mild frustration — 203
  - Moderate frustration — 204
  - Severe frustration — 205
  - Acute frustration — 206
  - Fundamental frustration — 207
- Explicit exit — 210
- Reticent resignation — 212
- Relentless resignation — 213
- Constant conflict — 214
- Peaceful patience — 216
- Aphonic acknowledgement — 219
  - Silent pact — 219
  - Deviated downward delegation — 221
  - Outrageous behaviour — 223
- Summary – steps 1–6 to become an enlightened subordinate — 227

8 Choices for an Enlightened Subordinate — 229

'How to' advice for subordinates — 229
- Take your freedom — 229
  - Subordinates who choose power — 230
  - Bypassing the no-decision manager — 232
  - Subordinates who choose fun — 233
  - With freedom you receive no support — 234

Learn from your no-decision boss	235
Three greats	235
Informal networks	235
Blandish the bosses	236
Handling of hierarchy	236
Protect yourself	237
Information	237
Informal networks	240
Measure the consequences	240
Career on hold	241
Never fired	244
How far do you help your no-decision boss?	245
Choose your level of enlightenment	247
1 Enlightened individual	247
2 Enlightened manager	247
3 Enlightened co-ordinator	248
4 Enlightened leader	249
Remember the dangers	256
Summary – steps 7–13 to become an enlightened subordinate	257

9 How to Manage a Team of No-Decision Managers — 259

Information on no-decision managers	259
Effect of no-decision managers on organisation	259
No decision managers are harmful to the organisation	259
Some toxic managers are successful	261
Why does top management accept no-decision managers in organisations?	262
1. Ignorance	262

2. Pivotal positioning	263
3. Too dear to dismiss	263
Summary of pivotal positioning	267
'How to' advice for bosses of no-decision managers	268
How to identify a no-decision manager	268
Annoying habits	270
Small incidents and minor complaints	270
Nothing gets decided	273
Spending time with your boss and headquarters	273
Accumulation and consistency	274
Aphonic acknowledgement	275
Reorganise the subordinates	275
Summary – steps 1–10 to manage a team of no-decision managers	280

10 Comprehending No-Decision Management — 282

Information on no-decision managers	282
Perpetual paradox	282
New management concepts	283
Deemed decision	284
Deemed instruction	285
Decision dilemma and survival point	285
Deviated delegation	286
Outrageous behaviour	286
Hiding in excellence	286
Decision principle	287
New management activities	287
Formal and fortuitous filtering	288

Focused filtering	288
Disclosure of decision avoidance tactics	289
'How to' advice for no-decision managers	290
Recognise the different emotions of your subordinates	290
Achieving perfection as a no-decision manager	291
Avoiding detection	291
Pivotal positioning	293
Final steps to becoming a no-decision manager	295
Decide on a motto	296
Your last decision	298
Summary – the final steps 32–39 to become a no-decision manager	298

List of Annexes

Annex 1	The No-Decision Manager Manual. The 39 steps required to become a no-decision manager	301
Annex 2	The Enlightened Subordinate Manual. The 13 steps required to become an enlightened subordinate of a no-decision boss	308
Annex 3	Manual on how to Manage a Team of No-Decision Managers. The 10 steps required to manage a team of no-decision managers	311
Annex 4	No-decision management glossary of terms	313
Annex 5	Bibliography	323
Annex 6	Additional reading	326
Annex 7	To make a decision or to take a decision?	331

List of Figures

Figure 1	The decision-making process for a no-decision manager (Chapter 2)	52
Figure 2	Action-Centred Leadership™ After John Adair (Chapter 2)	56
Figure 3	Action-Centred Leadership™ After John Adair representing a manager who neglects the circles. (Chapter 2)	56
Figure 4	The Managerial Grid adapted for no-decision managers (Chapter 2)	57
Figure 5	Manager's roles eliminated – no-decision roles added (Chapter 2)	60
Figure 6	Characteristics of management, no-decision management and leadership (Chapter 2)	63
Figure 7	The Five S's (Chapter 2)	67
Figure 8	The no-decision manager's roles (Chapter 2)	71
Figure 9	Updated decision-making process for a no-decision manager (Chapter 3)	93
Figure 10	The simple tactics of decision avoidance (Chapter 3)	106
Figure 11	The deemed decision (Chapter 4)	112
Figure 12	Final decision-making process for a no-decision manager (Chapter 4)	123
Figure 13	The complex tactics of decision avoidance (Chapter 4)	138
Figure 14	The no-decision-making System (Chapter 4)	140
Figure 15	The 'three greats' and other character traits a no-decision manager needs (Chapter 5)	163

Figure 16	Structured survival (Chapter 6)	167
Figure 17	The no-decision manager's internal informal information network (Chapter 6)	170
Figure 18	Separated specialised informal networks (Chapter 6)	176
Figure 19	Relationship rectangle (Chapter 6)	187
Figure 20	Herzberg's Motivation-Hygiene Theory for subordinates in fundamental frustration (Chapter 7)	209
Figure 21	Working for a no-decision manager: the emotional journey (Chapter 7)	225
Figure 22	Herzberg's Motivation-Hygiene Theory for enlightened subordinates in aphonic acknowledgement (Chapter 7)	226
Figure 23	Career choices of subordinates (Chapter 8)	242
Figure 24	Action-Centred Leadership ™ After John Adair with an impaired team (Chapter 8)	255
Figure 25	Action-Centred Leadership ™ After John Adair, with adapted Belbin Team Roles (Chapter 9)	276
Figure 26	Organisation chart of the perfect team to manage a no-decision boss (Chapter 10)	279
Figure 27	The no-decision manager's roles in pivotal positioning (Chapter 10)	294
Figure 28	The Managerial Grid in pivotal positioning (Chapter 10)	294
Figure 29	Herzberg's Motivation-Hygiene Theory applied to a no-decision manager (Chapter 10)	296

'The Government simply cannot make up their minds or they cannot get the Prime Minister to make up his mind. So they go on in strange paradox, decided only to be undecided, resolved to be irresolute, adamant for drift, solid for fluidity, all powerful to be impotent.'

Winston Churchill

Churchill Walking in Destiny, 2018,
Andrew Roberts, Penguin Books (p. 519)[1]

---

1 Taken from Ed. Robert Rhodes James, *Winston S. Churchill: His Complete Speeches*, published in New York in 8 volumes in 1974 V1 p. 5809

Preface

This book is my attempt at light-hearted satire. Its aim is to expose and ridicule managers who never take decisions. But to criticise them successfully, I first had to analyse and understand them.

I have analysed their characteristics, their behaviours, their functional strategies, how they become successful in organisations and where they operate. I have either experienced the behaviours and tactics of these managers first hand, or their subordinates have communicated their behaviours directly to me. I have also analysed their subordinates and their bosses, trying to show how to work effectively with these managers who never take decisions.

Have I carried out rigorous academic research on these no-decision managers? Not at all. I did not place a chair beside the no-decision managers' desks eight hours per working day to observe them. Nor did I spend my time discussing and recording the comments of their subordinates and colleagues. I had my job to do, my teams to manage, and businesses to run – all of which took priority over my interest in these managers who never take decisions.

After categorising their behaviours, I discovered resemblances. They all adopt similar behaviours because their working lives are organised around not making decisions. Likewise, their subordinates have common emotional attitudes towards a boss who never makes a decision. I found this all quite astonishing.

To make fun of these managers, I resort to invention and exaggeration, mixing this into a serious nonfiction 'how-to' format, using well known experts in management theory. Initially the use of invention arose from my total inability to answer the question:

How can managers who never take decisions and who have never met each other use the same tactics and have the same behaviours?

My answer to this question is simply that there must be a movement somewhere helping them. This I have called the 'no-decision movement'. My next invention follows on quite logically. It assumes that this movement has created a specific organisation to protect and instruct these managers. This I have called the 'Shelter'. You will see that they are useful mechanisms to explain and formalise the behaviours and strategies of managers who never make decisions.

I exaggerate, for instance in Chapter 9, where I explain how to set up teams of managers who never take decisions. Who would ever want to have this type of manager on their team? I can think of no one. However, some of these managers are protected by their organisations, so I explain how to work around them and still have a functioning team. And it is here I explain how to detect them.

I do not exaggerate when I describe the tactics these managers use to avoid decision-making. Their behaviours, coming from these tactics, can go all the way up to the ludicrous, which is actually the truth – it is the way these managers sometimes behave. Those who have worked with managers who never make decisions will recognise these behaviours, especially the ludicrous, and easily separate the truth from the imaginary and distinguish the satire from the reality. For those who are unsure if they have encountered a manager who never decides, this book will help you to identify and understand them regardless of my exaggerations.

Right from the title of the book, my intention is to show you that I am not always serious. It is ridiculous to want to become a manager who never makes decisions, but in learning to become one, you can actually understand in detail how they behave. Becoming enlightened as a subordinate is another exaggeration of mine, but by following this path to enlightenment, you will see how to deal with these managers and discover the choices you can make while working with them.

My use of experts in management theory reflects the serious nonfiction 'how-to' format I have chosen to use. I have adapted their theories to explain what these managers and their subordinates do – exaggeration perhaps, but invention on my part again. Many thanks to the experts who allowed me to use their theories and findings, especially those who went further, and adjusted their models to include managers who never make decisions. For those who refused my requests for permission, I comprehend with disappointment.

Why did I not write a straightforward book on 'How to understand managers who never decide', subtitled 'How to work with them' and 'How to detect them'? It would have been so much easier. This book would have been one of the first to analyse this type of manager in depth, and might even have made a contribution to management literature on the subject. But I consider that mere disclosure of their behaviour is not enough. They deserve, as I have already said, to be criticised and ridiculed. They are, after all, toxic to their subordinates and toxic to their organisation. This is my humble attempt to transfer some scorn and ridicule onto them.

Grant Tait

1

Introduction

Managers who never make decisions – it's almost impossible to believe that they exist in organisations. Decision-making, after all, is one of the critical tasks of any manager in any organisation, whether it be in business or government, so by definition they cannot exist. Only a person who has worked directly for a boss who never decides can understand that they *do* exist and even persevere and prosper. Some of these managers who never take decisions, whom I call no-decision managers, are even promoted into top management.

Only someone who has worked for a no-decision manager can understand the frustrations that arise when trying to get them to decide something. These subordinates go through a journey of frustration but, often without realising it, they have choices while working with this type of boss. Some choose to stay in states of negative emotion, others decide to be positive and take advantage of the freedom that working for a no-decision boss gives them. This book explains the emotional journey and the choices subordinates can make.

It also attempts to answer the question of why management accepts no-decision managers in organisations and describes ways that bosses can detect them. Above all, it shows how to work effectively with these managers who never make decisions.

Summary of the book

Chapter 1 sets out the way my analysis of no-decision managers was carried out, including some conventions that had to be created to facilitate understanding. It also summarises references to people who find it difficult to decide and to research on 'decision fatigue'.

Chapter 2 gives some definitions, explains where and how no-decision managers work, and describes the first steps to becoming a no-decision manager.

Chapters 3 and 4 cover mastering the basics and the complexity of the different tactics no-decision managers use to avoid decision-making, from the simple universal ones used by them all to the sophisticated and devious used by the more experienced. Potential no-decision managers must learn, memorise and apply these tactics.

Chapter 5 explains how to become not just an ordinary no-decision manager but a great one.

Chapter 6 outlines the strategies no-decision managers have devised to survive long-term in organisations.

Chapters 7 and 8 are for subordinates who work for a no-decision boss. These chapters describe the different states the subordinate can take and give advice on how to become enlightened while working with a no-decision manager.

Chapter 9 is for bosses who might want to have no-decision managers in their teams. It explains how to detect them and how best to manage and work effectively with them.

Chapter 10 gives more background on no-decision management and explains the final steps in becoming a no-decision manager.

Methodology

The methodology used in this book to study no-decision managers is based on Jean Piaget's study of children, described in *The Origins of Intelligence in Children*, published in English in 1952, but in its original French version in 1936.

Wallace E. Dixon, in his *Twenty Studies that Revolutionised Child*

Psychology, explains Piaget's methodology even more precisely than Piaget himself:

> The participants for this book were two girls and one boy, all siblings. They were essentially observed several times a day every day from birth to about two... So from Jacqueline's birth through the time Laurent reached two, Piaget made detailed recordings of at least one kid pretty much constantly for at least 3,000 days! Although this would be a Herculean effort for anybody, Piaget's efforts were reduced somewhat because the three siblings were his own children. At least the participants in his study lived in the same house!

My study of no-decision managers has a similar methodology. Again, Wallace E. Dixon would no doubt be able to explain it better than I could myself.

Dixon might say something like this:

> The participants for this book are eight no-decision managers. They were essentially observed several times a day every day while in the same organisation as the author, without detailed recordings made of each manager pretty much constantly for sometimes several years. Although this would be a Herculean effort for anybody, this author's efforts were reduced somewhat because almost all of the eight managers were either his own boss or one of his colleagues. At least the participants in the study worked in the same organisation as the author!

So Piaget observed three children (his own) several times a day from their birth over two years to arrive at his conclusions, i.e. he studied a very small sample over a long period. I have done the same. I observed eight no-decision managers (my own) several times per working day for periods between one and five years, depending on how long we were together in the same organisation. Piaget made his study of children in the present. I made this study, however, in hindsight, based on recollections of the events after they had occurred and sometimes many months after, so without Piaget's level of rigour.

Studying no-decision managers

Objective

The objective of the study is to use my observations of no-decision managers as a basis to determine how ordinary managers can become competent, even great, no-decision managers themselves. What characteristics and behaviours are required? Is there a process? What are the key elements required to be successful? How do they survive in organisations?

Sample size and representation

As a sample size, why eight? Why not ten or more? Or just three, similar to Piaget? Simply because I met eight no-decision managers during my working career. Piaget had three children and studied all three. If he had only two children, he would have studied the two and still would have written his book. It is a personal choice that I have included all eight in the study and not three chosen at random to conform exactly to Piaget.

There is some evidence that the sample size is too small to be relevant. Standard calculations on an unknown size of the total population of no-decision managers indicate that a sample size a little over 100 no-decision managers would be necessary to obtain a 90% value for the confidence level and a 10% value for the margin of error. These eight managers have a confidence level of 34% and a margin of error of 34%. This is discouraging.

However, the Piaget model does not require large numbers. The sample size of the no-decision managers is 2.67 times greater than Piaget's sample size. The periods under study are similar to those used by Piaget. The wide recognition of the Piaget model by psychologists today with a much greater sample size of eight using the same model cannot now be contested, even if some would still argue that the sample size is too small.

Further, when the sample is broken into two groups – experienced no-decision managers in place for more than 15 years and no-decision managers with less than 15 years of no-decision experience – the statistical significance of some behaviours goes up to 100%. This is clearly significant.

The sample is, however, too small to study other variables such as different cultures, nationalities or ages. These variables are not explored. Gender differences, if any, also are not studied.

Method of observation

Piaget had no established methods available at the time to measure the evolution of thinking in babies, so he made them up as he went along. There are no available methods either to measure behaviours of no-decision managers, so I have used three simple tools: observation, provocation and a dose of common sense. I simply observed the no-decision managers' actions, discussions and behaviours, and then remembered them.

Provocation of the 'non-decision' was sometimes used, to stimulate no-decision managers into using different behaviours. With the help of my subordinates and colleagues I was able to provoke managers into 'decision situations' that they had to avoid, thus increasing the number of tactics that I could study. In this way it was possible to observe in greater detail the decision avoidance tactics and more easily classify them into the different categories. Common sense was then used to analyse and compile the data into an easy-to-understand format.

Means–end task

Piaget invented and used the principle of the means–ends task. A similar but slightly modified task was used to study no-decision managers. The clearest definition again comes from Wallace E. Dixon's book, where he explains this method:

> In the typical means–end task, babies are observed to see whether they can perform one action in order to do a second action.

Adapted to a no-decision manager the 'means–end' task becomes a 'means–beginning' task and this definition becomes:

> In the typical means–beginning task, no-decision managers are observed to see what different **first** actions they can perform, in order to perform the second action: that of not making a decision.

The second action changes frequently for babies but not for the no-decision manager. It is a constant. It is a non-action, that of avoiding a decision. What is being observed in no-decision managers' behaviours are the many different types of first action, a sort of 'means–beginning task', performed by them to avoid the second action.

Analysis of data

Once collected, the data relating to each no-decision manager was compared with that of the other no-decision managers, and categorised into different types and groups. Any similar behaviour observed from at least three different no-decision managers was considered to be standard no-decision management behaviour and is included as such in the book.

There is no statistical justification for choosing to categorise only behaviour shown by three or more no-decision managers – it is an arbitrary decision. However, if the same behaviour from four different no-decision managers had been chosen as the 'standard no-decision management behaviour', the number of different behaviours would have been so few that this book could not have been written. There would have been nothing to write about, because the number of relevant tactics to avoid decisions would have been almost non-existent.

It is therefore significant that all no-decision managers without exception used the two behaviours that I have called 'instinct-based behaviours'. Other behaviours were classified into two categories:

'simple' and 'complex'; and called 'decision avoidance tactics'. The 'simple' tactics were broken into two groups, the first of which were the tactics that were used most often by no-decision managers. The three 'complex' tactics were generally used only by the more experienced no-decision managers in senior positions.

I invented all the names of the tactics and different groupings that make up what I call the 'No-decision-making System'. The no-decision management glossary of terms in Annex 4 summarises these invented terms and expressions.

Hypotheses

The main difference between Piaget's study and mine is that there is no main hypothesis to prove. The proof is known at the outset – that of the second action, namely that no-decision managers avoid decisions in all circumstances, except (as will be discovered) in just one instance.

The first actions, those designed to avoid decisions, were observed simply to explain and categorise them. They were then used to describe ways to become an effective no-decision manager.

There are, however, two secondary hypotheses that my study seeks to validate. These are:

1. No-decision managers are dismissed on discovery.
2. No-decision managers survive long-term in organisations.

Limitations

The most severe limitation in studying no-decision managers is the same as Piaget's with his children. It is conversation, or the lack of it.

One cannot have a conversation with a baby. One can have an exchange or an interaction, but not a conversation. It is the same with no-decision managers. One can never have a conversation with no-decision managers about their inability to decide. They systematically refuse to talk about anything relating to their no-decision working life, except, I suppose, to their fellow no-decision managers.

One can of course have conversations about other topics with them, but never one on the topic of no-decision management. Non-verbal exchanges on decision avoidance are, however, encouraged and even non-verbal interactions with no-decision managers are allowed.

Findings

In addition to the 'decision avoidance tactics' explained above, my study found that no-decision managers have three common skill sets. While these skill sets are also common to normal managers, their level of sophistication and degree of excellence in no-decision managers are exceptional enough to be considered as particular to no-decision managers.

As a bonus, I discovered seven new concepts in management and organisational behaviour while studying these no-decision managers. These are explained in Chapter 10.

Fifty percent of the no-decision managers were fired during the time they were being studied. There is anecdotal evidence, but no clear proof, that the reason for these dismissals was the discovery that they were no-decision managers. The hypothesis that no-decision managers are dismissed when discovered is considered valid by this statistic, despite the lack of formal proof.

The remaining 50% were still in place at the end of the study and in a brief follow-up after 10 years were found to be either still in place or to have retired. Thus the other secondary hypothesis that no-decision managers survive in the long term is also validated.

Studying the subordinates of no-decision managers

Objective

While studying the no-decision managers, I also talked to their subordinates. The objective was to study their behaviours and opinions when working with their no-decision bosses and from this to come up with recommendations of how to become enlightened while working with a no-decision boss.

Sample size and representation

From the eight no-decision managers, more than 41 of their subordinates, out of a total of approximately 65, accepted to talk to me about their no-decision bosses.

There is some evidence that, as with the no-decision managers, the sample size of subordinates is too small and that a sample size of over 100 would be more representative. However, the findings revealed that all 41 subordinates without exception fell into one of six different 'emotional states' while working with their no-decision manager and this represented such a precise pattern that there is no doubt that this sample is representative of subordinates who work for no-decision managers.

It may be that a larger sample would reveal more 'emotional states' than the six who were discovered. However any others, if they exist, are likely to be marginal.

Method of observation

As with the no-decision managers, I observed subordinates' actions and behaviours, but, unlike no-decision managers, I was able to discuss in detail their feelings, opinions and motivations while working with their no-decision bosses and compare them with my own.

Analysis of data

Once collected, the data of each subordinate was compared with the others and they were categorised into different types and groups. No exclusions or limitations were required.

Hypotheses

There is no hypothesis to prove for subordinates. The study was concentrated on the reactions, attitudes and behaviours of subordinates following repeated decision avoidance of their no-decision bosses.

Limitations
There were no significant limitations. Subordinates were talkative and eager to share their experiences and emotions while working with their no-decision bosses.

Findings
Subordinates revealed a common pattern of emotions and a range of behaviours and attitudes resulting from the daily contact with their no-decision bosses. These have been categorised into six different 'emotional states' that subordinates adopt while working with these managers.

Subordinates did not remain in one of these 'emotional states', except those who chose to stop working for their no-decision boss and leave. They moved from one state to another.

However, employees of no-decision managers in middle management, especially younger subordinates, genuinely suffered and ended up working in frustration, anger or resignation with their no-decision bosses. Subordinates of senior no-decision managers seem to suffer less or not at all. They had the experience to choose the way they want to work with their no-decision boss and adjust their careers in their own time.

I invented all the names of the behaviours of the subordinates and the different ways to work with no-decision managers. The 'No-decision management glossary of terms' in Annex 4 summarises these invented terms and expressions.

Discussion
The three 'emotional states' where negative emotions prevail in the working relationship with no-decision bosses cover nearly half of subordinates. This is significant. It is not known whether these states were actively chosen or whether subordinates just fell into them thinking that their state was a natural one for them. There is some evidence, however, that many were not aware that the two more positive states even existed, despite working alongside colleagues who had chosen to work in them.

Studying the bosses of no-decision managers

Objective

During the study of no-decision managers, a limited review was carried out on their bosses. The objective here was to discover why top management accepts no-decision managers in their organisation. This information was combined with the findings regarding the no-decision managers and their subordinates, described above, to map out a way to manage no-decision managers.

Sample size and representation

The eight no-decision managers had in total twelve bosses. There is no evidence that these bosses are generally representative of managers who have no-decision subordinates, and there is no evidence available that they are not, but I knew and worked with them all, so I have first-hand experience.

Method of observation

Bosses of no-decision managers were observed at a distance and no attempt was made to discuss directly why they allowed a no-decision manager to work in their team.

Limitations

Conversations are impossible with a baby, impossible with no-decision managers and finally impossible with their bosses as well. Bosses of no-decision managers never discuss the weaknesses and failings of their no-decision subordinates. And they certainly would never discuss them with me when I was a subordinate of these bosses. Further, it was impossible to find out whether or not any boss in question was aware that their subordinate was a no-decision manager.

Hypotheses

As with no-decision managers and their subordinates there is no primary hypothesis to prove. The study was concentrated on obtaining as much information as possible on the bosses of no-decision managers in relation to their no-decision subordinates.

Findings
Despite these severe restrictions, four reasons were found why these bosses tolerate and even accept no-decision managers in their organisation. These four reasons were deduced from the behaviours of these bosses and the comments of their colleagues and subordinates, but never openly admitted by the bosses themselves. They are explained in Chapter 9.

Other research
No serious academic research has been carried out on no-decision managers, for many of the reasons given above. But the main reason is problems with identification.

First, no-decision managers are unlikely to volunteer to come forward to be examined. And second, researchers let loose in organisations in search of no-decision managers are unlikely to be welcomed. Interviews would have to be done without the knowledge or the consent of the no-decision managers themselves. And then the researchers would have to reveal the no-decision status of the people they found. These three reasons make research on no-decision managers from people outside any organisation almost impossible.

Research on 'decision fatigue'
Research, has, however, been done on 'decision fatigue'. In an article in the *New York Times* on 17 August 2011, 'Do You Suffer From Decision Fatigue?', John Tierney commented on research done by Jonathan Levav of Stanford and Shai Danziger and Liora Avniam-Pesso of Ben-Gurion University on decision-making by judges on parole boards. The decisions they made at the beginning of the day were different to the decisions at the end. He concluded:

The more choices you make throughout the day, the harder each one becomes for your brain, and eventually it looks for shortcuts, usually in either of two very different ways. One shortcut is to become reckless: to act impulsively instead of expending the energy to first think through the consequences... The other shortcut is the ultimate energy saver: do nothing. Instead of agonising over decisions, avoid any choice.

No-decision managers use this same shortcut, albeit on a permanent basis every time a decision comes up to be made. They do nothing – as Tierney calls it, 'ducking a decision'. It is, for them, a natural behaviour.

The finding that no-decision managers behave like people with 'decision fatigue' is not a coincidence. Nor is it a coincidence that it is an instinct or impulse that forces the people with 'decision fatigue' to do nothing: a similar instinct of no-decision managers.

No-decision managers are in a sort of permanent but acute state of 'decision exhaustion' without having expended any energy or effort and without having made any decisions! With this comes the paradox that it takes as much energy to ignore the repeated requests for decisions from their subordinates, even by doing nothing, as it does to make decisions.

The Stanford and Ben-Gurion researchers also discovered that decision-making can be broken down into three phases: the pre-decisional phase, the decision phase and the post-decisional phase. They showed that only the decision phase is tiring and causes 'decision fatigue', not the pre- or post-decision phase. It is not a coincidence, either, that no-decision managers, as will be shown, excel in the pre- and post-decision phases.

Research on mentally ill patients

Research has also been done on mentally ill patients or patients with brain damage who are unable to make decisions. Antonio Damasio discovered, while studying people who had damage to the prefrontal cortex of the brain, that some are unable to make decisions but keep intact most of their other mental capacities. In his book *Descartes' Error: Emotion, Reason and the Human Brain* (2005), he goes much further than just concentrating on lack of or faulty decision-making. He shows that lack of decision-making of these patients was accompanied by lack of emotion, which was the basis for his 'Somatic-Marker Hypothesis'.

However, at least two patients in his book had similar characteristics to no-decision managers.

The first patient 'had the requisite knowledge, attention and memory; his language was flawless; he could perform calculations; he could tackle the logic of an abstract problem. There was only one significant accompaniment to his decision-making failure: a marked alteration of the ability to experience feelings.'

What is interesting in this patient in relation to no-decision managers is the combination of three conditions:

1. Lack of decision-making
2. Sound reasoning
3. Lack of emotion

The first two characteristics are present in all no-decision managers, who also show complete lack of sympathy for the wellbeing of their subordinates.

In an anecdote about the second patient, Damasio describes what happened when the patient is presented with a decision to make:

> I was discussing with the same patient when his next visit to the laboratory should take place. I suggested two alternative dates, both in the coming month and just a few days apart from each other. The patient pulled out his appointment book and began consulting his calendar... For the better part of a half-hour, the patient enumerated reasons for and against each of the two dates: previous engagements, proximity to other engagements, possible

meteorological conditions, virtually anything that one could reasonably think about concerning a simple date…but we finally did tell him quietly that he should come on the second of the alternative dates. His response was equally calm and prompt. He simply said: 'That's fine.'

It is quite remarkable that this behaviour of a mentally ill patient exactly mirrors the behaviour of a no-decision manager confronted with a decision to make: first, extensive and excessive analysis, and second, immediate acceptance of a proposed decision from a person in authority. This example is a patient–doctor relationship, but it precisely describes what happens when the boss of a no-decision manager suggests a solution to a no-decision subordinate: immediate and total acceptance of the suggestion.

In citing this research, there is no suggestion that no-decision managers suffer from mental illness, brain damage, lesions to the prefrontal cortex, damage to any part of the frontal lobe, brain tumours or any other of the mental ailments discussed in Damasio's book. Nor do any of them have an iron rod 'pierce the base of the skull, traverse the front of the brain and exit through the top of the head', as does the unfortunate Phineas Gage, the first patient described by Damasio in his book.

Conventions used in this book

1. No-decision manager

To keep it concise in this book, the two words 'no-decision' have been added before the title, so a president becomes a 'no-decision president', a boss becomes a 'no-decision boss', a finance director becomes a 'no-decision finance director' and so on.

However, before I arrived at this simple title I had considered many other options. 'Decision evasion manager' was one of the first favourites. 'Managers who abstain from decision-making' was another, but was eliminated as being too cumbersome. The frivolous was also envisaged, for instance 'decision ducking manager' or 'decision ducking director', or even 'decision dodging director'.

In the end, I decided this continuous mocking would undermine the seriousness of the subject for both managers and subordinates. 'Decision shunning supervisor' and 'decision boycott boss' were also envisaged for a short time. 'Negation' and 'negatory' were considered but were deemed too complicated. Many pages of the book were first written with 'No Decision Manager' in capitals before the simple choice of 'no-decision' to describe a manager, boss, president, subordinate, or director.

After having spent all this intellectually creative time thinking up a name, I discovered that Rajiv Rajendra in his book *Lead 3D: The Future of Leadership is Here*, had already noted, 'A no decision manager is not a leader and he creates chaos on what next to do one level below'. So the credit goes to Rajendra, as does the opinion that a no-decision manager is not a leader. Not to copy Rajendra, but more to recognise a true compound adjective, a hyphen is added to 'no decision' so that these managers here become 'no-decision managers'.

2. Structure of chapters

Where relevant, each chapter has been structured in three sections.

One section is usually information related to no-decision managers under the heading 'Information on no-decision managers'.

A second is called '"How to" advice', and gives practical advice on how to become a no-decision manager, advice for subordinates, tips on how to work with a no-decision boss, and guidance for bosses on how to oversee no-decision managers effectively.

At the end of each chapter is a summary of the steps recommended for those involved in no-decision management: the no-decision managers themselves, their subordinates and their bosses. These come under the headings:

> Steps to become a no-decision manager
> Steps to become an enlightened subordinate
> Steps to manage a team of no-decision managers

Annexes 1, 2 and 3 also summarise these steps.

3. Case studies

The case studies tell the stories of the eight no-decision managers who are the main protagonists of this book. To ensure their total anonymity, as well as that of their subordinates and bosses, each of the 49 case studies features a different no-decision manager.

The name, title, location and often gender of the managers discussed have all been changed. First names in the case studies have been chosen at random from one of the lists of the 100 most popular first names given to boys and girls in the UK in 2017.

The only reality in the case studies is the content of the storyline. All are situations that subordinates of no-decision managers have recounted to me, or that I have personally witnessed during my corporate life. So the case studies are not works of pure fiction. None of the case studies are untrue. Characters and incidents are not products of my imagination and are not used fictitiously.

Where necessary, a section called 'Comments on case study' follows each case study, which explains the situation from a no-decision manager's point of view. Here I try to explain what is going on, how they feel, and why they act like they do. It also compares their behaviour to that of normal managers. Normal managers in this context are managers who take decisions. They may also be other types of manager: for instance an incompetent manager, a lazy manager, a brilliant manager or whatever, but the moment they take a decision in the case studies they are a 'normal manager'.

4. To 'make a decision' or to 'take a decision'

I use the phrases to 'make a decision' and to 'take a decision' because I sometimes take a decision and other times I make one. The *Oxford English Dictionary* clearly states that these two phrases mean the same thing: to decide; and this is their exact meaning throughout the book. There is some debate that 'make a decision' and 'take a decision' have different meanings, so I explain in Annex 7 what this debate is about.

5. Impartial and unbiased

Every attempt has been made to present the situation of no-decision managers in an impartial and unbiased manner. It may seem that no-decision managers are being continually criticised or presented in a one-sided negative manner, but that is not the intention. They behave as they do because they avoid making decisions.

It is acceptable to feel sorry for subordinates of no-decision managers but not for no-decision managers themselves. Their actions are centred on not making decisions. They are happy to go through a career with this as their primary objective, regardless of the consequences to anyone around them.

No-decision managers may behave like someone with a reflective personality who needs to gather information based on fact and needs to have adequate time to make decisions. They may be careful and prudent and not want to be impulsive. They might have other more important concerns not indicated in a case study and should not be pressured by subordinates. Personality clashes between the no-decision boss and their subordinate may also cause conflict in their working relationships. All or some of this might be true, but in the end there is one unique constant: no-decision managers never decide. They never explain what they are doing. It is this which drives the actions and feelings of their subordinates.

If, for instance, a manager says to a subordinate, 'I know you think that I am asking for too much information, but for this decision I want to be sure of the facts,' or, 'You must think that I am being slow with this decision, but let me take my time on it. It is too important,' then they are probably not a no-decision manager, but a prudent and careful manager, or just one who is slow to make decisions. But in the end, if there is never a decision, then this manager is a no-decision manager.

Not deciding is a way of life for no-decision managers and does not need defending. No-decision managers don't feel the need to defend themselves. They think they have done nothing wrong. They consider that they are acting in a normal way and not in a way that needs a defence or even an explanation.

References to people who find it difficult to decide

There is extensive information on the 'indecisive manager', but this describes only a limited number of the tactics of no-decision managers and often focuses on how these managers can be helped by their subordinates to make decisions more often. Some management manuals even advise indecisive managers on how to become decisive and make decisions easily and quickly in the future.

But as we've already learned, no-decision managers are distinguished by never making, or wanting to make, a decision – ever. The focus on 'indecisive managers' keeps attention away from the true no-decision manager. Experienced business writers have in common the systematic omission of the true no-decision manager.

Literary references

Indecision may be a state we all find ourselves in from time to time. But chronic indecision is a different matter. It can blight someone's whole life. One of the earliest serious references to this condition was by the philosopher William James in his book *The Principles of Psychology*, originally published in 1890 in the USA. He noted:

> There is no more miserable human being than one in whom nothing is habitual but indecision.

James was writing about personal habits, such as lighting cigars, going to bed and which 'trouser-leg' is 'put on first'. He argues that personal habits are learned before the age of 20 but professional ones are learned between the ages of 20 and 30:

> the period between 20 and 30 is the critical one in the formation of intellectual and professional habits.

So this human being remains miserable with his indecision, in both his personal life and later in his intellectual and professional life. It is interesting that indecision is immediately associated with a negative term –'miserable' – just as the modern no-decision manager is associated with the equally negative 'frustrating' as far as his subordinates are concerned.

But the similarities do not end there. William James goes on:

> the great thing…is to make our nervous system our ally instead of our enemy. It is to fund and capitalise our acquisitions and live at ease upon the interest of the fund.

James associates indecision with the nervous system and Jean Piaget some 45 years later associates it with reflexes or instincts (hereditary equipment and the 'natural inborn inability' of no-decision managers). Whoever is right about its real origin, both consider indecision to be so ingrained in the personal system that it really does not matter whether it is part of the nervous system, an instinct or a reflex.

James, through an interesting change of style, is the first to write about indecision in business. While writing mainly about personal habits, he suddenly includes financial metaphors: 'fund', 'capitalise', 'acquisition' and 'interest', to illustrate the move out of the personal into the business and professional.

Thirty years on, the Irish author Brendan Francis makes another reference to indecision, this time specifically to decision avoidance. He says:

> Some persons are very decisive when it comes to avoiding decisions.
> (Source: izquotes.com)

This sentence could be the definition of a no-decision manager. Here we have a deliberate action to avoid decision-making. It is the first recognition that no-decision people do in fact make decisions but only decisions designed exclusively to enable them to avoid making decisions. In the no-decision management jargon this is now known as 'delay decisions' (explained in Chapter 3).

Not only are these people decisive in not making decisions, but they have set up a whole new process, revealed by a basketball coach, Mike

Krzyzewski, in his book with Donald T. Phillips in 2000, *Leading with the Heart: Coach K's Successful Strategies for Basketball, Business, and Life*. He writes:

> The truth is that many people set rules to keep from making decisions.

This is the first public acknowledgement that no-decision managers have set up a whole system of rules and tactics to avoid decisions now called in modern management jargon the 'No-decision-making System'. It is described in Chapters 3 and 4.

Krzyzewski's quote also reveals that no-decision managers survive in all types of organisations, even in the world of professional sport, which is often considered to be so competitive as to eliminate any possibility that the no-decision manager could exist there.

Political references

For more recent evidence, quotes from a former prime minister of the UK and a former United States Secretary of Defence provide more information. These two eminent, famous and successful politicians bring us clear confirmation that no-decision managers thrive in the higher echelons of democratic government and in their civil services or administrations.

James Callaghan is quoted to have said, not without exasperation, in the 1970s:

> Some people, however long their experience or strong their intellect, are temperamentally incapable of reaching firm decisions. (attributed to James Callaghan by finedictionary.com)

Here Callaghan is explicitly stating that not only do such people exist and survive in the long term, 'however long their experience', but amazingly they are both experienced and intelligent. They have been admitted into, or have infiltrated, the British Civil Service and government at high levels of responsibility.

Donald Rumsfeld, former US Defence Secretary, went further in his quote:

> If in doubt move decisions up to the President. (Source: Donald Rumsfeld (2001). Public Statements of Donald H. Rumsfeld, Secretary of State, 2001)

Here Rumsfeld reveals one of the most favoured tactics of the no-decision manager. While one cannot accuse him of being one, here he is as Secretary of Defence admitting that it is normal to use the principal weapon of the no-decision manager: get the boss to decide. The experienced no-decision manager spends most of his corporate energy and managerial life trying to push decisions that they should take themself up to their boss.

It would be quite ludicrous to conclude anything from quotes gathered from three countries on two continents taken out of context over two centuries, from a former United States Secretary of Defence, a former British prime minister, an American philosopher, an Irish author and an American basketball coach. However, these five people, who are not no-decision managers themselves, collectively acknowledge that people who never make decisions exist in all types of organisations – even at the highest levels of government – they survive over time, they are intelligent, and they have an organised system of decision avoidance. They are also generally despised.

Business and managerial references

Starting in the late 20th century, business literature begins to describe managers who have difficulty making decisions. They give guidance on how to work with them and how to help them make their decisions.

Various rather odd names have been invented for these managers. To name but five:

a) Indecisive Stallers, *Coping with Difficult People* by Robert M. Bramson (1981)

b) Fickle Terrible Office Tyrant, *Tame Your Terrible Office Tyrant* by Lynn Taylor (2009)
c) The Avoider, *Surviving and Thriving When Your Boss is a Jerk* by Marsha Evans, Elizabeth Gaynor and Colt George (2014)
d) No-Boss Boss, *A Survival Guide for Working with Bad Bosses* by Gini Graham Scott (2005)
e) People who are Fickle, *Working with the Enemy* by Mike Leibing (2009)

But generally these managers are called either indecisive or procrastinating. Annex 6, 'Additional reading', has more detail.

These managers, though, are not true no-decision managers. They take on certain characteristics but not all. They are what I call 'pseudo no-decision managers'. They specialise in a few selected tactics borrowed from the no-decision movement.

Some of these managers, according to these authors, are afraid that their decisions will hurt someone. Others are looking for the perfect decision and cannot choose which one is the best. Some are just anxious. But in the end these managers will eventually make a decision, especially when subordinates are clever enough to prepare a favourable environment to help them. A true no-decision manager, however, will never make a decision.

No books have yet referred to the true no-decision manager. I have found only one article that describes a true one. This article, called 'Strategies to Deal with Indecisive Bosses', is posted in www.employmentcrossing.com. The author, who is anonymous, is clearly someone who has worked extensively with a no-decision boss.

Apart from explaining several different tactics the indecisive boss uses to avoid decisions, the article reflects the deep, distressing frustration the author still feels when looking back on the experience, and the profound lack of respect that lingers when writing about this particular manager. This frustration, anger and disrespect reflect accurately what subordinates feel when they choose to stay in a state of negative emotion while working with no-decision managers. While giving advice on how to get away from such a manager, the writer claims to have worked with this no-decision manager for six years in a constant state of distress.

The author of the article makes several claims about this manager:

    a) that she only made decisions through her subordinates,
    b) that she always took the credit for the good work done by others,
    c) that she was frightened and insecure,
    d) that the author lost all possibility of advancing a career because of her,
    e) that she never defended her subordinates,
    f) that subordinates never confided in her.

The author describes the action he took to 'build allies' in the company to make sure that senior management was aware of his own achievements.

    The article comprehensively explains the behaviour of no-decision managers and the feelings of subordinates working for them. The author calls his former manager an 'indecisive boss', but she has all the characteristics of a true no-decision manager.

2

The World of the No-Decision Manager

Information on no-decision managers

What is a no-decision manager?
No-decision managers are simply managers in any type of organisation who never take decisions. They avoid decisions at all times. They have expelled decision-making from their managerial life. Decision avoidance is their primary objective.

A true no-decision manager is not just indecisive. Indecisive managers will make a decision in the end even if slowly or too late – often with the help of their subordinates. No-decision managers do not just procrastinate. Procrastinating managers put off decision-making until later but will, in the end, make a decision, again too slowly or too late.

A true no-decision manager will never take a decision.

The no-decision manager's definition of a decision
At what stage in a decision is it that no-decision managers find themselves unable to act? They need to know precisely what parts of the process they can perform and what parts they cannot. But the definition of a 'decision' is complicated because it is a process where, in some parts, no-decision managers perform well.

Decision-making, according to the *Oxford English Dictionary*, is a process in three steps:

> The action, fact, or process of deciding or bringing to an end a contest, controversy, etc.; judgement with regard to a matter in dispute; settlement, resolution. Also: an instance of this.

> The action, fact, or process of arriving at a conclusion regarding a matter under consideration; the action or fact of making up one's mind as to an opinion, course of action, etc.; an instance of this.

> The result of this action or process; that which has been decided; a conclusion, a judgement, a resolution; a choice.

All no-decision managers recognise this. Relying on this definition they can clearly understand their position in the decision-making process. They are able to participate in the process at the beginning and at the end but miss Step 2: 'the action of deciding'. It is this that does not exist in their decision-making repertoire.

Figure 1: The decision-making process for a no-decision manager

Step 1	Step 2	Step 3
Preparation of the decision	Act of deciding	Implementation of the decision
Oxford English Dictionary 'The process of deciding regarding a matter under consideration'	*Oxford English Dictionary* 'The action of deciding'	*Oxford English Dictionary* 'The result of this action or process; that which has been decided'
	Missing from a no-decision manager's repertoire **The act of deciding does not exist**	

Figure 1, The decision-making process for a no-decision manager, summarises and simplifies the definition of a decision as stated in the *Oxford English Dictionary* highlighting that Step 2: the act of deciding, does not exist for no-decision managers.

The act of deciding is missing from a no-decision manager's repertoire. For them, it does not exist. But contrary to all expectations not only do no-decision managers actively participate in the preparation of the decision, Step 1, and its implementation in Step 3, they also become experts in these two steps of the process.

The no-decision manager's definition of a manager

Now we have explained what part of the decision-making process is missing from the no-decision manager's repertoire, we need to know what the 'manager' part is in a no-decision manager. Or more precisely, what types of managers do not come under the heading no-decision manager.

The *Oxford English Dictionary* defines a manager as follows:

> A person who organises, directs or plots something; a person who regulates or deploys resources;

> A person who manages (a department of) a business, organisation, institution, etc.; a person with an executive or supervisory function within an organisation, etc.

No-decision managers have borrowed freely from the *Oxford English Dictionary's* definition of 'manager' and 'decision' for their own definition of a no-decision manager:

> a person who supposedly manages a team and pretends to control, direct or administer a business, an organisation, a government administration or a public or private institution or any part, and who refuses to arrive at an opinion or conclusion about a matter under consideration or who refuses to make a decision regarding a

question or issue, on which there is doubt or dispute especially after considering several alternatives.

Or, to put it more simply, it is a manager who never takes a decision. A person who works on his own with the title of manager without subordinates is not considered a manager in the no-decision management environment.

Where do no-decision managers work?

No-decision managers are everywhere. They can be in all positions and in all types of organisations. They can be supervisors with just one subordinate up through middle management responsible for a large department until they get to top management with international responsibilities in charge of a division with thousands of employees. They exist in all types of organisations: private or public, large or small, commercial, industrial or service oriented, for profit or not for profit, even in government.

They prefer, and flourish in, positions where their immediate boss is physically as far away as possible. The best scenario is when the boss works on a different continent, usually in top management, or in a different country or in a different town. It can even be in the same country or town, as long as it's in a different building. The worst position for a no-decision manager is one where they have to work in the same building as their boss. A different floor might be manageable, but having the boss close by on the same floor can be complicated. Proximity gives the boss direct, rapid and continuous access to the subordinates of the no-decision manager, so the boss can verify in more detail, and more often, any information directly with them.

With experience, when given the time to gradually learn survival and the tactics of delaying decisions, no-decision managers can hide in any type of organisation. There are, however, organisations where it is easier to hide. Some even encourage no-decision managers. In organisations public or private where time is not a key factor in decision-making, no-decision managers can build a career more easily.

In organisations where committees take all the important decisions they can thrive in numbers. Corporations, where consensus decisions are the norm, encourage no-decision managers. Finally, they exist in all countries and cultures.

Never the top job

Although no-decision managers are found almost everywhere, they cannot have the top job in any organisation. In commercial and profit-oriented organisations the top position is usually the Chief Executive Officer (CEO) or president. In government it is the president or the prime minister.

The top job often reports to a committee, a board of directors or a board of trustees. People in these positions make decisions all the time, so no-decision managers exclude themselves from going too high in an organisation into positions that by definition require decision-makers.

At the next level down in the hierarchy, however, no-decision managers can and do survive.

Impact of no-decision managers on people in organisations

John Adair's Action-Centred Leadership model shows how a competent manager is able to build a team, develop individuals and carry out the tasks in harmony, with all members working towards a common goal. His model in Figure 2 below shows tidy overlapping circles representing the team and the individuals working together on common tasks.

The action words Adair describes to connect and overlap the circles, with words like 'develop', 'build', 'maintain' and 'achieve', are far removed from no-decision management. The only achievement no-decision managers are interested in is not making decisions and they disregard all three circles, do not achieve the task, nor build a team nor develop an individual. These interlocking circles become an organised blot of nothing in particular in Figure 3, which fairly represents the management of no-decision managers: 'nothing in particular.'

Figure 2: Action-Centred Leadership™ after John Adair

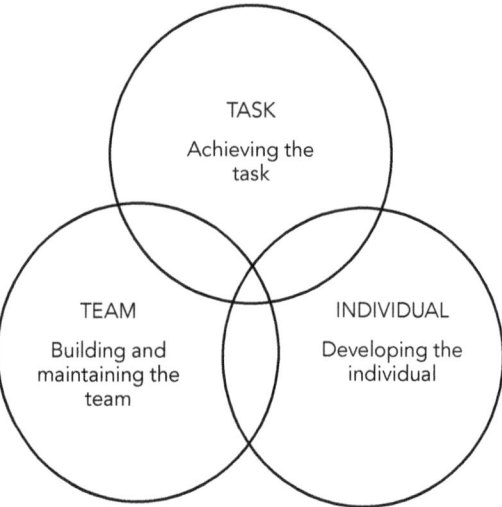

Reproduced with the permission of Adair International. Copyright © Adair International

Figure 3: Action-Centred Leadership™ after John Adair, representing a manager who neglects the circles

The three interlocking circles are blotted out to represent a manager who ignores the circles, one who is not interested in the task, nor in building a team, nor in

developing individuals. This blot represents a no-decision manager whose sole interest is to avoid decision-making. The circles overlap and stay connected. They do not fragment or crack. They continue to exist, ready to be picked up by a future leader.

Reproduced with the permission of Adair International. Copyright © Adair International

Figure 3 shows what happens when no-decision managers are in charge of a team: they do nothing. Individuals become lost with lack of direction and attention and the teamwork disintegrates, represented by the black blot.

Another equally effective image of the impact of no-decision managers on subordinates can be seen by adapting The Managerial Grid of Blake, Mouton, Barnes and Greiner. This grid shows, on the vertical axis, where different manager types are positioned on a scale of 'Concern for people' and, on a horizontal axis, 'Concern for results'. Figure 4, The Managerial Grid adapted for no-decision managers, shows where the no-decision manager is positioned.

Figure 4: The Managerial Grid adapted for no-decision managers

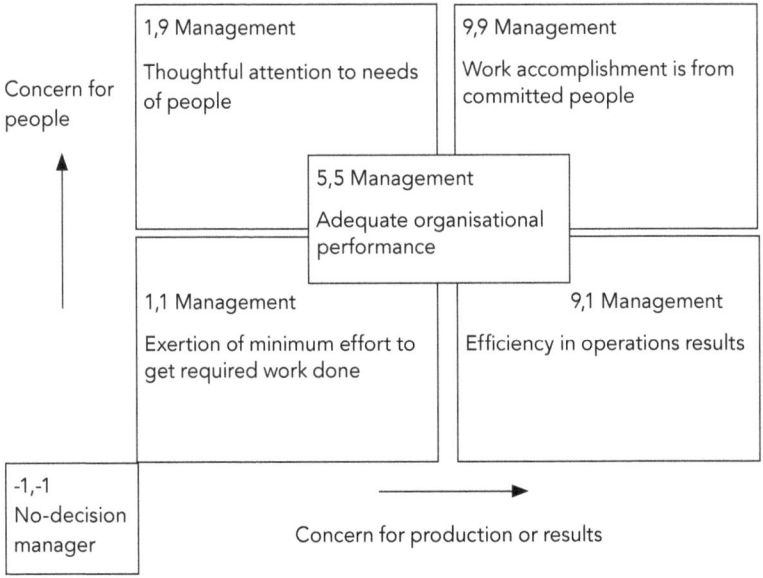

Borrowed from the article 'Breakthrough in Organisation Development' by R. R. Blake, J. S. Mouton, L. B. Barnes and L. E. Greiner (*Harvard Business Review*, November 1964) and adapted to include the no-decision manager.

Reproduced and amended by permission of *Harvard Business Review*. Original Copyright © 1964 by Harvard Business Publishing: all rights reserved.

Explications of the Managerial Grid

1,9 Management
Thoughtful attention to needs of people for satisfying relationships leads to a comfortable, friendly organisation atmosphere and work tempo. Sometimes called the Country Club Manager, because these managers are not at all interested in the results of their department or subordinates, who more or less do what they want with little control and direction from their manager.

9,9 Management
Work accomplishment is from committed people; interdependence through a 'common stake' in organisational purpose. Leads to relationships of trust and respect. Sometimes called the Team Manager who takes care of his subordinates and closely control the results of his department.

5,5 Management
Adequate organisational performance is possible through balancing the necessity to get out work while maintaining morale of people at a satisfactory level. Sometimes called the Middle of the Road Manager because everything is just average.

1,1 Management
Exertion of minimum effort to get required work done is appropriate to obtain organisation membership. Sometimes called the Impoverished Manager, who is not interested in either results or the welfare of subordinates.

9,1 Management
Efficiency in operations results from arranging conditions of work in such a way that human elements interfere to a minimum degree. Sometimes called the Authority-Obedience Manager, who is only interested in results at the expense of the feelings and opinions of subordinates.

-1,-1 No-Decision Manager
The no-decision manager does not exist in the original Managerial Grid and has been added to show how poor a manager he or she is, in both concern for people and for concern for results.

The no-decision manager has no concern for people or for results, so he or she has the unique privilege of being the only manager type who is outside the grid. They are below the line for 'concern for people' because of the high levels of frustration that they generate among their subordinates and below the line in results because decision avoidance takes priority. They are worse than the worst manager defined by the grid – the Impoverished Manager.

These adaptations of two well-known management theory charts clearly show the impact of no-decision management on people in organisations.

How can no-decision managers work with this inability?

There is no doubt that decision-making is one of the key roles of a manager and an integral part of management. And of course there is much management literature and research supporting this.

Here are two examples out of thousands:

Peter Drucker in his book *Management* in 2012 states:

> The first managerial skill is, therefore, the making of effective decisions.

Not a contentious statement.

Marcia W. Blenko, Michael C. Mankins and Paul Rogers in their article 'The five steps to better decisions' go further:

> No company can reach its full potential unless it makes good decisions quickly and consistently and then implements them effectively.

Not a statement that is likely to be contested.

If decision-making is so important, an inborn inability to make decisions must clearly put no-decision managers at a severe disadvantage compared to their decision-making managerial colleagues, and should be a serious handicap for advancement in whatever career they happen to have fallen into.

But it is an inability that successful no-decision managers learn to overcome – not by learning to make decisions but by building up other factors and abilities to hide behind and eventually to compensate for it.

Henry Mintzberg and John Kotter, while using different concepts and contrasting analyses, are able to explain how no-decision managers function despite this managerial inability.

Mintzberg's managerial roles for no-decision managers

Henry Mintzberg in his article in the *Harvard Business Review* in 1975, 'The Manager's Job: Folklore and Fact', illustrates the different roles a manager has, and the importance of the 'decisional roles' that describe the different types of decisions a manager must make.

His chart of the 10 managerial roles has been adapted in Figure 5, Manager's roles eliminated – no-decision roles added, to show how no-decision managers have abandoned the four decisional and two other – the role of leader and the role of disseminator – roles used by normal managers.

Figure 5: Manager's roles eliminated – no-decision roles added

Formal authority and status		

Interpersonal roles	Informational roles	Decisional roles
Figurehead	Monitor	~~Entrepreneur~~
~~Leader~~	~~Disseminator~~	~~Disturbance handler~~
Liaison	Spokesperson	~~Resource allocator~~
Survival	*Secrecy*	~~Negotiator~~
	Negotiator	*Decision avoidance*

Borrowed from Henry Mintzberg's Article 'The Manager's Job: Folklore and Fact' (*Harvard Business Review*, July-August 1975) and then adapted to include three new roles for the no-decision manager: secrecy, decision avoidance, and survival, and to exclude the six unnecessary roles for which no-decision managers have no need.

Reproduced and amended by permission of Harvard Business Review. Original Copyright © 1975 by Harvard Business Publishing; all rights reserved.

The four decisional roles shown in the figure are by definition obsolete for no-decision managers, so they have been crossed out. No-decision managers do not make decisions, so these roles are not part of the daily activity in their management lives. There is, however, one exception relating to the fourth decisional role, namely that of 'negotiator'.

As Mintzberg says:

> Managers spend considerable time in negotiations, [which] are an integral part of a manager's job.

This is also true for no-decision managers, but with one major difference. No-decision managers spend endless time discussing in negotiations, but in the end never decide anything. While discussing, they do not have to make decisions, and because they never decide, the negotiations take much longer. So for the no-decision manager, the negotiator is no longer a decisional role, but an informational role under the Mintzberg criteria. It has accordingly been moved to the Informational roles' box in Figure 5.

No-decision managers also ignore the disseminator role, where the manager communicates information downwards in the organisation to their teams and subordinates. This action enables normal managers to function effectively. A common characteristic of all no-decision managers is the complete absence of downward information given to subordinates. No-decision managers have no concern for their subordinates and even less attachment to whether their team is functioning correctly. They generally consider that they do not need to communicate any information to subordinates.

No-decision managers cannot perform Mintzberg's leader role, because leaders must make decisions on the direction and strategy of their department or organisation. This role is inaccessible for no-decision managers.

Kotter on managers vs. leaders with no-decision managers

John Kotter, in his 1990 book *Force for Change: How Leadership Differs from Management*, has a different approach to Mintzberg, with a table setting out the characteristics of a manager compared to those of a leader. The table can be used to explain how the characteristics of a no-decision manager differ from both a leader and a normal decision-making manager. See Figure 6, Characteristics of management, no-decision management and leadership.

Using Kotter's scheme of reference, Figure 6 shows that the main characteristic of a no-decision manager would be decision avoidance and the preservation of the status quo. Any change to the actual situation in which a no-decision manager finds themselves requires them to make a decision, which they will never do. By making no decisions they leave everything as it is.

It can be seen from Kotter's table that leadership invokes action words such as 'change' and 'movement'. Action requires decisions. Leaders by definition lead, and in leading they make decisions. No-decision managers do not make decisions so cannot be leaders. Management, according to Kotter's table, looks for 'order' and 'consistency'. These are action words in this context, so no-decision managers do not fit this definition. Their first priority is decision avoidance, which maintains the status quo.

In terms of people management, no-decision managers give priority to managers in their hierarchy and generally ignore their teams and subordinates. Although not an objective in itself, the result of this focus on subordinates is to increase their frustration, which no-decision managers make no attempt to reduce. In contrast, decision-capable managers and leaders align and organise their people with actions.

Figure 6: Characteristics of management, no-decision management and leadership

Management: Order and consistency	No-Decision Management: Decision avoidance resulting in preservation of status quo	Leadership: Change and movement
Planning/budgeting • Establish agenda • Set schedule • Allocate resources	**Status quo** • Adopt No-Decision-Making Process • Leave existing strategies in place • Leave resources alone	**Establishing direction** • Create vision • Clarify the big picture • Set strategies
Organisation/staffing • Provide structure • Make job placements • Establish rules and procedures	**Handle the hierarchy** • Concentrate on what the boss wants • Develop relationships with the boss's team, their hierarchy and headquarters • Ignore teams and subordinates	**Aligning people** • Communicate goals • Seek commitment • Build teams and coalitions
Controlling/problem solving • Develop incentives • Generate creative solutions • Take corrective action	**Frustrating and exasperating** • Bore and discourage • Frustrate subordinates • Systematically ignore unmet needs and certainly take no corrective action	**Motivating and inspiring** • Inspire and energise • Empower subordinates • Satisfy unmet needs

Adapted with permission from: *A Force For Change: How Leadership Differs from Management* by John P. Kotter, Copyright © 1990 John P. Kotter Inc. Reprinted with the permission of The Free Press, a division of Simon & Schuster Inc. All rights reserved and adapted and republished with permission of Sage College from *Leadership Theory and Practice* by Peter G. Northouse, Sage Publications Inc. Copyright © 2004; permission conveyed through Copyright Clearance Center Inc.

Through their behaviour no-decision managers manage to bore, discourage and frustrate their subordinates and then go out of their way not to take any corrective action. Effective managers and leaders, on the other hand, are inspiring and energising and develop incentives to ensure that subordinates progress.

'How to' advice for no-decision managers

Become a member of the Shelter

With this background you are now ready to start the process of becoming a no-decision manager. The first thing you have to do is find one. As already explained, they are everywhere and there is undoubtedly one working in your organisation. Just ask around. The more senior they are the easier they are to find.

Now you have your first complication. No-decision managers never talk about no-decision management or admit to being no-decision managers except to other no-decision managers. Secrecy is primary. Nothing can be put in writing.

So you cannot simply go up to a no-decision manager you have just found and say, 'Hey, I heard that you are a no-decision manager. I am interested in becoming one. Can you tell me something about them?'

Instead you must declare your allegiance to no-decision management and ask to become a member of their organisation. If they believe you, he or she will ask you to meet another no-decision manager and it is this second one that will start the membership process for you.

You will be asked to make the oath of secrecy below:

No-Decision Management – Oath of Secrecy

I, Percy, a no-decision manager, solemnly undertake never to disclose to any third party, except to other recognised no-decision managers who owe allegiance to the Shelter, any information admitting to be a no-decision manager nor to put anything in writing which relates to the no-decision movement. I further solemnly undertake never to reveal any detail of the four pillars of the Shelter: Secrecy, Survival, System and Skills. Finally I agree to abide by the rules of, and to give exclusive jurisdiction to, the Shelter and its rulings in the event of (a) any dispute with another no-decision manager or (b) any non-compliance with the Shelter's rules.

Note: This is the first time this Oath of Secrecy has been published and therefore goes against the rules of the no-decision management movement, leaving the author open to whatever redress for damages the Shelter decides to seek.

Take the oath, and you become a member.

You are now officially a no-decision manager BUT do not stop taking decisions yet – wait until you know a little more.

Case study 1 – Following the Secrecy Rule
Amelia is a senior no-decision manager who works in Europe. Noah, a consultant who has worked with her for many years, is having lunch with some of her ex-colleagues. He tells them:

'I will be having dinner with Amelia tonight to let her know what product decisions she should be making. She will listen and probably say that she agrees with my analysis, but will then do nothing. It is very frustrating, Amelia never ever makes any decisions, but I have to help. It is part of my job.'

The day after, Noah's story is a little different:

'I had a big argument with Amelia last night. She would not accept or even listen to me telling her that she never takes a decision. She usually agrees with me but then never decides. This time she fought back. I know, however, that she will decide nothing, despite her strong opinions last night.'

Comments on case study 1
Amelia is a long-serving, experienced, senior no-decision manager. Many people in her organisation know that she is a no-decision manager, yet she refuses to admit even to a close friend that she never makes decisions.

> Her behaviour here can be interpreted in several ways. She might be refusing to accept criticism of a management weakness coming from an outside consultant, even if he is also a close friend. She will not reveal the secret that she is a no-decision manager, following the Shelter's rules. She might make decisions that Noah doesn't know about, or she simply does not accept Noah's advice. It might be one or several of these reasons. Only she knows.
>
> However, it is not a secret in her organisation that she is a no-decision manager and she is keeping to her oath as one.

This is not the moment to completely abandon decision-making. You are just starting on the road to becoming a no-decision manager and there are many more steps to take. Your next one is to become a member of the Shelter to be informed of the process and tactics of no-decision management. You now have the chance to learn everything about no-decision management before actually switching over to full decision avoidance. With this knowledge you will have a considerable advantage over natural, instinctive no-decision managers, who make no decisions right from the start of their careers and then have to learn the process on the job.

It is strongly recommended that you stop decision-making only at the end of the learning process, not now. But it is up to you. When you reach the last step you will have all the elements to become a great no-decision manager, with the knowledge that you are secure in your new position and new status. You could move to a no-decision mode at any time from now on. You are after all officially a no-decision manager.

Memorise the definition, learn the rules and roles

Your next step is to go back to the section above, 'The no-decision manager's definition of a manager, and memorise the definition it gives of a no-decision manager. You should be able to repeat it at any time without forgetting the three key words: 'supposedly', 'pretends' and 'refuses'.

Below is a reminder of the definition:

> a person who supposedly manages a team and pretends to control, direct or administer a business, an organisation, a government administration or a public or private institution or any part, and who refuses to arrive at an opinion or conclusion about a matter under consideration or who refuses to make a decision regarding a question or issue, on which there is doubt or dispute especially after considering several alternatives.

Memorise the three rules of the oath and the four pillars of the Shelter. The three rules are simple:

1. Nothing is ever put in writing.
2. Meetings of the organisation are limited to a maximum of two no-decision managers at any one time.
3. Publications on no-decision management are not permitted.

The Shelter and its four pillars, Secrecy, Survival, System, and Skills are known collectively as the Five S's and are shown in Figure 7.

Figure 7: The Five S's

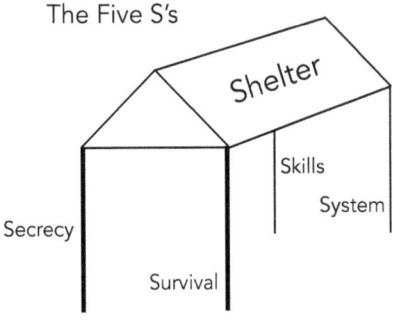

New no-decision managerial roles

The Shelter's set-up, believe it or not, was inspired by Mintzberg. Having decided to adopt his managerial roles for their movement and then eliminate the six which were not relevant to no-decision managers, there was not much left for no-decision managers to do. They quickly realised that their very existence could not be guaranteed with just the remaining Mintzbergian roles so they had to design some more specific ones adapted to no-decision managers.

Secrecy role

The first is easy. It is the 'secrecy' role that you now follow given that you have taken the oath. You must manage secrecy throughout your no-decision career. You need to make sure that your boss and top management in your organisation never know that you are a no-decision manager. To do this you need to control the information that flows up the hierarchy and you need to monitor secrecy levels at all times. Advice on how to do this is given in later chapters.

Decision avoidance role

The second role is also straightforward. It is the 'decision avoidance' role. This is a collection of decision avoidance tactics designed by no-decision managers with the unique objective of ensuring decisions never have to be made. You will need to learn these by heart. They are explained in detail in Chapters 3 and 4. There are five different categories for decision avoidance that no-decision managers have developed, which, together with their two instinct-based behaviours, they blatantly call the 'No-decision-making System'

Survival role

The third role specifically invented for no-decision managers is the 'survival' role. The Shelter has designed a whole survival system called 'structured survival' to help no-decision managers enjoy long careers in organisations. This is explained in detail in Chapter 6 and is an important role that you must also master.

As you can see from the drawing of the Shelter in Figure 7, these three roles are pillars of the Shelter, but there is another pillar called 'skills'. This is not important enough to be considered as a role on its own, but is a series of optional skills that are useful for no-decision managers. These are explained in Chapter 5.

Modification of managerial roles

The Shelter eliminated six of Mintzberg's managerial roles from his article in the *Harvard Business Review* in 1975, 'The Manager's Job: Folklore and Fact', and has added three others specifically for no-decision managers. But then they went back and examined the four remaining roles to see how relevant they were to no-decision managers:

1. Figurehead role
2. Liaison role
3. Monitor role
4. Spokesperson role.

The Shelter decided that these roles needed expansion and adaptation for no-decision management. As a no-decision manager you need to understand the changes that were made and master them completely.

1. The figurehead role

This is the ceremonial role and you as a no-decision manager must learn to love ceremonies, if only because, as Mintzberg explains, they involve 'no important decisions'. In fact ceremonies involve no business-related decisions at all.

You will find that as you become more senior as a no-decision manager you will be making more and more speeches and will even seek out opportunities to do so, and eventually become a recognised expert. Some people will argue that speaking involves many decisions in organisations, especially when it comes to writing down what you want to say. True, but this activity for a no-decision manager is equivalent to a 'delay decision', which is explained in the next chapter.

2. The liaison role

No-decision managers are good at liaising. If you are not, then you will have to learn. Normal liaising involves being the link between people and speaking to people to get them to work together. This generally does not involve decision-making and so no-decision managers excel at it. It also involves exchanging information, and here you will learn how to collect information without giving any out. This role has been expanded by no-decision managers into a sophisticated collecting and processing (not giving) of information through networks, which is explained in Chapter 6.

3. The monitor role

The Shelter has reduced the monitoring role to two activities. First, you, as a no-decision manager, must monitor the emotional state of your frustrated subordinates who will be tempted to complain about you either directly to your boss or through Human Resources. The second monitoring activity is secrecy. Is the secret that you are a no-decision manager safe? Is it being contained? You will need to monitor this, and the ways to do it are explained in Chapter 6.

4. The spokesperson role

According to Mintzberg, again from the same article in the *Harvard Business Review* in 1975, 'The Manager's Job: Folklore and Fact', this role has two functions. The first is for the manager to send 'information to people outside the unit', and second, to 'inform and satisfy the influential people who control the organisational unit' in which they work.

The Shelter has eliminated sending information outside the unit, as this is too close to making a decision – in fact just choosing what information to send outside is a decision. The role becomes one of only *receiving* information from outside the unit. This rule is easy to apply.

The second rule is important:

> Every manager must inform and satisfy the influential people who control the organisational unit. (Source Henry Mintzberg, 'The Manager's Job: Folklore and Fact' (1975) *Harvard Business Review*).

You will need to identify the influential people in your organisation and make sure they are adequately informed and satisfied, and then get their support. Without it you will realise that you cannot survive in the long term. Not making decisions is a serious handicap for you in any organisation, so you need all the support you can get.

You should memorise Figure 8, The no-decision manager's roles, which summarises the different roles of no-decision managers based on the Shelter's reworking of the Mintzberg table.

Figure 8: The no-decision manager's roles

Formal authority and status

Interpersonal roles	Informational roles	Decisional roles
Figurehead	Monitor	**Decision avoidance**
Liaison	Spokesperson	
Survival	**Secrecy**	
	Negotiator	

Adapted from Henry Mintzberg's article 'The Manager's Job: Folklore and Fact', (*Harvard Business Review*, July-August 1975) to fit the no-decision manager.

Reproduced and amended by permission of *Harvard Business Review*. Original Copyright © 1975 by Harvard Business Publishing; all rights reserved.

Origins of no-decision managers

It was Jean Piaget who unwittingly discovered the origins of the no-decision manager. In *The Origins of Intelligence in Children* (1936) he explains that, before thinking starts, there exist common biological factors, which he calls the 'hereditary equipment' of a child.

The 'hereditary equipment' of the no-decision manager could be said to be a 'natural inborn inability', a sort of affliction genetically programmed at inception. Some people are born with natural abilities, others with natural inabilities.

Or, as Shakespeare might have written:

> Some are born indecisive, some achieve indecisiveness and some have indecisiveness thrust upon them...

No-decision managers, though, have more than just indecisiveness; they have the natural inborn inability never to make decisions. It is the biological factor common to them all.

Instinct-based behaviours

This inability generates two 'instinct-based behaviours' for no-decision managers, which they use when presented with any new decision to be made. All true no-decision managers have both.

The first of the two instinct-based behaviours is called in no-decision management jargon 'permanent procrastination', a pompous title for simple non-action: doing nothing. When presented with the request for a decision, the no-decision manager will say nothing and do nothing. They will just wait. The second is inelegantly called 'imposing incremental information', or more simply 'the three i's'.

Curiously, these behaviours only occur successively. Permanent procrastination always comes first, and may be repeated, but only then it is followed by imposing incremental information when subordinates demand, for the second or third time, that their no-decision manager make a decision. Imposing incremental information never comes first.

Permanent procrastination

Often in the early stages of permanent procrastination, the no-decision manager will not even reply or acknowledge that they have heard the request. Subordinates may be surprised and bewildered by this first encounter with this type of behaviour.

> **Case study 2 – An introduction to permanent procrastination**
> Oliver is an experienced marketing manager who has been working in his division for many years. Jack, his no-decision boss, has just been appointed. The first review of the quarterly results is due the week following Jack's promotion. Both know the process well.
>
> In the very first one-on-one meeting with Jack, Oliver reminds him:
>
> 'As you know, the quarterly review with headquarters is on Friday next week at 9 am in Munich. Would you like me to prepare the presentation? Who in the team would you like to attend?'
>
> No reply from Jack.
>
> Oliver continues: 'I'll prepare the first draft and review it with you on Monday next week.' No reply.
>
> On the Monday, Oliver discovers that Jack is out of the office all week. He prepares his proposal for the presentation and sends it by email to Jack to get his approval. No answer. On Wednesday he sends his completed presentation. The answer comes in a short email on the Thursday morning: 'I am already in Munich. Meet you tomorrow at nine for the meeting.'
>
> The email says nothing about the presentation.
>
> Oliver turns up early and alone at headquarters in Munich on the Friday morning in the hope of meeting quickly with Jack to see what he thinks of the presentation. No Jack. Two minutes

before the meeting, Jack arrives, and, settling in to his seat in the conference room, says to Oliver: 'You make the presentation today.'

Comments on case study 2
The lack of a coherent reply to Olivier's questions is pure permanent procrastination. Jack is letting events take their course without interfering, regardless of the consequences. He never comments on Oliver's proposals. He never tells him what he thinks of them. He never answers his emails. He essentially, in Oliver's eyes, just does nothing.

This scenario involves a deadline, associated with multiple minor decisions:

- what subjects to include in the presentation,
- what to omit,
- how to explain issues,
- what numbers to show in the forecast,
- and many others.

These are all small decisions, but nevertheless decisions that should be made by the boss – in this instance by Jack and not Oliver.

As a true no-decision manager, Jack does not take any of these decisions. He is in his second week in his new position. He considers he is not at risk. Had the presentation been a failure Jack would easily have been able to blame Oliver because none of the actions presented in the review were under his responsibility, but under his predecessor's. A normal manager would use this moment to impress their boss and would have reviewed the presentation with Oliver, thus taking responsibility for it. Not a no-decision manager. If, for instance, the forecast is not accepted, he could

> jump in and say he would look into it immediately, coming up with an excuse. If the forecast is accepted, Jack has successfully used permanent procrastination not to make a decision on the forecast, and to have it accepted by his boss.
>
> Jack, though, when questioned by Oliver on his lack of feedback has a perfect reply:
>
> 'Yes, thanks for your different versions during the week. It was very useful. Of course had I found anything wrong, I would have contacted you and would have let you know.'
>
> Oliver has knowledge of the concept of successful no-decision management. Jack's reply confirms to Oliver that his new boss is a no-decision manager.

Reminders from subordinates will keep coming: 'Have you decided yet?' 'When will you decide?' 'The deadline is approaching.' 'Just a reminder that we need to have a decision.' However, the no-decision manager will hope that the need for a decision will just go away. Wait long enough and sometimes it does.

Robert M. Bramson has noticed this tendency and has coined a name for those who show it:

> I call them stallers because of their tendency to stall off major decisions until they go away.

Bramson's 'Stallers', in his 1981 book *Coping with Difficult People*, are pseudo no-decision managers who have difficulty making decisions and wait until the decisive moment goes away. They do, however, use some of the tactics of no-decision managers, but they do not make decisions because they are afraid that their decision will hurt someone; very different from no-decision managers.

Imposing incremental information

The second instinct-based behaviour is imposing incremental information.

After receiving repeated reminders and realising that sitting back and doing nothing in permanent procrastination is not working, no-decision managers will instinctively call for more information. Subordinates are sent back to find more information to present, with or without an explanation that the no-decision manager needs this additional information to make the decision.

Meanwhile, no decision is made. No decision will ever be made. Subordinates are initially unaware of this. No-decision managers can put in requests for incremental information several times, interspaced with periods of permanent procrastination.

Practising the instinct-based behaviours

If you are to be a truly effective no-decision manager these two behaviours must become second nature, so you will need to practise with your current team both permanent procrastination and imposing incremental information. Because this is a major change to the natural way of managing, this new behaviour will take time to become second nature. You should start practising now.

This will involve inventing and then memorising two or three standard phrases to accompany the new behaviour of permanent procrastination. For instance, if a subordinate asks:

'Can you sign the purchase order for the new equipment that we have already discussed?'

You could reply:

'I am going to headquarters tomorrow.'
'I have a meeting in five minutes.'
'I am working on my presentation for next week.'
'I am waiting for a call.'

You do not need to add anything more. Nor does the comment

have to be true. The implication in these replies is that you will sign the document when you get back from headquarters or after the meeting or when you have finished your current task. Let your subordinates infer what they like, but for you, imprecision is a tool. A 'you are disturbing me' tone also works well.

Silence is effective, but you need a lot of practice to pull it off without provoking insistence from your subordinates.

Choose phrases and behaviours that come naturally to you. Practise them and see what works best for you and your subordinates. You might also want to invent a few standard phrases for imposing incremental information.

Remember that at this stage of the process, you are not yet a fully fledged no-decision manager. You have been accepted into the movement but this doesn't mean you should feel obliged to stop making decisions. There is nothing to prevent you from continuing to make decisions while you learn. You, after all, know how to make decisions. A natural no-decision manager does not.

Summary – steps 1–9 to become a no-decision manager

Step 1 Find a no-decision manager.

Step 2 Declare your allegiance to the no-decision movement.

Step 3 Request membership of the Shelter.

Step 4 Take the oath of secrecy and become a member.

You are now officially a no-decision manager BUT do not stop taking decisions just yet – wait until you know a little more

Step 5 Memorise the definition of a no-decision manager:

a person who supposedly manages a team and pretends to control, direct or administer a business, an organisation, a government administration or a public or private institution or any part, and who refuses to arrive at an opinion or conclusion about a matter under consideration or who refuses to make a decision regarding a question or issue, on which there is doubt or dispute especially after considering several alternatives.

Step 6 Learn the three rules of the Shelter:

1. Nothing is ever put in writing.
2. Meetings of the organisation are limited to a maximum of two no-decision managers at any one time.
3. Publications on no-decision management are not permitted.

Step 7 Learn the four pillars of the Shelter: Secrecy, Survival, Skills and System.

Step 8 Memorise Figure 8, The no-decision manager's roles. Learn the three new roles and the four amended ones specially adapted:

New Roles

1. Decision avoidance
2. Secrecy
3. Survival.

Amended Roles

1. Figurehead
2. Liaison
3. Monitor
4. Spokesperson.

Step 9 Discover, learn and above all practise the two instinct-based behaviours of permanent procrastination and imposing incremental information until they become second nature.

Annex 1 summarises the steps required to become a no-decision manager.

3

Understanding the Simple Tactics of Decision Avoidance

'How to' advice for no-decision managers

Read, understand, reflect, experiment and remember

Whatever your personal learning process may be, to become a no-decision manager you will need to be able to implement each of the decision avoidance tactics shown in the sections on active avoidance and delay decisions below. You must read each tactic carefully. There are nine in all. You must make sure that you understand them.

Then you should start reflecting in what circumstances you should use each of these tactics. Some might, for instance, be more effective with certain subordinates compared to others. You might think that some are more appropriate for certain projects or situations compared to others. When your preliminary list is completed you should make a note of each of them.

Next you need to start experimenting. This should be done discreetly over time to ensure that subordinates do not become bewildered by your change in behaviour. After each experiment with a tactic you should record its effectiveness. At the end of this process you will need to go through your records, noting which tactics are effective and with whom. If a tactic did not work well the first time, try it out on another subordinate to see if it's more effective. Some tactics may have to be discarded as not being relevant for your organisation or your position in the company.

When your notes are complete and you are happy with the choices you have made, memorise them. You now have an effective list of your personal basic tactics of the No-Decision-making System ready for immediate use when you make your final decision to become a no-decision manager. After this you should destroy your notes. Remember: keep no written records of no-decision management.

Simple tactics of decision avoidance

Active avoidance

No-decision managers learn early in their careers that they have to live with their 'natural inborn inability' to make decisions. But the two related 'instinct-based behaviours' described in Chapter 2 can't be relied on as the only decision avoidance mechanisms they can use. Young and inexperienced no-decision managers may find these avoidance mechanisms work for them for many months, but eventually they recognise that they require sophistication to keep subordinates at a distance to prevent decision-making over longer periods.

Other mechanisms will be added over time, which the no-decision movement has formed into a complex decision avoidance system called the 'No-decision-making System'.

The first reference to this system in the business context was made obliquely by Robert M. Bramson in *Coping with Difficult People*. Bramson's no-decision managers are called 'stallers', and he notes:

> Stallers do not simply prolong the decision-making process, they avoid it, sometimes to absurd and unproductive limits.

The combined 'absurd and unproductive limits' have now, decades later, been collected and formalised into the current No-decision-making System.

These mechanisms are generally called decision avoidance tactics. They are all deliberately and consciously applied by no-decision managers depending on the organisation they work in, their level in the hierarchy, the type of decision to be made and the emotional state of the subordinate or subordinates requesting the decision. No-decision managers leave nothing to chance.

The system has five different groups of decision avoidance tactics to prevent decision-making. The first group is called 'active avoidance' and includes five tactics with a simple level of complexity and sophistication:

1. Judicious absence
2. Ignoring
3. Physical barriers
4. Artificial agreement
5. Meaningless meetings

Active avoidance tactic 1: Judicious absence
The first, simplest and most popular active avoidance tactic is absence. While they are absent, no-decision managers decree that they cannot make decisions. This way they put themselves in a position not to be available for any decision. Absence signifies being out of the office, usually in an unknown location with the mobile telephone turned off and with no apparent access to emails.

Mere absence on its own, however, is too primitive, so no-decision managers have stolen the concept of 'judicious absence' conceived by Charles Reade in 1870, but they have refined and adapted it to make it more relevant to the no-decision movement.

Judicious absence was invented by the mother of a character called Henry Little in Reade's novel *Put Yourself in His Place*, to describe Henry's forced retreat from an unwanted conversation with his love rival Mr Coventry:

'Judicious absence is a weapon,' said Henry Little's mother. 'And I must show you how and when to use it.'

To be truly judicious, the no-decision manager selects the appropriate timing, fixes a duration and chooses a type of absence. Timing in its simple form is the choice of the most suitable moment to be absent. Absence too soon is a waste. Absence too late means subordinates will increase the pressure for a decision, and so supplementary tactics will have to be used. The ideal duration is as long as credibly possible in the circumstances. But the most important factor is the choice of the appropriate type of judicious absence for each no-decision occasion.

Types of judicious absence

For no-decision managers in senior positions two types of judicious absence are popular. The first is absence without explanation – often called 'judicious abrupt absence' – and the second is absence via travel. Judicious absence through sudden illness is popular for middle managers, and is usually used for important meetings or presentations where a decision will be required. The bout of ill health will start shortly before the meeting.

> Case study 3 – Judicious absence in action
> Oscar is the no-decision director of a large retail store that is part of a national chain. He has been the no-decision store director for many years. His financial controller Sophia has to bear the brunt of Oscar's no-decision tactics.
>
> Whenever head office calls a meeting, Sophia knows that she will almost always attend alone. Her boss invariably calls in with a sudden illness, applying judicious absence to avoid the decisions that he might be called upon to make at the meeting.
>
> Oscar's other favourite trick is to take his holidays at the most critical moments in the year. As he's in retail this means late

September, when orders for the Christmas period have to be filled, or in December, the busiest time of the year when the store is open seven days a week, and, finally, when the annual budget has to be prepared in March.

Oscar never tells his team in advance. But they know that he will take sudden, unannounced, but for them predictable, holidays in September, December and March: judicious absence via holidays.

Comments on case study 3
Of course normal managers sometimes do not turn up to important meetings for various reasons, leaving their subordinates in complicated situations. They might be genuinely ill, incompetent or lazy.

But Sophia knows Oscar is never around when he is most needed. It has become an office joke. She also knows that his repeated, almost systematic absence is just a way for him to get out of decision-making.

Case study 4 – The champion of judicious absence
The champion of judicious absence is Miriam. She is a senior no-decision project manager in charge of several teams implementing new business software in Europe.

She manages to convince her hierarchy to send her to the USA for six months on a top management development course. She leaves her teams for six months, without a boss and with no supervision while she is away. Miriam pushes Henry Little's mother's concept of judicious absence to an extreme level.

Comments on case study 4

> Miriam is considered to have potential for promotion to top management in the future. She has exceptional personal relationships with her boss and key decision-makers who collectively allow her to be absent for six months. She is successful in hiding from her superiors that she is a no-decision manager, despite having been in the company for many years. And on a personal level, being absent, she can legitimately avoid decisions for six months.
>
> Any normal manager would set up a temporary organisation in their department to ensure that it continues to work normally during their absence, for instance appointing a manager to run the department or organising regular calls with the team so that decisions are made.
>
> Miriam just left without organising anything, leaving her team to fend for themselves without a boss for six months.

Other types of judicious absence are of course numerous: visiting headquarters or consulting the boss, attending a congress or exposition, or talking to suppliers or clients, whether these absences are necessary or not.

Active avoidance tactic 2: Ignoring

Following on from judicious absence, no-decision managers use ignoring as the second tactic within the active avoidance arsenal. Ignoring subordinates is a simple and logical follow-on from judicious absence, again recommended by Henry Little's mother. On Henry's return from his judicious absence from Mr Coventry, she next advises disregard. She says to Henry:

> 'Go back to the room with me and put on an imperturbable good humour and ignore him: only mind you do that politely or you will give him an advantage…'

While it would be preposterous to suggest that no-decision managers stole the tactic of disregard from Henry Little's mother, there is no doubt that they have refused to adopt her secondary advice. No-decision managers never ignore subordinates with politeness. They never ignore them with an air of 'good humour'. And they are not concerned about giving anybody any advantage.

The psychology of ignoring is most developed in parenting, where it is used to counteract complaining and tantrums in young children in the hope that consistently ignoring a particular behaviour will encourage them to stop. No-decision managers hope that this tactic will also encourage subordinates to stop making requests for decisions, but the real reason is to avoid indefinitely and delay decision-making.

When their boss comes back from a judicious absence impatient subordinates, eager to get on with their work as quickly as possible, think their no-decision bosses will at last take the long-awaited and urgent decision. However, they systematically ignore these subordinates; they remain unrecognised in the corridor or unacknowledged in meetings, without even a good morning greeting. Their no-decision boss lets them know that they do not exist.

Ignoring, as a tactic in management, is known and well documented. Lynn Taylor in her 2009 book *Tame Your Terrible Office Tyrant* invented a type of manager who does just this, the 'TOT Ignoring Boss', who is always absent and does not reply to emails, with the result that no decisions are made.

More recently, in 2014, Marsha Evans and Elizabeth Gaynor in their book *Surviving and Thriving When Your Boss is a Jerk!* portray a similar type of manager called the 'Avoider' who ignores subordinates totally – no greeting, no eye contact – and makes them feel that they do not exist.

Ignoring is an easy way for no-decision managers to delay decision-making. It can be disruptive because it is such a contrast to their normal friendliness and approachability, but this only makes it more effective.

Active avoidance tactic 3: Physical barriers

After ignoring comes the simple but effective tactic of constructing a physical barrier and positioning a guard to prevent access. The old-fashioned barrier is the door of the no-decision manager's office (if they have one). The guard of course is their secretary or personal assistant.

Nowadays no-decision managers have to invent other more modern barriers such as hiding in a conference room, switching off their phone, an automatic 'out of the office' or 'unavailable for the moment' response to emails, wearing headphones in an open-plan environment, and many others.

Saying, 'I have a conference call in two minutes,' or, 'I am busy at the moment,' is a form of invisible barrier that is the modern equivalent of a physical one.

No-decision managers have a habit of closing the doors of their offices when they are inside, combined with a policy that forbids entry when it is closed. Where an office is not available, they will try to position themselves in a remote part of the building with difficult access far from their team and direct subordinates.

If the no-decision manager is senior enough to have a personal assistant, the assistant is an effective weapon in decision avoidance. The personal assistant can be well-organised, calm, have a professional manner, act with tact and discretion and carry out multi-tasking. But above all no-decision managers need a personal assistant who is trained as a watchdog to protect them from people in the organisation who want them to make decisions: someone fierce, vigilant and faithful.

The no-decision manager will give the PA two lists. First is a list, updated daily, of people who are to be refused entry and whose calls are to be blocked. These are the people in the organisation who are pushing the no-decision manager for a decision.

The second list, also updated daily, names people who are to be allowed entry. These are the people who are currently not asking for a decision to be made. The PA has strict instructions to ensure that the no-decision manager can be only disturbed by these people.

This behaviour is part of the new exaggerated 'liaison role' identified by Mintzberg (see Chapter 2) that has been adapted by the no-decision management movement, where the no-decision manager invites 'interpersonal relationships' with as many people as possible: employees, peers, subordinates and the hierarchy as well as people outside their organisation. Lunches, dinners, one-on-one meetings, or just informal conversations are all used extensively. The no-decision manager grabs any excuse to talk to people to fill the day, knowing that no decision will be possible while they are playing this role.

Active avoidance tactic 4: Artificial agreement

Having exhausted the simple tactics of 'active avoidance', described above, no-decision managers turn to more devious and underhand tactics. For example, to neutralise a request for a decision they will announce that they agree with the subordinate. This tactic is called the 'artificial agreement' and comes in three variations: the 'agree with conditions', the 'vaguely agree' and 'outright agreement'.

Agree with conditions

The no-decision manager will say: 'I agree with your proposal but I need to talk to my boss,' or, 'I need to talk to headquarters.'

They have no intention of speaking to the boss or headquarters, or with anyone else, concerning this potential decision. The objective here is to divert attention away from the no-decision manager to someone else to gain some time.

The subordinate will move on from asking, 'Have you decided?' and will ask, 'Have you talked to your boss or headquarters?' or, 'Have you had the time to talk to your boss yet?'

The no-decision manager can then forget to talk to the boss or promise to talk to them 'next week' or 'next month' or 'next time I see him' or whenever.

Vaguely agree

The 'vaguely agree' response comes in the form of statements like:

'I need more time to think.'

'I agree with your proposal but we must be careful.'

'I agree but we must not rush the decision,' or any other suitably vague excuse avoiding a commitment to act.

Time is not specified. 'Careful' is not defined. A 'rush' is not detailed. The objective is to divert the conversation away from the potential decision to gain more time.

Agree outright

The truly devious response is the outright agreement: 'I agree with your proposal.' It's devious because to the no-decision manager this is just an opinion. And opinions can change.

To the subordinate, though, it is not only an agreement to the proposal but a decision. The subordinate thinks that if the boss has said, 'I agree with your proposal,' that means the boss will make the decision. A decision has at last been made! He or she should know better, but hope is so high and so much effort has been put into getting a decision that any sign from a no-decision boss is accepted, exaggerated and interpreted as such. The subordinate will then prepare the contract for signature or the order for authorisation, but the no-decision manager will not sign it. A signature is a real decision.

The natural consequence of these kinds of 'artificial agreements' will be angry subordinates, who will surely let their no-decision boss know about their displeasure, probably in a passionate exchange. Why does the no-decision manager behave this way, knowing quite well that they will have to face an angry subordinate shouting in outrage? The reason is simple: they'd rather put up with angry shouting than make a decision.

Not making decisions inevitably generates negative emotions in subordinates, so dealing with them is part of the no-decision manager's normal managerial life. In contrast, making a decision is not.

But it goes further: not making the decision is the high point in the daily managerial life of a no-decision manager. They relish these moments of non-decision. A normal manager will be happy to analyse a problem, make a decision and implement it, and will take satisfaction from the successful outcome. A no-decision manager is happy to analyse a problem, avoid the decision but take satisfaction in both the success of the avoidance and the manner in which the avoidance was achieved.

Active avoidance tactic 5: Meaningless meetings

The 'Informational role' is also important to no-decision managers. Mintzberg notes that 'The processing of information is a key part of the manager's job'. No-decision managers do this through the active use of 'information meetings'. Their stated aim is to gather and exchange information, but in reality this is secondary.

Decisions are banned at the outset of the meeting and only an exchange of information or opinions on a subject is expected. So organisations that have too many meetings, or have a culture of management through meetings, are great places for no-decision managers to thrive and grow.

In fact any type of meeting where a decision is not required is actively promoted by no-decision managers.

> **Case study 5 – Meaningless meetings for no-decision managers**
> Jackson, a no-decision manager, is a specialist at organising 'information meetings'. He usually starts with the statement:
>
> > 'Today we are holding an information meeting to ensure that everyone has the same level of information. We will not take any decisions. Everyone please take 20 minutes to update the others on what is going on in your department.'
>
> Jackson's team are exasperated with the number of 'information meetings' he organises. They believe they're a waste of time. Some have stopped attending. They deputise colleagues to go to the meeting in case they can pick up any useful information, which is then shared.

Comments on case study 5

Of course, it is normal to have meetings to share information within a team. When they are legitimate and helpful they do not come under the heading of 'meaningless'. Nor are meaningless meetings restricted to no-decision managers. Any manager can fix a meeting that turns out to be meaningless.

However when they are repetitive, numerous and useless, holding meaningless meetings is a sign of either an incompetent manager or a no-decision manager. This is because they are not useless to no-decision managers. They are an effective method of decision avoidance.

Case study 6 – Devious weekly meetings

James is the no-decision director of a large distribution warehouse. He has a meeting with his management team every Monday morning. His team want the meeting to be a decision-making one where all the unresolved operational issues of the past week can be discussed and decided.

James allows open discussion, but never organises the team's priorities. He refuses to arbitrate differences between team members, fixes no limits on behaviour and decides nothing. The meeting invariably ends up in general chaos.

Comments on case study 6

James is using the weekly meetings to show his boss that he's going through the motions of normal management. He is showing that he is a normal manager. But the real reason for the meeting is to avoid making decisions.

But James is an organised and canny no-decision manager. His meetings have an objective: to discuss and resolve operational

> issues. They have an agenda, a regular schedule and specific attendees. His intentions seem to be the same as any normal manager's.
>
> The inconclusive result, though, is a direct consequence of systematic decision avoidance. It is here that a no-decision management strategy is in evidence. James goes through the actions of a normal manager, but with no results and no decisions.

More disorganised no-decision managers will arbitrarily invite attendees to unprepared meetings with no clear agenda, no stated or obvious purpose, and at irregular intervals, and then, like James, let the meeting run its course with no direction well past the allocated time. Some no-decision managers fill up their day with meetings; the more unproductive and inefficient they are, the better.

Delay decisions

'Delay decisions' are trivial, inconsequential decisions designed to delay the moment of deciding. But because they are decisions in themselves, they do not come naturally to no-decision managers. Some will learn this technique on their own. Others have to be taught by other trained no-decision managers. After some experience they can become experts in these delay decisions.

You will recall from Figure 1 in Chapter 2 that the decision-making process has three steps and no-decision managers do not perform the second step: the act of deciding. The Shelter, however, quickly realised that the first step; the preparation of the decision, was an important phase for no-decision managers.

The Shelter decided that no-decision managers would become experts in preparing the 'matter under consideration'. During their analysis of management literature to help them formalise and become experts in the preparation of the decision, the Shelter came across two books whose ideas they have partly adopted and then modified to help no-decision managers.

Figure 9: Updated decision-making process for a no-decision manager

Step 1	Step 2	Step 3
Preparation of the decision	Act of deciding	Implementation of the decision
Oxford English Dictionary 'The process of deciding regarding a matter under consideration'	Oxford English Dictionary 'The action of deciding'	Oxford English Dictionary 'The result of this action or process; that which has been decided'
A no-decision manager excels in the preparation of the decision	Missing from a no-decision manager's repertoire. The act of deciding does not exist	

The first book is *Principles of Management and Administration* (2004) by D. Chandra Bose, who states:

> The managers have to take a large number of decisions daily to run an organisation.

The no-decision manager does of course make decisions during their busy day, but their 'large number of decisions daily' are not made to 'run the organisation', only to make delay decisions to avoid the final decision.

The no-decision manager's version of Bose's quote becomes:

> No-decision managers have to take a large number of delay decisions daily, not to run an organisation, but to avoid the act of deciding.

Delay decision 1: Incremental information improved

The first of these delay decisions is an extension of the second instinct-based behaviour described in Chapter 2, namely that of the imposing incremental information. No-decision managers find this strategy is not effective enough on its own and they need to try something more systematic and formal, so they've come up with a more sophisticated version called 'incremental information improved'.

This concept has been taken directly from the second book chosen by the Shelter for guidance, namely *Principles of Business Management* (2000) by Arun Kumar and Rachna Sharma. The Shelter was searching for the most comprehensive method in the process of decision-making to turn upside down and to use to delay decision-making.

There is much advice in management literature on the different steps of making a decision. Most commentators see it as a seven-step process, others a six- or five-step one. The more practical guides, usually written by managers themselves, have only four steps: identify, analyse, evaluate alternatives and then just make the decision.

But on page 249 of *Principles of Business Management*, there is a more complicated, complete and clear nine-step decision-making process, as follows:

1. Problem identification
2. Classification and gathering data
3. Diagnosing the problem
4. Developing alternatives
5. Analysing alternatives
6. Evaluation of alternatives
7. Selection of the best alternative
8. Implementation of decision
9. Follow-up.

No-decision managers follow the recommendations in the first six steps of the process precisely.

Many other books were reviewed by the Shelter before they chose Kumar and Sharma – even books written by 'celebrity gurus'. But these gurus use fewer steps and for no-decision managers this is too simple and concise, offering few opportunities to delay making decisions.

Instead of two steps, Kumar and Sharma have constructed five: points three to seven above. This model is attractively comprehensive for no-decision managers and more detailed. It takes so much longer to reach the moment of deciding, which Kumar and Sharma call

'Selection of the Best Alternative'. Just what no-decision managers are looking for! Let's examine how they deal with each of the steps.

1. Problem identification

'Problem identification' is easy for no-decision managers. They clearly do not decide on their own but wait for someone else to identify a problem for a future decision. Pressure will come from somewhere in the organisation – either from their team who get together to try to force an issue that needs addressing, or from the boss.

The response will be to make a delay decision, such as saying that they will set up a committee or appoint someone to study the problem and come up with recommendations. This way they gain time while their team works on the next five steps.

2. Classification and gathering data

This step involves classifying the problem and gathering information. It should answer the questions:

- Who should take the decision?
- Who else needs to be taken into confidence?
- What information is needed and where can it be found?
- Which specialists should be consulted?

The key step here is the third one: finding out what information is needed.

The Shelter has homed in on this as the point at which the decision can be delayed for the longest time, by using the new three i's. The Shelter has decreed that incremental information improved should be exaggerated and extended to include four levels of information that no-decision managers must obtain in this part of the non-decision process.

The first is 'indispensable information', which is the normal level of information that any ordinary manager would need before taking this type of decision. It is not specific to no-decision managers.

The second level is 'insignificant information', usually information that is interesting for the decision-maker but unnecessary. The volume of information requested can be immense, but must be insignificant in terms of its importance to the decision.

The third level, 'ineffective information', sometimes called 'inutile information', is information that has no direct relevance at all to the decision under study. Even if it is totally inappropriate to ask for inutile information, the no-decision manager should request it anyway.

Finally, the no-decision manager will sometimes request the ultimately absurd level of information, 'inept information' – a term invented by the no-decision movement to convey information not related to the decision under study but requested anyway by the no-decision manager. The reasons for this request are explained in detail in Chapter 4.

'Classification and gathering data' is, however, complicated for no-decision managers. In the world of normal managers many decisions would be made in this phase. An organisation needs to be set up, people need to be chosen for the team, a timetable should be developed – a whole process needs to be explained and put into place.

Clearly, it is complex for the no-decision manager to make any of these mini-decisions, even if they are assimilated into a bigger delay decision. Usually, given the pressure and the urgency of the problem, a volunteer will come forward to manage the process. The no-decision manager will normally just let the volunteer go ahead – with, or even better *without*, any explicit approval. If the problem has been handed down from the no-decision manager's boss, they will try to get them to decide on a team leader.

3. Diagnosing the problem
This is left to the team in place. No action is required by the no-decision manager, who is at peace during this phase of the project.

4. Developing alternatives
It is at this point that the no-decision manager can increase the number

of alternatives to be studied and reported on, guaranteeing delay. Members of the team might sit up and wonder why their no-decision boss is suddenly making intelligent suggestions for alternatives to be studied, not realising that this is simply a ruse to delay the process, by giving out more work.

5. Analysing alternatives

What has made Arun Kumar and Rashana Sharma real favourites for no-decision managers is their recommendation in the section 'Analysing Alternatives':

> Again, where none of the alternatives is found suitable to get the expected results, all alternatives should be discarded and a fresh attempt should be made to trace undiscovered alternatives.

While this is of course standard advice in any normal decision-making process, no-decision managers have exaggerated and corrupted the meaning to their own ends. 'Wow!' they say. 'Discard everything and start afresh to develop new alternatives!' This is the ultimate delay decision tactic.

This idea of 'starting afresh' has been a boon for no-decision managers. It clearly indicates that decision-making is not a linear, logical process to be applied in a given order. Until this idea cropped up, no-decision managers had applied their decision avoidance tactics in order: first instinct-based behaviours, then active avoidance before moving on to delay decisions. Since the publication of Kumar and Sharma's book in 2000, no-decision managers have been encouraged to mix their delay decision tactics and go back and forth using them randomly according to which tactic is the most relevant.

6. Evaluation of alternatives

In this phase no-decision managers are active. First, they make sure the number of alternatives is as high as possible and each one is analysed and reported on thoroughly. Second, the alternatives are 'presented without prejudice'. They do not bring preferences into the analysis, as managers are supposed to do. Normal managers will recommend a preferred alternative. No-decision managers do not care which solution is chosen as long as they are not the ones who have to make the choice. And anyway, giving a definite proposal of a preferred solution actually requires a decision to be made.

7. Selection of the best alternative

'Selection of the best alternative' is decision time. The instinct of permanent procrastination will usually reappear for most no-decision managers at this moment. Doing nothing is the easiest option, at least for a while.

Chandra Bose's definition of a manager in *Principles of Management and Administration* (2004) includes this description of their role:

> To come up with solutions to difficult problems and to follow through with their decisions even when doing so may be unpleasant.

No-decision managers never come up with any solution to a problem, difficult or not – nor do they follow through with a decision, whether unpleasant or not.

Accordingly, at the end of the consideration of alternatives, no-decision managers decide nothing. They consider the report on the various alternatives to be completed and push it up to the boss for a decision. 'Selection of the best alternative' is not considered part of their job.

Once the decision has been made by someone else, no-decision managers are ready to move on to the next two steps of the process.

8. Implementation of decision

Implementing the decision is a whole new opportunity for decision avoidance that will be described in the next chapter.

9. Follow-up

Follow-up, sometimes called monitoring of the results of the decision, is optional for no-decision managers. Since they did not make the decision in the first place, they can use their superior analysing skills to lay out the positive and negative impact of the decision without any personal bias.

Delay decision 2: Announce an action

The second delay decision tactic is for the no-decision manager to announce an action in the future that is designed to encourage the subordinate to think that a decision, if not imminent, will eventually be made. An illusion, of course.

This announcement will often come, however, after the no-decision manager's subordinates have pressured them heavily to decide.

Set a deadline

In its simplest form 'announcing an action' occurs when the no-decision manager sets a deadline, or apparently sets a deadline, maybe saying something like: 'I will make the decision next week.'

Next week comes and goes and no decision is made. Meanwhile the no-decision manager has had a week of peace without being pestered for a decision.

It takes time to understand that a no-decision manager is never stressed by a deadline for a decision. No amount of pressure to hurry an urgent decision will affect them. A deadline exists only to be postponed and rescheduled after they have enjoyed the moment of missing the first deadline. Effective no-decision managers will be able to change deadlines three or four times before finally not making the decision.

Case study 7 – Announcing actions

Freddie is a no-decision regional manager in a small construction company in the north of England. Two of his subordinates are in conflict: Isaac, a site manager, and Finley, the sales manager. Grace, the Human Resources manager, intervenes to inform Freddie of the conflict in his team. She recommends that he set up a meeting with the four of them to resolve the conflict.

Freddie, as an experienced no-decision regional manager, does nothing. He hopes there will be no follow-up, no reminder, and that the issue will just go away.

When Grace comes back to remind him, Freddie announces to Grace that he will first talk to Isaac and then get back to her. He does not talk to Isaac and does not get back to her.

When next reminded by Grace, Freddie announces that he will set up the meeting she recommends with Isaac, Finley and Grace to discuss the matter within the next few weeks. He does not set up the meeting.

Finally, in frustration, Grace calls the meeting herself. Freddie lets Isaac and Finley air their feelings, discusses reasons for the conflict, agrees that there is a problem that needs to be resolved – and then does nothing.

Grace is back to where she started, with an understanding that help will never come. Giving help would be a decision for Freddie, which he is never going to make.

Comments on case study 7
Freddie promises actions twice. First, he says he'll talk to Isaac, then he says he'll set up a meeting. But he does neither. When Grace sets up the meeting, he decides nothing.

With an open discussion in the presence of the boss and Human Resources, a conflict situation might resolve itself. Freddie, though, is a true no-decision manager, and does not arbitrate. Nor does he tell Grace to find a solution. For him, this would be a decision. Nor does Grace propose to resolve the issue herself.

Decision meeting

Ironically, no-decision managers often use decision meetings as a decision avoidance tactic. They may say: 'Let's have a meeting next month to decide.'

Until the meeting is held, the no-decision manager has some respite from being pestered for a decision.

During the meeting, there is an active discussion on the pros and cons of the alternatives. Subordinates give their opinions freely and at the end of the meeting turn to their no-decision boss for a decision. They do not decide.

Sometimes they give a reason:

'We need more information,' or
'This particular point was not well documented.'

Sometimes they do not give a reason. They may even set a date for another decision meeting. But even at that meeting they do not decide.

Case study 8 – Using decision meetings

Sienna, a no-decision manager, likes to organise 'decision meetings' where each member of her team gives a structured opinion, laying out the advantages and disadvantages. This is followed by a free discussion. Having heard the different points of view, everyone expects Sienna to arbitrate and make a decision, but she announces: 'No decision will be made today.'

Her team is angry that she won't decide, so Sienna fixes another 'decision meeting' and requests a more detailed analysis of two or three points that she says have not been investigated enough.

At the end of the second decision meeting, she again announces that no decision will be made at the meeting. This time the reaction of her team is not as strong as before, so Sienna formally ends the meeting and avoids the decision for ever.

> *Comments on case study 8*
> In many instances a normal manager might have quite legitimate reasons to request additional analysis on any of the points discussed at this type of meeting. So Sienna's request is one that any manager might make.
>
> However, normal managers will eventually make a decision when the information is sufficient and the analysis is complete. No-decision managers do not. Sienna, as a no-decision manager, will still not decide, however many meetings she calls.

Delay decision 3: Task force

Task forces are normally set up to help decide a complicated management issue that needs to be resolved. But no-decision managers in top management set up task forces to avoid decision-making.

> **Case study 9 – An ingenious task force**
> Sophie is the no-decision manager of Eastern Europe for a corporation. Her direct boss is the CEO of Europe but through her manufacturing plants also has a dotted line responsibility to the vice president of Manufacturing in the corporate headquarters, a sort of secondary boss in the head office.
>
> Sophie receives a question from headquarters:
>
> 'How will you rationalise production? We have three plants: one in Austria, one in Poland and one in Russia, all making essentially the same product. What plans do you have to improve efficiency and productivity and lower production costs?'
>
> Sophie faces a dilemma. She must send a clear proposal to headquarters. She innovates by creating a permanent task force headed up by one of her managers, Daniel.

The objective of this permanent task force, Sophie tells Daniel, is to study the important questions brought up by her boss or by headquarters.

As a true no-decision manager, she gives instructions to Daniel not to make recommendations but to come up with the maximum number of alternatives possible in a formal written report for the manufacturing project.

Daniel and his team can take as much time as they need, but they must be ready to make interim reports at short notice, in the event that Sophie's boss or headquarters become impatient. While the team is working, Sophie has a period of peace from being pestered for proposals from headquarters.

Sophie of course never makes any specific proposals based on Daniel's reports. She just sends the reports up to headquarters and waits for a reaction.

Comments on case study 9
By setting up a permanent in-house task force headed by Daniel, Sophie is doing what a normal manager might do. While the task force is working, she does not need to make decisions. And when the analysis is complete, the report is sent up to headquarters for a decision without a proposition.

Sophie innovates by institutionalising a delay decision tactic and setting up a permanent task force, effectively creating a new structure in her company.

Delay decision 4: Consultant

Instead of only using people from inside the company, no-decision managers can also draw on outside consultants to artificially extend the time frame or postpone the decision-making moment. Consultants can take many months to prepare and send in their report. While they are working, no-decision managers have a period of peace. The solution the consultant proposes is of no consequence to them. Conclusions from consultants make it easier for the no-decision manager to push the decision-making up the hierarchy.

> **Case study 10 – Misusing a consultant**
> Liam works as a consultant with Zackary, a senior no-decision sales manager. In his region Zackary has two types of salespeople: those who sell products made by the company and those who sell products from independent manufacturers.
>
> Because the margins are lower for the products purchased from independent manufacturers, headquarters asks Zackary how to increase profitability of the sales of these products.
> Liam's report comes up with four scenarios for the 'development of alternatives':
>
> 1. Eliminate all products from independent manufacturers,
> 2. Keep only the two most profitable products from independent manufacturers,
> 3. Keep all products from independent manufacturers, or
> 4. Develop an independent manufacturers' business to increase their numbers throughout Europe to get economies of scale to improve profitability.
>
> Zackary has the authority to decide alone on scenarios 1 to 3, but relies on the fourth scenario to explain that the decision is a corporate one regarding the strategy of the group and not one that Zackary can make.
>
> *Comments on case study 10*
> Zackary successfully pushes the decision up to corporate headquarters, using a consultant's involvement, and then just

waits for the decision. In this case corporate headquarters decide on scenario number 1 – to stop selling products not manufactured by the group.

Zackary then just implements the decision. Simple!

Senior managers use consultants to help them make difficult decisions. Zackary is doing exactly this with his consultant Liam. But in this instance Zackary has the authority to make decision number 1 on his own, which is in line with corporate policy to phase out products from independent manufacturers. He doesn't need a consultant for this decision. But Zackary is a no-decision manager and cannot make a decision, so he has to find another way.

A normal manager would have made a recommendation based on the consultant's report. Zackary does not. If a normal manager made decision number 3, he might for instance present number 4 as a strategic alternative for the group, even if it was not part of corporate policy. Zackary, as a no-decision manager, just sends the report up to headquarters and waits.

Business decision vs. delay decision

Setting up a task force is a business decision. Appointing a consultant is a business decision. For no-decision managers, though, these are not business decisions, they are delay decisions that will enable them to avoid the ultimate decisions.

Setting up a task force diverts valuable resources from the organisation. Appointing a consultant takes up employee time, is usually expensive and can have consequences for the financial situation of the organisation. However, no-decision managers aren't worried about coming up with a successful solution to the problem at hand. Their objective is simply to delay the final decision for as long as possible and, through the written report, find someone else to make the decision in their place.

Figure 10, The simple tactics of decision avoidance, summarises graphically the two instinct-based behaviours, the five active avoidance tactics and the four different delay decisions that make up the decision avoidance repertoire of the no-decision manager.

Figure 10: The simple tactics of decision avoidance

Instinct-based behaviours	Active avoidance	Delay decisions
Permanent procrastination Imposing incremental information	Judicious absence Ignoring Physical barriers Personal assistant Artificial agreement Meaningless meetings	Incremental information improved Announce an action Task force Consultant

Summary – steps 10–11 to become a no-decision manager

Step 10 Read, understand, reflect, experiment and remember the five active avoidance tactics.

Step 11 Read, understand, reflect, experiment and remember the four different delay decisions.

Annex 1 summarises the steps required to become a no-decision manager.

4

Understanding the Complex Tactics of Decision Avoidance

'How to' advice for no-decision managers

Now that you have mastered the basics, you need to learn three more sophisticated and devious methods to delay and even eliminate decision-making:

1. Deviated delegation
2. Implementing decisions of others
3. Outrageous behaviour.

The first method is a deviated form of delegation in which you systematically search your organisation for someone to make your decisions. The second is implementing these decisions after you have found another manager to decide. And the third and most sophisticated method is to use 'outrageous behaviour' to send messages to subordinates.

Deviation of delegation

Managers generally see delegation as a way to get things done more quickly and a motivational tool to help develop the skills of their subordinates. Most of the definitions of delegation in management explain it as a transfer of power from the boss to the subordinate. A boss gives his subordinate an act to carry out or a decision to make but keeps the accountability for the outcome, regardless of what the subordinate does or decides.

And this delegation involves three conscious actions by a manager:

1. Giving authority to the subordinate to make a decision
2. Keeping full responsibility for whatever decision is made
3. Monitoring and helping the subordinate through the decision-making process.

Most dictionaries use words like 'assign', 'share', 'transfer', 'entrust', 'commit' or 'deliver' to describe the act of delegation. You as a no-decision manager will never do any of this, because these actions require a decision on your part. You must forget how to delegate. Instead you need to learn how to 'deviate delegation'.

Deviation of delegation 1: Deviated downward delegation

To 'deviate delegation' to a subordinate you need to learn three new rules:

1. You must wait for the subordinate to take the initiative. It is always the subordinate, never you, the no-decision manager, who takes the initiative on a task normally delegated by the manager or to make a decision normally made by the boss.
2. You renounce all responsibility for the decision, unless your boss considers it to be an excellent one, in which case you personally take the credit.
3. You monitor nothing and never help a subordinate.

These are the fundamentals of 'deviated downward delegation'. You must learn them and make them second nature.

Subordinates refer to this kind of situation as 'take it anyway'.

This is because whatever happens the subordinate always decides without any intervention from you, their no-decision boss.

> **Case study 11 – Working with deviated downward delegation**
>
> Emelia is an experienced no-decision director. Jamie works in her team as a senior marketing manager.
>
> Jamie wants to convert his annual magazine and newspaper advertising into a short three-month TV advertising campaign for a new product to be introduced in September. For this radical change in the marketing strategy he needs a decision from Emelia. He knows, however, that he is not going to get one.
>
> Jamie prepares a new marketing plan including all the elements required for a TV campaign: market research, an analysis of the competition, the timing of the spots and TV channels. He chooses an agency to help him with filming, booking and final tracking.
>
> When the report is complete, he arranges a meeting with his boss Emelia together with the advertising agency to present his analysis and proposals to her. Jamie organises the meeting as though a decision has been made by them both.
>
> Instead of saying, 'This is my proposal, what do you think of it?' Jamie says, 'This is what we have decided to do for the launch of our new product in September.'
>
> Any opposition to Jamie's plan is a decision for Emelia, which she will not make. An approval is also a decision. Emelia neither agrees nor disagrees, so Jamie decides in her place and the advertising campaign goes ahead.

Having discovered the tactic of deviated downward delegation, the Shelter soon found out that delegation solely to subordinates was too restrictive. So they extended deviation upwards, sideways and diagonally in organisations. In fact anyone is welcome to make a decision that should normally be taken by the no-decision manager.

The Shelter's definition of deviated delegation becomes:

> Deviated delegation is the invisible acceptance of a decision taken by anyone in the organisation that should have been made by the no-decision manager, who silently refuses any accountability for the outcome of the decision unless the decision is approved by management.

With this new definition, you are now able to move deviated delegation into different directions within the hierarchy. When you move it to the boss it is called 'deviated upward delegation'. When you move it to a colleague it is called 'deviated sideways delegation'. When you move it to someone in headquarters it is called 'deviated diagonal delegation'.

But you must never explicitly give the authority to make a decision on your behalf. This is Rule Number 1 above. Nor must you explicitly offer such authority. The initiative always comes from the other person – never from you.

Deviation of delegation 2: Deviated upward delegation
Deviated upward delegation is clearly the most convenient, elegant solution for you. Not only is the decision made by the boss, but the boss automatically takes direct responsibility for it. You must spend a lot of your time and invent as many ways as possible to convince your boss to make decisions for you. You need to find a process to persuade him or her to make as many decisions as possible in your place.

The behaviours relating to deviated upward delegation are

explained by Gini Graham Scott in her book *A Survival Guide for Working with Bad Bosses*, where she devotes a long section to what she calls the 'No-Boss Boss' – a manager who allows someone else to make a decision. This tactic is the same as the one used by no-decision managers on their bosses.

Deemed decision

But the Shelter is intelligent enough to know that the boss will never make all decisions all the time, especially the simple, trivial ones. So they have developed the concept of the 'deemed decision':

> Give information to the boss and watch the reaction.

A positive comment or reaction from the boss is a clear instruction to decide. A negative comment is an instruction not to make this decision. But (and this is the essence of a deemed decision), no reaction to a pending simple or trivial decision is considered to be an instruction from the boss to go ahead.

For the more important decisions that the no-decision managers must make alone, the deemed decision concept only applies to negative reactions or comments from the boss. Here, as with the trivial decisions, a negative comment from the boss is an instruction not to proceed. No reaction to information on a pending important decision is considered to be a 'wait, do nothing' sign. A positive comment is not sufficient to be a deemed decision so you must not make a decision on that basis. You must wait until you receive a direct order from your boss.

The Shelter has prepared Figure 11, The deemed decision, as a memory aid to help no-decision managers learn by heart its application.

Figure 11: The deemed decision

Type of decision that the no-decision manager wants the boss to take	If the reaction of the boss is the following:	Then the no-decision manager acts as follows:
Simple or trivial decision	No reaction	Take the decision as a deemed decision of the boss
Simple or trivial decision	Favourable reaction	Take the decision as a deemed decision of the boss
Simple or trivial decision	Unfavourable reaction from the boss on the decision to be made	Do not take the decision
Important decision	No reaction from the boss on receiving the information relating to the important decision	Wait, do nothing – no reaction means that no decision has yet been made by the boss
Important decision	Favourable reaction to the information relating to the important decision	The reaction is not sufficient to be a deemed decision. The no-decision manager must wait for a direct order from the boss
Important decision	Unfavourable reaction to the information relating to the important decision	Do not take the decision

Some examples of what to do for some typical trivial decisions are given below.

Travel

You need to give your subordinate Patrick permission to travel but as a no-decision manager you do not decide, so you get your boss to decide for you. You just need to say to your boss:

> 'Patrick has made a request to travel to Rome to negotiate prices with supplier X.'

Then you wait for a reaction.

Both the decision for Patrick to travel and the choice of the supplier X are decisions you would normally make on your own, without approval from your boss.

No reaction from your boss is a deemed decision and an approval for Patrick to travel.

A positive comment such as: 'Yes, that supplier is very professional,' is equivalent to two direct orders from your boss. The first is, 'Let Patrick travel to Rome'. The second is, 'Work with this supplier.' So if Patrick comes back from his trip to Rome with a proposal to work with this supplier, you implement the deemed decision of your boss and inform them:

'We have chosen to work with supplier X and have negotiated lower prices with them.'

However, a negative comment from your boss such as, 'I have never liked supplier X,' would again be equivalent to two direct orders: 'Patrick must not travel to Rome,' and 'You must not work with this supplier.'

A semi-negative comment such as, 'Supplier X has always been expensive in the past,' is again equivalent to two direct orders to you, the no-decision manager. The first is, 'Let Patrick travel to Rome,' and the second is, 'Do not work with this supplier.'

All this is part of the no-decision tactic to 'move decisions to the boss'. Whether the decision is relevant for the business is not important. If your boss agrees, then you agree. If the boss does not agree, you take his lead and disagree as well.

Expense reports

An exchange between you and your boss on expense reports could go like this:

> 'I have to sign the expense reports later this week, but travel expenses are well above budget this month.'

The reply might be:

> 'Well, make sure that next month you do not have the same problem.'
> 'But overall expenses are on budget.'
> 'But this month you had an important convention, didn't you?'

These comments are all neutral comments relating to a minor decision that is not really important for your boss. But according to the concept of the deemed decision they mean that you have been ordered to sign the expense reports.

Now it is natural even for a normal manager to try to get the opinion of their boss. This is especially true of important or difficult decisions, but the no-decision managers take this much further and pester their bosses even in the case of the minor, trivial ones.

Important decisions

You must remember that the deemed decision concept does not work with important decisions. For these you need to obtain a direct order from your boss.

Case study 12 – Working with important decisions

Hugo works as a no-decision section head in a large research and development department. Hugo's direct boss is the vice president of the whole department.

During the preparation of the strategic plan, Hugo and his boss have many important decisions to make. Strategic choices have to be made, and a detailed roadmap must be drawn up with future dates for the introduction of new products. Options and choices are numerous. They have to take into account the limitations of manpower, money and time. Hugo as a no-decision manager is not able to propose anything for his department.

His tactic therefore is to take his team's propositions and arrange a meeting with his boss to get him to decide. Luckily for Hugo, his department is so important to the overall group that his boss decides for him. Hugo simply has to carry out the boss's instructions.

Comments on case study 12
It is normal for a manager to consult their boss before an important decision, especially one as critical as a strategic plan, and this is what Hugo does.

What is less normal is that Hugo just puts together his team's proposals without any of his own input. Then he waits for his boss to make the important decisions for him.

Deemed instruction

A second concept that the Shelter has developed is the 'deemed instruction'. Any guideline received from corporate headquarters is deemed to be an instruction to follow. It is equivalent to a direct order from your boss. You can often use this when you have to determine annual salary increases or the annual budget.

Annual budget
Most budgets will come with corporate assumptions. You should treat them as 'deemed instructions' to be followed when preparing your budget.

If, for instance, headquarters' guidelines specify that sales should increase by 40% and profits by 60%, this will be what you present as your budget. Whether it is possible to carry out is irrelevant. Whether it is realistic is also irrelevant. You present what headquarters wants to see.

Some normal managers also use this tactic, so it is not specific to no-decision managers. But most normal managers will present what they think they can do and argue their case with the boss before applying the corporate guidelines. You might have done just this before you decided to become a no-decision manager. But doing this involves making a decision, so you absolutely must not take this course of action. You must forget the past.

An annual budget without guidelines, however, will be a real problem for you. When you're faced with this you must find out what your boss expects for your division or department. These expectations can then be considered as corporate instructions or deemed decisions and you can use them in your budget. Whether it is possible to carry them out is irrelevant. Whether they are realistic for the next year is also irrelevant.

Salary increases

When it comes to salary increases, bosses are often given guidelines; for example, 'Salary increase should not exceed 2% for the year.' If you are in middle management in charge of a department you just need to make a proposal to increase the salary of each employee in your team by 2%. Ordinary managers often call this the 'communist commendation'. All employees are equal so should get the same increase in salary.

If you are more senior you just wait for your managers to give you their salary increase proposals. If the total increases exceed the 2%, you reject them all and tell them to revise them downwards, several times if necessary, until they come to less than or equal to the 2% guideline from headquarters. This then becomes your proposal. You are following the headquarters guideline as an order: the 'deemed instruction'.

If, however, there is no guideline your life becomes more complicated yet again and things may even get dangerous. You will have to search for an opinion from your boss. You can do this by looking for a deemed decision from your boss giving some information on the salary increase process so far, by saying something like:

> 'My team has proposed the salary increases. I have not changed anything. The overall increase for my department is 3.5%. Two

people have been recommended for an increase of more than 6%, and three others for no salary increase at all.'

You can treat no comment from your boss as a deemed decision, so you are now free to make these proposals for the salary increases in your department. You can treat any other comments from your boss as direct orders to change the proposal.

This information-giving process is not that different from what goes on between a normal manager and their boss. A normal manager would also be seeking the boss's opinion on their proposal to see if in principle the boss was in agreement before the final decision was made. A 6% increase might be excessive. The boss might want to know who the subordinates who have a zero increase are, and why zero is proposed. He might think that an overall 3.5% increase is too much.

A normal manager, though, would have actually decided these increases and would be testing them out on his boss. A no-decision manager has decided nothing. They have just put forward what their own managers have proposed in the hope that this will be sufficient.

Deviation of delegation 3: Deviated diagonal delegation
Deviated diagonal delegation is your next best option if your boss does not decide. This involves persuading a colleague of your boss or someone in headquarters to make it. This option is useful if you work in a company where managers often have multiple bosses, i.e. in a matrix organisation and 'dotted line' responsibilities or in an organisation with a prolific headquarter staff.

> **Case study 13 – Discovering deviated diagonal delegation**
> Logan is an experienced no-decision sales manager working in a matrix organisation where product managers in headquarters have a dotted line responsibility for sales in his country.
>
> Hillary (who is not a no-decision manager) is one of the headquarter product managers who has a new product to

introduce worldwide. Thomas is a regional sales manager in Logan's team. He does not want to introduce this product for many reasons, which he lays out in a detailed and convincing report.

The decision to introduce the product is Logan's to make with Thomas, while Hillary's responsibility is to influence and recommend but not decide. However, she is adamant that the product be introduced in all regions of the world without exception.

Logan agrees with Hillary and lets her decide. The product is introduced but fails miserably.

Comments on case study 13
In this instance Logan has a 50% chance of acting as a normal manager who might agree with Hillary or agree with Thomas.

But Logan is a no-decision manager, so he has only one option. Hillary is a senior manager from headquarters who is encouraging him to introduce the product in his region. He has found someone to make a decision for him, so he capitulates and allows Hillary to decide.

He has deviated delegation diagonally to the dotted line boss. Resistance to Hillary's opinion is anyway a decision, which he would not make. A no-decision manager like Logan will systematically agree with all proposals made by headquarters.

This does not mean that normal managers who agree with someone in Hillary's position are automatically no-decision managers. But if they systematically agree with all propositions from a person in Hillary's position and they never make their own decisions then they are no-decision managers.

Crisis

A crisis is another occasion for you to deviate delegation diagonally. Crises need experts and these experts can become the decision-makers.

> ### Case study 14 – Managing a crisis with deviated diagonal delegation
> Henry is a no-decision country manager. Mitra is his IT manager.
>
> A flood in the computer room paralyses Henry's company. The warehouse and the manufacturing plant come to a standstill and none of the office staff can use their computers. Henry calls the senior IT manager at headquarters, who naturally takes over the problem and manages it directly with Mitra.
>
> Henry as a true no-decision manager just sits back and does nothing.
>
> *Comments on case study 14*
> At a first glance Henry's action could be the natural behaviour of any normal manager. After all, Henry does not have the technical expertise to manage the IT department in such a crisis.
>
> But this crisis is not technical. It is a business crisis. The boss needs to give direction to the IT team on which department has priority in the plan to start the computers. Should manufacturing be started before distribution? Are some clients or products to be given priority over others? Should the backup system be activated? If so, for which parts of the business? Should manual processes be introduced in some business functions? These and many other decisions must be made.
>
> The boss here is Henry. As a no-decision manager he does nothing. He lets his managers negotiate directly with the senior

> IT manager, who in turn decides on the priorities for the business after these discussions. A normal manager would be active in the decision-making process, evaluating different alternatives to decide which was best for the business.
>
> Henry deviates delegation diagonally to the senior IT manager from headquarters and lets his team sort out the problem.

In a crisis situation no-decision managers often create an impression of serenity and calm. So you need to adopt this sort of attitude. You need to show that you feel no pressure to resolve the crisis. Resolving it yourself will involve decisions, but your main concern is the opposite – avoiding decisions. You need to find a decision-maker through deviated delegation.

If you cannot find a decision-maker then set up meetings. If, for instance, a strike looms, a major customer goes bankrupt or a supplier reneges on a contract, you go in to the talks appearing friendly, seeming to understand the situation, giving clear opinions and finally promising an action.

Coming out of your meeting the participants should feel reassured, confident even, that an agreement has been reached or the solution has been found. However, as a follow-up you should just do nothing and decide nothing.

Deviation of delegation 4: Deviated sideways delegation

Deviated sideways delegation is another way you can avoid a decision. Here you persuade a colleague to make a decision in your place. However, it's not often possible to move a decision sideways to another manager at the same hierarchical level. If you have a common project it might be possible for the other manager to take the lead and make the key decisions. If you are a senior manager you will find this option almost impossible, though, so it is best not to spend too much time searching. If you are in middle management it is easier.

Case study 15 – Skilful use of deviated sideways delegation

Evelyn is a no-decision sales and marketing director. She is responsible for fixing sales prices in her region. A new product is being introduced and so Evelyn must decide the new sales price in each of the regions.

Her team calculates the proposed prices taking into account corporate guidelines, ensuring that prices are consistent between regions, checking that gross margins are in line with those of the budget after consulting each regional marketing manager. The final decision is Evelyn's to make. But being a no-decision manager she does not make it.

She goes to her colleague, the regional finance director, and asks:

'Can you give your OK for the prices of the new product line? We need your signature before we issue the formal price list and instructions to the region.'

The regional finance director signs off and Evelyn now has her decision made for her by someone else. She has successfully used deviated sideways delegation.

Comments on case study 15

In most organisations it is normal that Finance participates in price changes. So there is nothing odd about Evelyn's request to the regional finance director.

The only sign that Evelyn is a no-decision manager is that she waits for the authorisation from Finance before she agrees to the price increase. Her manoeuvre is subtle and discreet to ensure that she seems as normal a manager as possible.

Remember that the key rule in deviated delegation is always to wait for someone to come forward. You can hint or imply, but you never make a direct request and you certainly do not delegate in the usual manner. Remember, too, not to take any responsibility for the decision made unless your boss thinks it is a good one. Monitor nothing, and never help in the decision-making process.

Do not forget the two new concepts in deviated upward delegation, which will help in getting decisions made for you: the deemed decision for the simple decisions and the deemed instruction from guidelines coming from headquarters.

Implement the decisions of others

Having managed to persuade someone else to decide for them, no-decision managers excel at implementing the decisions of others. As a normal manager coming into no-decision management, this is not something you will find difficult. Remember that as a no-decision manager it is only the *act of deciding* that you cannot carry out. Implementation is OK. To illustrate the point more clearly, we need to go back to the definition of what a decision is.

Figure 12, Final decision-making process for a no-decision manager, shows the same table as Figure 9, but now the table is complete with the addition of the shaded text noting that no-decision managers excel in the implementation of decisions made by others. The table shows that no-decision managers are not able to perform Step 2 of the decision-making process, but are experts in Steps 1 and 3.

There are two simple things you need to remember when implementing decisions:

1. Implementing a decision can be used as a tactic to avoid other pending decisions
2. Decisions must be implemented precisely.

Figure 12: Final decision-making process for a no-decision manager

Step 1	Step 2	Step 3
Preparation of the decision	Act of deciding	Implementation of the decision
The Oxford English Dictionary 'The process of deciding regarding a matter under consideration'	*The Oxford English Dictionary* 'The action of deciding'	*The Oxford English Dictionary* 'The result of this action or process; that which has been decided'
A no-decision manager excels in the preparation of the decision	Missing from a no-decision manager's repertoire The act of deciding does not exist	**A no-decision manager excels in the implementation of decisions made by others**

Tactic to avoid other pending decisions

It is important to remember that the main objective of implementing decisions of others is to avoid making decisions yourself. And you need to spell it out to your subordinates that when you are implementing you cannot make decisions in other areas at the same time. Appropriate responses to decision requests are:

> 'Wait until I have implemented these decisions, then get back to me.'
> 'I am busy implementing this important decision from headquarters, so please wait until I have finished before bringing up any other issues.'

You now have a valid excuse to put off all the decisions on the waiting list. Implementation then becomes in itself a sophisticated form of decision avoidance. In reality your business or department is effectively shut down while you are implementing decisions.

Case study 16 – Avoiding decision-making by implementing the decisions of others

Hannah is the no-decision regional manager responsible for Spain and Portugal. She has just been promoted following a take-over, with an objective to reorganise four merged companies into one covering the two countries. She now has four IT managers, four logistics departments, four financial directors with their respective teams, four HR directors, and four buildings in two countries.

Hannah has many important decisions to make in a relatively short time but her instructions from the integration committee at headquarters are clear. She must create one department out of the four existing ones. She needs to choose the manager to run it. Then she has to fire most of the others. Her company in Spain is to take over everything and only the managers of her company in Spain will survive. Buildings of the company taken over are to be closed down and sold. All of the processes or systems of the company taken over are to be abandoned. The merger is to be completed within 12 months.

But as a no-decision manager Hannah has no decisions to make. All she has to do is follow the instructions of the integration committee, which are:

1. Keep your organisation in Spain
2. Close down all the others
3. Keep your managers in Spain
4. Dismiss all others

With this she obtains a year's holiday from making other decisions.

Many of Hannah's close managers do not realise that she

is a no-decision manager at all. She appears to be making important decisions at an incredible rate, while in reality she is merely following instructions.

Comments on case study 16
In this type of situation, no-decision managers are indistinguishable from normal managers. Each carries out both orders from headquarters.

On closer examination, however, it's possible to see some differences. A normal manager will take initiatives in the integration process, adapting them to the local situation. Hannah as a no-decision manager does not. This task is so important that she easily postpones and avoids decision-making in her other areas of responsibility. She uses it as a tactic to avoid these other decisions.

Implement decisions precisely

You must learn to become an expert in implementing the decisions of others. What you will find different, though, is that you will have to implement the decisions precisely and to the letter regardless of the consequences for the business or organisation. Nothing should be questioned.

If, for instance, the most recent hires are all in one section of the manufacturing plant and firing them would seriously disorganise overall production, you must nevertheless implement the lay-offs as requested. As a no-decision manager, the consequence of the decision is not important to you.

A normal manager, when faced with a counterproductive order from above that would damage the local organisation, would inform their boss of the possible harmful consequences before implementing the decision. A competent manager would inform headquarters and propose an alternative or amended decision before doing anything. You just implement. Informing headquarters is a decision, as is proposing an alternative. You simply carry out the instructions and implement the decision regardless of the consequences.

Advantages of implementing but not taking decisions

New position

For a normal manager starting a new job is pretty challenging. There are so many things to learn, other managers and employees to meet and evaluate, networks to set up, and often new technology to understand. It is an intense and stressful time.

No-decision managers find this process easy. They go through the motions of a new manager but have no decisions to make and just implement those of their boss. Their status as a true no-decision manager is invisible to their subordinates. The initial reaction from their direct reports will naturally be favourable. No one knows that the decisions being made are coming directly from above. For no-decision managers this happy state can sometimes last for many months.

A rewarding activity

Implementing important decisions is rewarding for no-decision managers. As these important decisions often take a long time to implement, they suspend the pressure from subordinates for other pending decisions. These are often organisational or strategic.

They may come in the form of instructions from top management to:

'Reduce the headcount by 10%.'
'Transfer production to Eastern Europe.'
'Outsource administration to India.'
'Consolidate and centralise marketing in Brussels.'
'Close down the manufacturing plant.'

But these top-down decisions need to come with precise instructions to follow to the letter without interpretation.

A precise instruction, for instance, would be, 'Reduce the headcount in manufacturing before the end of the year – recent hires to be fired first.'

This is precise enough and will be implemented with a rapidity and energy that will astound colleagues and subordinates, who are more used to inaction by their manager.

Some subordinates will start to doubt that they do in fact have a no-decision boss. This period of decision implementation will last a few weeks depending on the size of the project, but then the frenzy will end as abruptly as it started, with the no-decision manager returning to their decision avoidance routine.

Illusion of decision-making

No-decision managers in fact enjoy implementing the decisions of others. It gives them the illusion that they have made a decision themselves, and it gives the impression to subordinates that they have at last decided something. They try to show to the whole organisation that the decision is theirs, and this creates a moment of doubt over whether they are really no-decision managers.

As a novice no-decision manager you, however, will not have the same sensation. You might enjoy implementing decisions as a reminder of your previous life as an ordinary manager, but you do not need the illusion that you have made a decision, because you did actually make them before. Remember that a hereditary no-decision manager has had no experience of decision-making at all.

Subordinates may sometimes be persuaded that their no-decision boss has suddenly decided something. This situation is true for some of the people some of the time. But most subordinates are not duped. They know from the nature of the decisions that their no-decision manager has decided nothing and will know that the decision has probably come from above, but certainly not from their no-decision boss.

A chance to do something else

A period of intensive implementation gives you a chance to do something other than working the No-decision-making System. It is a chance to fill your day with activities that will move your business or department forward. Hereditary no-decision managers are intelligent enough to recognise that their non-decisions hold back their business or department, and this is a source of personal disappointment and deep desolation for some of them. You might feel the same way too, and this could turn out to be a major disadvantage of becoming a no-decision manager, but is just something you will have to accept.

Outrageous behaviour

As the ultimate decision avoidance tactic, no-decision managers resort to 'outrageous behaviour'. This you will find difficult to learn and understand. It will not come naturally to you, so you must be cautious when first applying it.

'Outrageous behaviour' is behaviour both outside the usual norms of management and totally out of character. It is unexpected, sudden – often fierce with a high emotional charge. It will surprise everyone. In its simplest form it is just anger or an explosion of rage. It could be shouting, storming out of meetings or something more calculated such as a blatant change of opinion, a request for something ludicrous to be done, or even lying.

'Outrageous behaviour' was first identified as a specific managerial behaviour by Robert M. Bramson in 1981 in *Coping with Difficult People*. He calls it 'overload', and it arises when indecisive managers, called in his book 'Indecisive Stallers', become angry because of too much pressure from subordinates to make a decision.

All types of managers can become angry. What is different for no-decision managers is the action following the anger. In the example described by Bramson the 'staller' lost his temper with his subordinates and made an unfair decision that was hated by everyone. A normal manager might punish the subordinate or give them some sort of official blame for the act that made them angry. A true no-decision manager will of course never make a decision, even after a bout of anger. They will sit back and wait for a reaction from the subordinate.

When you are a no-decision manager you must realise that 'outrageous behaviour' has three clear objectives. You must not use it as a mechanism to release an emotional charge, as a normal manager might do. For you, it is far more complex. The three objectives of 'outrageous behaviour' are as follows:

1. A tactic to delay decisions

At the simplest level 'outrageous behaviour' is just another tactic to delay decision-making. Your subordinates should be so surprised by the behaviour that they will stop asking you for a decision. It may only be for a short time until they get over their surprise. But stop they will.

2. A simple message to subordinates to stop insisting

At the next level 'outrageous behaviour' sends a message to your subordinates to stop pushing you to make decisions:

> 'Stop trying to get me to make a decision. Back off. I will not do it.
> You have gone too far this time.'

You of course do not say this, but this is what 'outrageous behaviour' means. Most subordinates will understand the message. They will at least back off and ask themselves what has suddenly changed to make you act so peculiarly. This will usually lead them to realise that they may have gone too far in pushing you for a decision.

3. A complicated message to subordinates asking them to work positively

The most important message of 'outrageous behaviour' is a complicated one: asking your subordinates to drop their aggressive attitude towards you as a no-decision manager and take on a positive attitude to no-decision management in general and you as a no-decision manager in particular. Your behaviour is sending the following message:

> 'Come out of your negative emotion and work with me positively.'

A more complicated version might be:

> 'I have gone to great lengths to do something stupid as a reaction to your pressure on me to make a decision. Recognise that I will never take this decision that you want. There is another more positive way we can work together.'

An obscure version might be:

> 'You know I am not mad. Why would I react in such a way? Think it through.'

Remember you cannot talk to your subordinates about no-decision management openly, so you have to resort to this baffling, unclear and confusing method of communication. Do not forget Step 4: your oath of secrecy!

As a no-decision manager, though, you must never actually lose control or lose your temper. You already have enough problems in management in general without adding this to your list. You can, however, pretend to lose your temper – in which case you plan it, control it and have clear objectives. You act it out. If you cannot be realistic when acting out extreme anger, don't use this tactic. Do something else. 'Outrageous behaviour' is not limited to a bout of anger.

You can choose almost anything as 'outrageous behaviour'. You can more or less do whatever you want. But it must be something that you are comfortable with and that has the necessary characteristics to be classified as 'outrageous behaviour'. It must be:

- Outrageous
- Out of character
- Unexpected

- Sudden
- Highly emotional for the subordinate
- A surprise to all.

And whenever you decide to use this tactic you must make a calculated, deliberate action, carefully timed to maximise surprise and the emotional reaction of your subordinates. Do not lose control.

Below are three examples of 'outrageous behaviour' that have been used by experienced no-decision managers in the case studies below, and which you can use as a basis for your 'outrageous behaviour' when the need arises.

Outrageous behaviour 1: Inept information

One of the most devious forms of 'outrageous behaviour' is the request for 'inept information'. It is requested by no-decision managers as part of the first delay decision discussed in Chapter 3 called incremental information improved. An example was given of a situation where subordinates are asked to collect information and make a report in preparation for a decision.

At the end of the process to collect information, which has taken subordinates many days or weeks and is virtually complete – certainly complete in the eyes of the subordinates who have prepared the report – the no-decision manager will ask for some 'inept information' to be included.

This information is unnecessary, irrelevant, useless for the report and certainly not needed to make the decision in question. It makes subordinates feel extremely negative. They start to use adjectives such as 'stupid' and 'pointless' to describe the information to be collected and 'incompetent', 'crazy' and 'mad' to describe the no-decision boss who has asked for it.

Case study 17 – Requesting inept information
Sarah's no-decision boss Elisabeth puts her in charge of a task force to choose which of two office locations should become

the new headquarters of the group. Elisabeth instructs Sarah to make a formal report and propose the best location.

Sarah tracks the home addresses of every one of the 500 employees at each site, plotting not only the distance from their homes in miles but also the time they take to travel to and from each site in the rush hour. She checks the availability of public transport for each employee – bus or train – and makes complicated statistical calculations of costs per category of personnel to determine which of the locations is the best. The report takes her three months to prepare. All criteria point to one location.

Elisabeth, as a true no-decision manager, does not monitor Sarah's progress while the report is being prepared. In fact she refuses to discuss it with her during its preparation. So Sarah sends it in to Elisabeth with her recommendation and waits.

Meanwhile Sarah calls a colleague to see if any information on the new buildings has leaked out. Her colleague says: 'Headquarters made the decision on the location of the new offices six months ago. Didn't you know? I don't understand why they even asked you to prepare a report.'

Sarah has just become a victim of 'outrageous behaviour', cleverly organised by her no-decision boss. She is asked to prepare a report that is not needed. Her recommendation is unnecessary. She is even publicly congratulated by Elisabeth for a conclusion she never makes, in a meeting to announce the location of the new premises to the employees.

Elisabeth's message to Sarah is:

'Hey I am your no-decision boss. I just gave you three months of useless work to do, without review or control. I ignore your recommendation without giving you an explanation. I didn't tell you that the decision had already been made by headquarters. It is however an excellent report. Put aside your frustration with me and come on board.'

Comments on case study 17
Sarah is of course frustrated and angry, but she is an inexperienced young manager and does not get the hidden message. She never asks herself the question, 'What has made this usually sane, intelligent person act in such a totally irrational way?' The hidden message is too sophisticated and too complicated for her. Elisabeth's communication with Sarah fails in this instance, but the 'outrageous behaviour' remains.

Outrageous behaviour 2: Blatant change of opinion
One of the severest forms of 'outrageous behaviour' is a blatant change of opinion. A case study is the best way to illustrate it.

Case study 18 – Introducing a blatant change of opinion
Alice is a senior no-decision manager in charge of a worldwide product line with manufacturing in Ireland. Layia and Stanley both work for her. Layia is in charge of manufacturing and Stanley controls marketing. Alice asks them independently to work on a make or buy decision on the introduction of a new product. Stanley is in favour of the buy decision with an independent supplier. Layia is in favour of manufacturing the product in her factory.

Alice has two decisions to make: first, whether to introduce the new product, and second, where it should be manufactured. However, both Stanley and Layia assume that Alice has made the decision to introduce the new product since they are already working on the make or buy analysis. Alice, as a no-decision manager, has of course not decided anything.

Both set up their teams and work systematically through the process and come to Alice with their proposals, with Stanley going as far as identifying the best supplier for the buy decision and Layia the most efficient suppliers for the new equipment in her factory for the make decision.

Alice now has all the information she needs to decide. With no decision forthcoming Layia and Stanley lobby Alice to ask her to make the decision. As their frustration levels increase so does the pressure on Alice.

Early one morning after a meeting with Alice, Stanley comes triumphantly into a colleague's office with the information,

'Alice has at last agreed to my buy solution for the new product line.'

Later that same morning Layia tells Stanley that Alice has at last agreed on the make solution.

'No,' says Stanley. 'She has just told me that she agrees with the buy solution.'

Both Layia and Stanley are furious. Alice has given two opposing opinions, telling both, 'I agree with your proposal.'

For Alice this incident was simply a blatant change of opinion, first agreeing with Stanley, then a few minutes later agreeing the opposite with Layia.

She does not specifically say, 'I have decided to implement your solution.'

But only, 'I agree with your proposal.'
Layia and Stanley both think that when Alice says, 'I agree,' she also means, 'I decide.' But because Alice is a no-decision manager this is quite wrong. Here all she is doing changing her mind in agreeing first with Stanley then later with Layia.

Comments on case study 18
Alice of course knows that her two managers will talk to each other and be furious at what she's done, but she considers that they are ready for a strong signal to stop putting pressure on her for decisions.

But neither Layia nor Stanley understands the message. Or if they do, they refuse the invitation to come out of their states of negative emotion. Alice's 'outrageous behaviour' just increases their frustration.

This incident shows that 'outrageous behaviour' from no-decision managers is deliberate and calculated. It does not come about by chance. It is not loss of control. And the timing is important to give the highest element of surprise.

The new product is never introduced.

Outrageous behaviour 3: Outright lie
The most dangerous form of 'outrageous behaviour' is the outright lie. It is a strong signal – a warning – and is very out of character. These are some questions that a subordinate might ask when they realise their no-decision boss has told an outright lie:

'Why has my boss lied to me at this particular time?'
'What is going on? What is he trying to do?'

'Am I putting too much pressure on my boss to make a decision?'

> **Case study 19 – Using an outright lie**
>
> Parker, a no-decision European sales director, has to decide whether to renew a sales distribution contract in Russia for another five years or to appoint a direct sales force.
>
> He has full authority but he needs the authorisation of headquarters to sign a contract with a third party distributor – even the extension of an existing one.
>
> Generally, headquarters favours a direct sales force rather than distributors, but is open to a case-by-case analysis.
>
> David is in charge of sales for Eastern Europe and Emma is the European sales controller. They both know that Parker will never decide to employ a direct sales force on his own. So to help him out, they prepare a presentation for the European headquarters showing that it is more advantageous to continue with the distributor.
>
> Parker, as a no-decision manager, is now in great difficulty. For both options he must make a decision. Even sending a presentation to headquarters with one clear recommendation is impossible because it means having to make a decision.
>
> Parker tells David and Emma that he will present their proposal to headquarters on his next trip. After several visits and innumerable evasive excuses involving lack of time or absence of key managers, Parker has still not discussed the project with headquarters. So David and Emma start to put pressure on him. Meanwhile the distributor is furious that he is now working without a contract.

Parker suddenly announces to David and Emma that headquarters have given their approval to renew the contract with the distributor.

David hastily prepares the distribution contract, gets it signed by the distributor and presents it to Parker for signature. Again they hear nothing from Parker for several weeks.

Emma discusses the project with the European financial director at headquarters, who tells her that he knows nothing about a distribution contract for Russia, adding that anyway he is against the renewal of this contract.

Parker lied to his team. He never discussed the renewal with headquarters, even though he told his subordinates that headquarters had approved it.

Comments on case study 19
Parker's behaviour here is difficult to understand. He can easily get headquarters to make a decision in his place. He knows that the policy is to appoint a direct sales force in Russia and headquarters would instruct him to do this if ever he brought up the subject. But he doesn't. He invents an imaginary decision and lies to Emma and David.

It can only be a case of 'outrageous behaviour'.

And with it Parker risks the scandal and chaos that erupts between his team and headquarters. David goes into a blind fury with Parker when he discovers the lie. He informs headquarters and Parker's boss about both the lie and his own anger.

For both Emma and David, what little trust in Parker existed before vanishes completely. Nothing Parker says following this

> incident is credible any more. Whenever he makes a statement they assume that he's lying again.
>
> It seems that nobody benefits from Parker's behaviour: not Parker himself, not Emma, not David and not the distributor.
>
> And to this day the distributor in Russia is working without a distribution contract.

Take note that, apart from being unethical, dishonest and unprofessional, a lie would put you in more danger than you already are as a no-decision manager. For this reason, it's definitely not recommended that you take this extreme step to achieve 'outrageous behaviour'. There are many other more honest ways to achieve the same result.

Remember, as a no-decision manager, you are trying to communicate with your subordinates without talking to them directly about no-decision management because of your oath of secrecy. You cannot be precise and it is likely that they will not understand. You have to live with this.

Figure 13: The complex tactics of decision avoidance

Deviation of delegation	Implement decisions of others	Outrageous behaviour

Deviated downward delegation		Anger – lose control
Deviated upward delegation		Inept information
Deviated diagonal delegation		Blatant change of opinion
Deviated sideways delegation		Outright lie

The No-Decision-Making System

Now, as a no-decision manager, you are aware of the full range of tactics used by no-decision managers. This chapter has explained the final trio of tactics – deviation of delegation, implement decisions of others and 'outrageous behaviour'. These are summarised in Figure 13, The complex tactics of decision avoidance.

The two instinct-based behaviours are explained in Chapter 2. The six active avoidance tactics and the four delay decisions are explained in Chapter 3. There are, in all, 21 separate tactics that no-decision managers use regularly. These tactics and their groups have now been adopted officially by the Shelter and are now called the No-decision-making System, which is illustrated in Figure 14. This is now a formal system taught by the Shelter to young no-decision managers.

Summary – steps 12–18 to become a no-decision manager

Step 12 Memorise the definition of deviated delegation:

> Deviated delegation is the invisible acceptance of a decision taken by anyone in the organisation that should have been made by the no-decision manager, who silently refuses any accountability for the outcome of the decision unless the decision is approved by management.

Step 13 Learn the three rules of deviation downward delegation:

1. Wait for the subordinate to take the initiative
2. Renounce responsibility for the decision
3. Monitor nothing, never help.

Step 14 Learn deviation upward delegation and the two new concepts: the deemed decision (by using Figure 11, The deemed decision, as a memory aid) and the deemed instruction.

Figure 14: The no-decision-making System

Instinct-based behaviours	Active avoidance	Delay decisions	Deviation of delegation	Implement decisions of others	Outrageous behaviour
Permanent procrastination	Judicious absence	Incremental information improved	Deviated downward delegation		Anger – lose control
Imposing incremental information	Ignoring	Announce an action	Deviated upward delegation		Inept information
	Physical barriers	Task force	Deviated diagonal delegation		Blatant change of opinion
	Personal assistant	Consultant	Deviated sideways delegation		Outright lie
	Artificial agreement				
	Meaningless meetings				

140

Step 15 Learn deviation diagonal delegation, especially if you work in a company with a matrix organisation with 'dotted line' responsibilities or in an organisation with a prolific headquarters.

Step 16 Be aware that deviation sideways delegation is an option, even if not always practical.

Step 17 Make sure you use implementing decisions as a decision avoidance tactic and then become an expert in implementing the decisions of others, precisely and to the letter regardless of the consequences.

Step 18 Choose the 'outrageous behaviour' that you feel comfortable with and apply it in a calculated, deliberate way – carefully timed to maximise the surprise and emotion of your subordinates. Do not lose control.

Annex 1 summarises the steps required to become a no-decision manager.

5

How to Become a Great No-Decision Manager

'How to' advice for no-decision managers

Three core skills

As you may remember from Chapter 2, one of the four pillars that make up the Shelter is 'Skills'. All experienced no-decision managers without exception have three core skills, which you will have to master if you want to move on to being a great no-decision manager. These are known appropriately as the 'three greats': great analysis, great knowledge, and great understanding.

These are excellent skills for any manager to have and are not specific to no-decision managers; nor are they particularly different in execution when mastered by normal, competent managers. What you will find, though, is that *all* experienced no-decision managers have all three of these skills. They actively manage the three in a specific manner and use them in a different way from normal managers. If you have these skills already then you will have to adapt them slightly to take into account the no-decision aspects. If you don't have them then you will need to acquire them before you finally choose to become a fully fledged no-decision manager. You absolutely must become proficient in them. You have no choice.

A normal manager will use these skills as a foundation to become a better leader or excellent manager. No-decision managers have these skills for a different reason. They have such a major handicap in never making decisions that they need to show excellence in other aspects of management. They have chosen these three skills. Their objective is to become so proficient in them that it distracts top management's attention away from their decision avoidance. They are 'hiding in excellence' from their hierarchy. This is another new concept developed by the Shelter.

These skills will also give you another excuse not to make decisions. You can, for instance, tell subordinates that you are working on an analysis of the competition and that you will come back to them for their decision when you have finished your report.

These three skills will help you delay detection. Complaints from subordinates about the lack of decision-making will eventually filter up to your boss through Human Resources. However, if this apparent weakness is compensated by excellence in the 'three greats', the complaints will be overlooked until decision avoidance becomes more persistent and problematic.

Core skill 1: Great analysis

'Great Analysis' is the strict application of the three steps of decision-making discussed by Arun Kumar and Rachana Sharma in *Principles of Business Management*, where they explain how to develop, analyse and evaluate alternatives in the decision-making process up to the moment of the final decision. You need to read the relevant section of their book and reinterpret their advice to approach no-decision management in the alternative versions of the three steps, namely:

Developing alternatives
Analysing alternatives
Evaluation of alternatives

As you will realise, these three steps have already been explained in Chapter 3, as part of the first delay decision tactic of incremental information improved. Knowing about them is not enough – you now need to become an expert. First, you need to find out who in your organisation is the most competent in preparing decision-making reports. Not in making the decisions, but in preparing the reports and analysis.

For the step 'Developing alternatives', Kumar and Sharma's advice is:

> 'All possible ways should be identified and analysed.'

As a no-decision manager you can take away from this that the more alternatives there are, the longer it will take to prepare any report and the longer it will take to come to the moment of deciding. This is not at all what the authors meant, but it is just what you need as a no-decision manager.

For the step 'Analysing alternatives' the advice continues:

> After the various alternatives are identified the next step is to analyse each alternative which seems important in its pros and cons in relation to each other. Taking the time and cost element into account...

Again, this is perfect for you as a no-decision manager. You are encouraged to carefully extract the four elements to be analysed: pros, cons, time and cost; and then group them 'into class on some specific criteria important to decision making'.

This takes a considerable amount of work and time, which is what you want, but it also needs a thorough approach, and so will show your skills in analysing.

And then, in Step 6, 'Evaluation of Alternatives', you are told that: 'Each alternative... should be evaluated in terms of risk and resources available,' taking into account 'tangible and intangible factors'.

So in all there are another four elements that you must consider for every alternative: risk, resources, tangible factors and intangible factors. This gives you eight elements in all to analyse in each of your reports: pros, cons, time, cost, risk, resources, tangible factors and intangible factors. This vastly extends the time you can spend on preparing your evaluation!

But the Shelter has rejected one important piece of advice given by the authors in the step 'Developing alternatives': 'alternatives should not be considered which are not possible to be accomplished due to a limiting factor.'

If you eliminate any alternative at this stage it would be equivalent to making a decision, so you must ignore this advice, whether there are 'limiting factors' or not.

In fact the more alternatives that remain, the better your report will be, and the longer it will take you to prepare it.

> **Case study 20 – Masterful use of analytical skills**
> Edward has recently been promoted from marketing manager to country sales and marketing director in Scotland. Human Resources doesn't know that Edward is a no-decision manager.
>
> As marketing manager, he showed competence in his analysis of the market, including the competition, product positioning, pricing strategy and all other aspects of his position. He also showed skill in discussing, but not negotiating, contracts with important customers. His analytical and personal skills are appreciated throughout the company. He is the perfect candidate for promotion.
>
> In Edward's new position, his first task is to reorganise the sales force to adapt it to changes in the market. His analysis of the situation is impeccable, with a detailed assessment of the strengths and weaknesses of each salesperson, an exhaustive

explanation of 10 different alternatives for reorganisation, and a summary of the advantages and disadvantages of each.

Each alternative has its specific, strict but subtle strategy with original and orderly objectives. He places the members of his team in each alternative organisation depending on their skills. Those who do not have the required characteristics for a position are to be fired. Costs to set up each alternative are precise. He prepares detailed financial statements for the first three years in each alternative organisation. He includes a comprehensive comparison of the organisations of the main competitors, together with an analysis of market share by product segment. In short, he draws up a complete and competent report.

But as he is a true no-decision manager, he includes all 10 alternatives without considering any 'limiting factors' as required by Kumar and Sharma. He does not include his own recommendation for the alternative organisation that is, in his opinion, the best for the company, because he is a no-decision manager.

He simply lists them all, sends in his report, and waits, applying the first no-decision manager instinct of permanent procrastination. Given his exhaustive analysis, he is hoping that his boss or one of the managers in headquarters will make the decision for him.

Comments on case study 20
Here Edward is showing his inexperience as a no-decision manager. Simply leaving someone else to make a decision for him is too basic as a strategy. He should try to get some help from his boss through deviated upward delegation or from someone in headquarters through deviated diagonal delegation to make a choice on one of the 10 organisations

that he proposes. Instead he sends in his report without a recommendation. There is no attempt to hide his indecision.

Headquarters is disappointed with Edward because he has no proposal. It asks him for his preferred solution, which he cannot give. As a result, headquarters discovers that he is a no-decision manager and this is brought to the attention of his boss. Edward is no longer on an upward career trajectory.

Core skill 2: Great knowledge

To become a successful no-decision manager you will need to acquire 'great knowledge' of your business, the competition and the technology, especially if you are in top management. If you are in middle management you will need to become an expert in your field, especially in technology.

You should allocate time to becoming an expert in each subject. Much of your excellence, however, comes from your informal networks. From them you get the incremental information that repositions you from good to excellent. Where it concerns the competition this information is probably not in the public domain, and if it relates to technology it will come more from unofficial and unpublished sources than from official ones.

Core skill 3: Great understanding

You will need to develop a 'great understanding' of your organisation, your department and the people in them. There are four distinct reasons:

1. The Shelter considers great understanding a core skill in becoming a great no-decision manager
2. It is one of the amended Mintzberg managerial roles
3. To combat 'filtering'
4. To help you monitor information.

Great understanding: a core skill in becoming a great no-decision manager

As a middle manager, you should become expert in the working of your department and in the formal and informal roles of the staff, especially your direct subordinates. As a top manager you will need to develop a great understanding of the staff lower than you in the hierarchy: their roles, their motivations, and their skills.

As a no-decision manager you need to understand your staff and employees, but remember to do absolutely nothing to protect or help them. Giving help is an action and equivalent to a decision, so it's out of the question.

It is true that understanding one's staff but not helping them is also something that normal managers do. It is not specific to no-decision managers. Many managers protect themselves against their own subordinates, as you need to do as a no-decision manager, and normal managers will at times not help their subordinates. The only thing that is different for a no-decision manager is the motivation behind these actions. Helping subordinates involves making a decision and so cannot be done.

> **Case study 21 – Showing great understanding**
> Theo is a no-decision section manager. Jasmine is one of his subordinates who has been working in the company for many years.
>
> A new retention bonus is being prepared by Human Resources, designed to keep key subordinates with the best technical knowledge in Theo's section so that they will be there to work on an important contract over the next three years.
>
> When Jasmine receives the proposal for the bonus, she goes to see her boss, Theo, to tell him that she has decided not to accept the bonus.
>
> The first thing Theo says to Jasmine is not:
>
> 'Please explain why you have decided not to sign.'

But

'You must be insulted by the low amount of the bonus.'

This is exactly what Jasmine is thinking. Theo knew in advance that Jasmine would consider the bonus amount insufficient, even before talking to her.

Comments on case study 21
As a capable no-decision section manager, Theo knows exactly how his team members feel. But he does not contact his boss or Human Resources to tell them that that the proposed bonus is insufficient.

It is true that a normal manager might have the same reaction as Theo. He might not see the point in arguing with management and Human Resources on the size of the proposed bonus because he might be weak, lazy, have low morale himself or even just be an unsupportive manager without necessarily being a no-decision manager.

But, as a true no-decision manager, Theo systematically follows corporate instructions, knowing the bonus amount upsets one of his team. He makes no attempt to warn Human Resources or his boss of their inadequate new policy, not because he is a weak or lazy manager but solely because such action would be equivalent to making a decision.

He makes no attempt to recover the situation with Jasmine. Corporate policy is corporate policy to be applied as requested: a normal behaviour from a no-decision manager. He has great knowledge about his team but does not use it for their benefit or that of his company. Jasmine resigns six months later.

One of the amended Mintzberg managerial roles

Describing the 'monitor role' of managers, Mintzberg notes in his *Harvard Business Review* article 'The Manager's Job: Folklore and Fact' (1975) that:

> As monitor, the manager is perpetually scanning the environment for information.

No-decision managers scan not only the external environment but the organisation in which they work, the competition, the technology, clients and suppliers. They also become experts in gossip, hearsay and speculation as they collect information from their contacts. This of course is not a bad thing and should be done by all managers, but what is really important and different for you as a no-decision manager is the focus on the emotional state of your subordinates when 'scanning' – something that normal managers do not need to concentrate on.

Combating 'filtering'

Your 'real' reason for finding out the emotional state of your staff in the organisation is the very real danger of 'filtering'. Filtering happens when subordinates of no-decision managers become frustrated because decisions are not being made, and they start to complain. These complaints will eventually filter up through the hierarchy and ultimately reach top management. It is this danger that you need to constantly monitor.

At first, these complaints will come in the form of pointed remarks or comments, made through Human Resources, that their no-decision boss has yet again not made a decision. When the remarks are oral and informal they are called 'fortuitous filtering'. At this stage you can assume that the filtering is not dangerous for you, but you need to know it is happening so that you can monitor the possibility of an eventual escalation.

As frustration levels increase, complaints by subordinates will begin to be made in writing – a process known as 'formal filtering'. It is when filtering escalates from 'fortuitous' to 'formal' that you need to carefully monitor the emotional climate of your team and control what information flows up to your boss.

You never, of course, intervene to prevent it, because intervention is an action that requires a decision, but you need to have time to prepare a defence if a query then comes back down from your boss.

Helping you monitor information

By cultivating your informal networks – both upwards towards your boss, and downwards towards your subordinates – you will be able to find out what is going on in your organisation at all times.

> ### Case study 22 – Effective monitoring
> Zoe has worked beside Lewis as a colleague for many years. Lewis is a senior no-decision manager and they are talking one morning when Lewis says:
>
> 'Headquarters wants the presentation to be made in the last week of May.' And then he adds, 'If I am still in the company at that time.'
>
> Lewis has received some indications from his internal network that his bosses are not satisfied with his performance. They think he is a no-decision manager and are discussing whether to fire him in the next few months.
>
> *Comments on case study 22*
> In the end, Lewis is both right and wrong. He is right that he will be fired but wrong on the timing. His boss has discovered that he is a no-decision manager, but he lasts another nine months in his position before he is fired.
>
> No-decision managers like Lewis are able to get accurate and relevant information even about themselves while monitoring their survival prospects through their internal networks.

No-decision managers have expanded the monitor role out of all proportion to the level indicated in Mintzberg's definition. This role is used by no-decision managers to monitor information filtering up to the boss, the emotional state of the team, especially frustration levels, and all other information relevant to the no-decision manager's survival.

Other character traits required by no-decision managers

No-decision managers have three unusual traits of character, common to them all, which you will have to learn and present to your subordinates. It is very likely that you do not have these traits as part of your natural character, so you will need to contact other no-decision managers and get practical details of when and how to use them.

Please also note that these traits are directed almost exclusively at your subordinates and their teams. You should not use them with your boss or managers higher up in the hierarchy. The three traits are summarised below.

1. Clear but changing opinions

No-decision managers have clear and precise opinions on all subjects. But they can change their minds rapidly depending on the audience and circumstances. These opinions are only opinions of the moment.

You will need to prepare yourself to invent an opinion about any person in the organisation, any project, any decision made by others – more or less anything. And then be ready to change it. So in fact you should invent at least two different alternative opinions about people, projects and decisions that have been made and be ready to recite them at any time. These need not be totally contrary, just different.

But there is an important exception to this rule. As soon as you know what your boss thinks, on any subject, this must become your own opinion and it must never change thereafter, unless your boss changes their mind too.

Case study 23 – Discovering clear but changing positions

Scarlett is a no-decision manager. There is some debate within her team about the effectiveness of Jacob, who is one of the managers in charge of an important project.

Jacob's direct boss thinks he is an excellent manager who manages the project well and has made sure that the project is on time and within budget.

'Yes,' says Scarlett to Jacob's boss, 'He is working very well on this project.'

Later, in a discussion with Evan, another team member on the same project, Evan tells Scarlett:

'The project is late and will never finish in time. I have spoken to Jacob in person and explained to him in detail the two issues that will delay the project. He doesn't take them into account when he makes his plans.'

'I agree,' says Scarlett, 'The project will be late.'

Scarlett's boss, when discussing the same project, says to her:

'Jacob talks as though he is technically an expert but in reality he does not understand what he is doing. The project will fail with him as leader.'

Some weeks later Scarlett tells Jacob's boss:

'Jacob seems competent but is not. He talks too much and the project will fail with him as the leader.'

Scarlett is just repeating what her boss thinks of Jacob. This, her third opinion of Jacob within a few weeks, is now her final and unwavering opinion of him.

Comments on case study 23
Normal managers, when faced with these conflicting opinions, would make an effort to find out for themselves whether or not Jacob was an effective leader, and then come to their own opinion of him.

A no-decision manager like Scarlett just accepts her boss's opinion regardless of whether there is any truth in the opinion or not.

So, in summary:

- Have an opinion, it doesn't matter what.
- Change it whenever you want.
- When you know what your boss thinks, make your opinion the same.
- Watch out for when your boss changes their mind and then change yours again.

This is complicated, so you must learn these steps well and perform them naturally without hesitation and with absolute conviction each time. If it is complex for you to follow, think how bewildering it will be for your subordinates!

2. Friendly, but does not care
The second of three unusual traits of character common to no-decision managers is friendliness, coupled with disregard and indifference. No-decision managers are friendly, but do not care about their subordinates.

The Economist magazine wrote in 2008 that Rosabeth Moss Kanter had 'achieved genuine guru status' in management. In an interview with Bob Morris (Rosabeth Moss Kanter: An Interview by Bob Morris, June 2011, bobmorris.biz) she is quoted as saying: 'Friendly people are caring people, eager to provide encouragement and support when needed most.'

But this is only partly true for no-decision managers.

For them a more accurate description would be: 'Although friendly, no-decision managers generally neglect subordinates, are disinterested at best, never provide encouragement and never give any support when needed.'

What this means is that being friendly becomes a tactic for you. Friendliness establishes contact, contact gives conversation, conversation gives information, and information is what you as a no-decision manager are seeking. It is part of maintaining your great understanding of the company and the people. Remember, decision avoidance is the priority – not the feelings and emotions of your subordinates.

So, if you are not a friendly person you need to become one. But at the same time you must learn to disregard the feelings, motivations or opinions of your direct staff and employees. You must never encourage them and must never give any support.

This is Step 21 on your way to becoming a great no-decision manager and it is a critical one. If you really care and want to help your subordinates, reconsider your ambition to become a no-decision manager now and decide whether you want to continue. You can still change your mind and get out of the process.

You might not care about your subordinates but you do care very much about your boss. Do not confuse the two! Remember your boss has the power to dismiss you.

3. Selective shamelessness

No-decision managers are selectively shameless. Their standards of behaviour are different when dealing with their hierarchy than when dealing with their subordinates.

Subordinates think no-decision managers are shameless. Their bosses believe the complete opposite. This arises directly from no-decision managers' acts of 'outrageous behaviour' and their changing of opinions, both of which their bosses never see.

This is not something that you have to learn to do, because it is an automatic consequence of 'outrageous behaviour' and 'clear but changing opinions' and it is not one of the obligatory steps to becoming a no-decision manager. If you do feel shame about the way you treat your subordinates, fine. If you are shameless towards your subordinates, also fine. Just make sure that you never direct 'outrageous behaviour' towards your boss and never show any bosses that you constantly change your mind. What is important is ensuring that you perform 'outrageous behaviour' correctly towards subordinates, that you change your opinions appropriately and that you systematically disregard the feelings of your subordinates. That's all.

You can classify yourself as a great no-decision manager when you have mastered the three core skills and the three new character traits. However, the most important lesson is still to come: how to survive as a no-decision manager.

Co-operation with other types of manager

But first, it is useful for you to understand what is going on between the no-decision manager and other types of manager. It is not critical and you do not need to learn anything special, but it is relevant and interesting.

There is a close relationship between no-decision managers and five other management types, namely:

1. Procrastination manager
2. Indecisive manager
3. Liar manager
4. Incompetent manager
5. Normal manager

1. Procrastination manager

Procrastination managers work primarily on tasks and actions that they enjoy. They delay all other tasks until the last minute, but they do make decisions in the end. They have taken on the permanent procrastination technique under an agreement with the Shelter and then have adapted it to their own needs.

Instead of procrastinating only over decisions, as no-decision managers do, they procrastinate over everything: tasks, managerial activities, actions and decisions of course; and have changed the name of the technique to 'comprehensive chronic procrastination'. Procrastinating managers do decide something in the end, albeit too slowly and often too late.

2. Indecisive manager

Indecisive managers are the closest species of manager to the no-decision manager. Because they hesitate in the same way as no-decision managers do, they have borrowed many delay-decision and other decision avoidance tactics from the no-decision managers.

In the end, though, indecisive managers are fundamentally different because they will make decisions, usually after excessive pressure from subordinates and in rare instances with their help. A no-decision manager will not make a decision no matter what the pressure is from their subordinates.

Indecisive managers and the Shelter have been co-operating for many years.

3. Liar manager

The 'liar manager' is one of the rarest species of manager. Their habitat is worldwide. Liar managers are few in number, but spread thinly throughout the managerial world. They are threatened and endangered in the same way as no-decision managers, primarily because of the risk of their hierarchy discovering and eliminating them. Because of their rarity they have no need of a common organisation similar to the Shelter, but the two groups do co-operate.

The Shelter provides expertise to the liar managers on such things as structured survival and monitoring of information in the organisation. And the 'liar managers' advise no-decision managers on how to lie convincingly, with special emphasis on the techniques of mock sincerity and indignation.

You should be aware that when you use a lie during 'outrageous behaviour', you automatically become a liar manager. The techniques you learn from the Shelter are borrowed directly from liar managers.

It is obvious that lying techniques are necessary tools if you as a no-decision manager are to be convincing in acting out 'outrageous behaviour', especially the outright lie and irrational changes of opinion, but also in justifying to your boss that you are always right and your subordinates are invariably wrong.

Liar managers obtain management fulfilment by never, ever, telling the truth. They use the whole panoply of lying techniques that are available: half-truths, outright lies, omission and all other types of lies. They lie all the time, in every conversation with everyone in the organisation. They are perpetual liars.

Lies are graduated depending on the hierarchy and status of the person being spoken to. Members of the management team are told 50% truths. The boss, 75% or perhaps even 90% truths, others lower in the hierarchy maybe only 25% truths, while people outside the company, such as bankers, suppliers and clients, are generally told outright lies.

> **Case study 24 – Working effectively with a liar manager**
> Matilda is a liar manager in a senior position. Hugo is one of her subordinate managers who recognises early that Matilda is a liar manager and so, in an attempt to manage the permanent lying of his boss, changes the way he and his team work.
>
> Hugo instructs his team to recall and note all key issues that come up when talking to Matilda and people who work closely with her. He decides to have a special weekly meeting with his team, called 'comparison of truth meetings', where each team

member compares notes on their discussions with Matilda and others close to her.

They then adopt the following rules:

1. Information from Matilda with no independent corroboration is automatically considered false.
2. Contradictory information directly from Matilda is ignored.
3. Only duplicated and corroborated information from at least three people is considered true.

Relying on these rules, Hugo and his team manage to work effectively with Matilda and are able to confront her when she gives them inaccurate information.

Comments on case study 24
It is complicated working for a liar boss. While the above method works for Hugo and his team, this is clearly not the only way. What is important, though, is to recognise the issue and set up whatever solutions work for the manager and team in question. Continuing as though Matilda is a normal manager will never work.

Liar managers have a discreet method of identification among themselves – that of printing a particular quote on the back of their business cards. The quotation is taken from William Blake's 'Proverbs of Hell':

> Truth can never be told so as to be understood and not to be believed.

If you find this printed on the back of a business card, you know for certain you have discovered a 'liar manager'.

4. Incompetent manager

Incompetent managers also co-operate with no-decision managers. The Incompetents Club is run by retired incompetent managers. It is only when they retire at the end of their careers as incompetent managers that they are invited to become members of the Incompetents, at which time they are encouraged to become mentors for the younger members.

The Incompetents Club persuades the incompetent managers to choose one of the three core skills: great analysis, great knowledge or great understanding. The Shelter then offers special courses for each of the three subjects under the theory that if the incompetent managers can learn just one management skill to a reasonably proficient level, they can no longer be considered incompetent, and can become ordinary managers.

In return for these training courses, the Incompetents Club provides advice to the Shelter and to no-decision managers on how to get the most out of being fired. Incompetent managers are fired frequently and so have developed best practice on how to cope with dismissal, which includes, for instance, how to maximise indemnities, how to optimise legal proceedings against the employer, and how to negotiate dismissal indemnities and obtain quality outplacement assistance.

It is more difficult to persuade incompetent managers to put a specific quotation on the back of their business cards, given that they do not know they are members of the Incompetents Club until retirement, but their retired mentors do everything to persuade them that these quotes are a way of distinguishing themselves in the business community.

The Incompetents Club has chosen Woody Allen's statement as its motto:

> I have no idea what I am doing, but incompetence has never prevented me from plunging in with enthusiasm.

5. Normal manager

And then there is the normal manager, a group most managers fall into. It is from this source that the no-decision movement borrows some normal behaviours and minor management weaknesses. These are then transformed or deformed into either tactics for decision avoidance or actions for survival.

Some of these behaviours and weaknesses have already been discussed, but below is a summary of the more important ones.

Normal manager behaviours used by no-decision managers include:

1. Task force creation
2. Consultant engagement
3. Decision meetings
4. Weekly or monthly meetings
5. Getting the opinion of the boss.

The use of a task force or a consultant is a normal behaviour for senior managers. Task forces and consultants analyse complicated situations and help managers establish frameworks for making decisions. No-decision managers use these to delay decision-making or get someone else to make decisions in their place. Similarly, consultative managers use decision meetings to help them make decisions. No-decision managers use decision meetings to avoid decisions.

Weekly or monthly meetings with direct subordinates are other activities normally used for information-gathering and decision-making. There is no real need for no-decision managers to have these meetings, but by going through the motions of holding them they can show their bosses that they are normal managers doing a normal job.

There is clearly no harm in getting the boss's opinion on any subject. After all, as a normal manager it helps to know what the boss thinks and how far one can go without constraint. But as we have seen, the no-decision manager takes this to a different level with the concept of the deemed decision.

Normal manager weaknesses

Normal managers often have managerial weaknesses, but these are usually not serious enough to damage the department or organisation they work in. Subordinates of these normal managers can work with these bosses and either live in harmony with their weaknesses or find a way to work around them. Two examples are:

a) Changing opinions
b) Taking credit for work of subordinates.

Some managers change their minds before eventually making a decision. Some go further and even change their decisions several times before making a final one. For no-decision managers, changing their opinion is a way of decision avoidance, nothing else.

For normal managers, taking the credit for the work of subordinates is mere selfishness. But for no-decision managers it is a tactic for survival.

Some management weaknesses of no-decision managers may seem the same as those of normal managers, but they in fact come directly from decision avoidance. Giving no support to subordinates is the best example. Some normal managers have this weakness, for whatever reason. But no-decision managers never give support, because support is a decision for them. And they never make decisions.

At this moment in your quest to become a no-decision manager you are still a normal manager. You have taken the Shelter's oath but you have not yet made the ultimate choice to stop decision-making. As a normal manager you know what normal managers do in their daily managerial life. So, unlike natural no-decision managers you have nothing to learn from them.

Figure 15: The 'three greats' and other character traits a no-decision manager needs

When you finally become a full no-decision manager, you should continue with your 'normal manager' activities. If you have weaknesses, keep them. You can use them where appropriate to avoid decisions. Whatever other qualities or behaviours you may have as a normal manager, keep these too, unless they involve decision-making.

The three core skills needed to become a great no-decision manager and the four traits of character – three of which need to be taken on and one that is interesting but optional – are shown graphically in Figure 15, The three greats and other character traits a no-decision manager needs.

Summary – steps 19–23 to become a no-decision manager

Step 19 Learn and implement 'great analysis' – developing alternatives, analysing alternatives and evaluation of alternatives – whenever you have to compile a report for a decision.

Step 20 Acquire 'great knowledge' of your business, the competition and any relevant technology.

Step 21 Develop a 'great understanding' of your organisation, your department and the people in them, above all to detect as early as possible any complaints of decision avoidance that may filter up through the hierarchy and ultimately reach your boss.

Step 22 Develop the behaviour of 'clear but changing opinions' so that it becomes natural, and learn the four steps for this behaviour:

a) Have an opinion – it doesn't matter what
b) Change it whenever you want
c) When you know what your boss thinks, make your opinion the same
d) Watch out for when your boss changes their mind and then change yours again.

Step 23 Learn the attitude of being 'friendly but uncaring' and memorise the definition:

'Although friendly, no-decision managers neglect subordinates, are disinterested at best, never provide encouragement and never give any support when needed.'

You can classify yourself as a great no-decision manager after having mastered these five steps. However, the most important lesson is still to come: how to survive as a no-decision manager.

Annex 1 summarises the steps required to become a no-decision manager.

6

How No-Decision Managers Survive

'How to' advice for no-decision managers

There is no point in being a 'great' no-decision manager if you cannot survive in the organisation, so after 'secrecy', 'system' and 'skills', the last pillar, 'survival', is essential. Don't forget that the two major pillars of the Shelter are secrecy and survival. So not only must you address survival, you must become competent in managing it. If your boss discovers your true identity, you'll be dismissed immediately and you will have to start not making decisions all over again in a different organisation.

Fortunately, the Shelter provides a defence called 'structured survival' that is tailored to the organisation, matched to your people, and then supervised as you implement it so that it becomes second nature for you. It is made up of six parts:

1. Separated specialised informal networks
2. Blandish the bosses
3. Handling of hierarchy
4. The Rumsfeld resolution
5. Organisations that no-decision managers should avoid
6. Bosses that no-decision managers should avoid.

The six points of structured survival, represented by the six points of a hexagon, are shown graphically in Figure 16, Structured survival, summarising the way no-decision managers organise their survival.

Figure 16: Structured survival

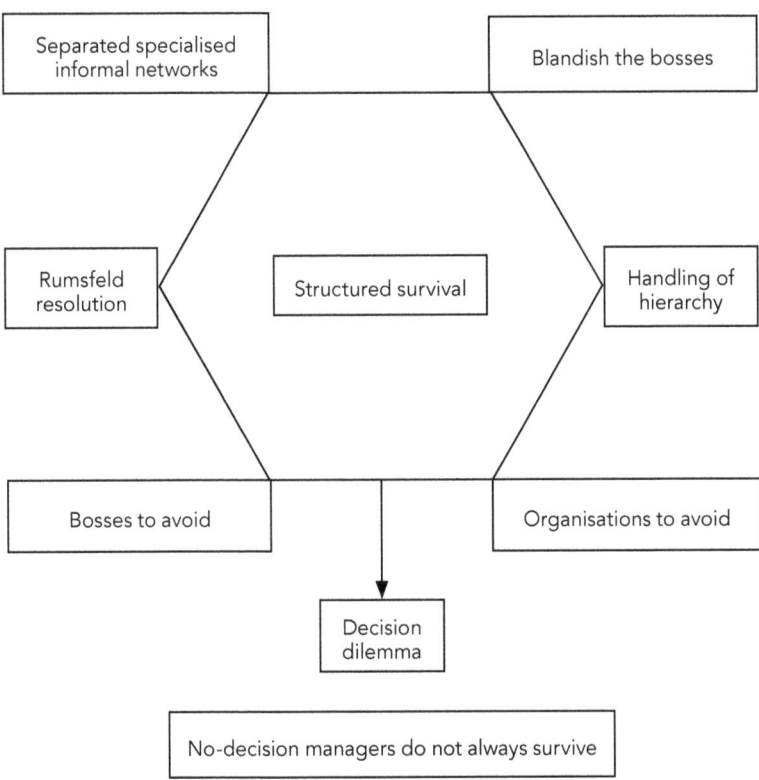

Separated specialised informal networks

Most no-decision managers are natural networkers. If you are not one already, you'll need to learn the necessary skills quickly.

If you are already in a senior position, you will have developed extensive networks, focused on your specific needs. If you are in middle management you will have to concentrate more on developing informal internal information networks. In both cases, whatever networks you may have, you will need to modify them to fit no-decision management and some might need to be abandoned. To become a no-decision manager, you must set aside the time to keep the right kind of networks active, relevant and productive.

Much has been written about informal networks in organisations: how they work, why they exist, what influence they have, how they can be controlled, and what type of information they generate, including some very sophisticated and often inventive analysis. You don't need to know any of this. You just need to have a few of the simple informal networks and adapt them to your no-decision management needs.

'Separated specialised informal networks' are an extension and expansion of Mintzberg's liaison role, adapted to include the required elements for survival of no-decision managers.

Regarding the liaison role, Mintzberg, in his article 'The Manager's Job: Folklore and Fact' (1975), writes:

> The manager makes contacts outside the vertical chain of command.

This is exactly what no-decision managers do when they set up specialised informal networks.

Rosabeth Moss Kanter remarks that informal networks are critical, especially in great companies. In her article 'How Great Companies Think Differently' (2011), she writes:

> Managers in great companies understand that formal structures can be too general or too rigid to accommodate multidirectional pathways for resource and idea flows.

You as a no-decision manager do not need to 'accommodate' anything, let alone 'multidirectional pathways for resource and idea flows'. In any case you cannot rely on formal structures in your organisation and you need to set up informal networks to survive.

Kanter goes on to say that:

> Informal, self-organising, shape-changing, and temporary networks are more flexible and can make connections between people or connect bundles of resources more quickly.

Your objective is not to change the shape of anything. In any case, as a no-decision manager, you probably have no reason to 'connect bundles of resources'. However, you can adapt the rest of Kanter's advice on networking to your own no-decision needs, that of survival:

> Informal, self-organising, and temporary networks are more flexible and can make connections between people more quickly to increase influence and above all to obtain up to date information for survival.

Five core activities of informal networks

Forget the conventional activities of informal networks, identified by social psychology, such as belonging, social relationships, identity or self-esteem. You need information and lots of it. You need networks for your survival and influence within the organisation. To take advantage of your networks, you must create two special no-decision management activities: monitoring and delegation. In all, you need to engage in five specific activities in your informal networks:

1. Information
2. Survival
3. Influence
4. Monitoring
5. Delegation.

1. Information

First, you need your networks for collecting information. A normal flow is usually in two directions: information in and information out. It is important to note that, as a no-decision manager, you are not interested in giving information, only in receiving it. You should only give information to two sets of people – the influential people in the organisation and selectively to Human Resources. If you give out too much you are wasting your time and reducing your capacity to influence.

Figure 17, The no-decision manager's internal informal information network, shows graphically where Leers, the CEO, Martin in HR and two other influential people are the only four to *obtain* information *from* Harris, the no-decision manager. All the others only *give* information *to* the no-decision manager.

Figure 17: The no-decision manager's internal informal information network

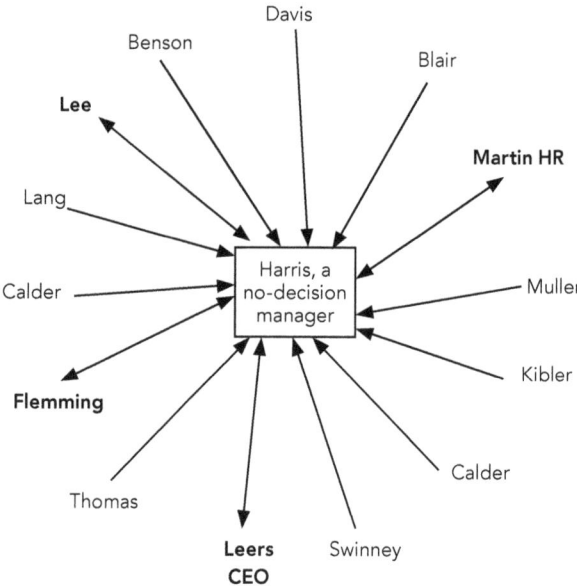

Based on the chart by David Krackhardt and Jeffrey R. Hanson (*Harvard Business Review*, July-August 1993) 'Informal Networks: The Company behind the Chart', and then adapted to no-decision management.

Only Martin in Human Resources, Leers the Chief Executive Officer (Harris's boss) and two influential managers, Flemming and Lee, get information from Harris the no-decision manager. All others in his informal network give information to Harris but get nothing in return.

Reproduced and amended by permission of *Harvard Business Review*. Original Copyright © 1993 by Harvard Business Publishing; all rights reserved

Now compare this to the information flow around Harris in the original chart in Krackhardt and Hanson's article, shown below:

The Advice Network Reveals the Experts

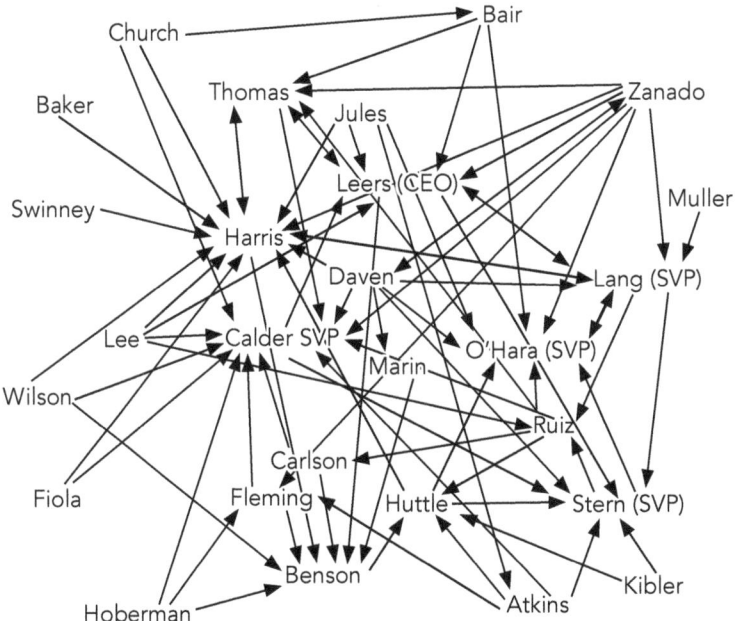

Reprinted by permission of Harvard Business Review. Copyright © 1993 by Harvard Business Publishing; all rights reserved

Figure 17 has been adapted from the *Harvard Business Review* article by David Krackhardt and Jeffrey R. Hanson, 'Informal Networks: The Company behind the Chart' (1993). Their original chart is also shown in Figure 17. When the two are compared, the simplification in the information flow is astonishing. Harris, the no-decision manager, becomes the centre and all other information flows in the company are irrelevant to him.

You should also use informal networks to generate information for the two core skills of great knowledge and great understanding that you need to become a 'great' no-decision manager. Internally this information is generated by your own informal networks, and externally it is generated by your exterior informal networks.

2. Survival

Your survival activity is very important. Through it you promote the concept of your hiding in excellence, emphasise your core skills and ensure that the secret that you are a no-decision manager does not get out.

3. Influence

With your 'influence' activities, you are not out to gain any political advantage in your organisation as a normal manager would. You are not seeking power or authority. Power and authority require decision-making, which of course is anathema to you. You, as a no-decision manager, simply seek to spread your personal influence in the organisation, specifically promoting yourself with two messages:

> 'I am a great manager doing a great job.'
> 'I am a great manager who knows our people well.'

You should give the first message to people close to your boss and the second to Human Resources.

In promoting yourself, you need to spread the message of your technical and people skills – especially relating to your knowledge of your industry, the technology and the competition – to the influential people in the company. You must not forget to show your understanding of the company and its people. This is an indirect way of showing people that you are a great manager doing a great job.

4. Monitoring

In your monitoring activity, you will need to watch out for secrecy and the emotional states of your subordinates. If you feel that your secret is being revealed you must take action immediately. You must also monitor the emotions of your subordinates by making enquiries through your colleagues and other employees.

5. Delegation

Finally you must be constantly on the lookout for people who can make decisions for you – especially people close to your boss and/or your colleagues. This activity, if you remember, is called deviated delegation and has already been discussed in detail in Chapter 4 as part of the No-decision-making System, but to be totally effective it needs to be complemented by special informal network activity.

Normal managers and the five activities

The five activities described above are similar to those which any normal manager might carry out, but there are significant differences. The most obvious ones relate to the last two activities, as normal managers don't need to spend any time monitoring secrecy or the emotional state of their subordinates, or looking for people to make decisions for them. They decide for themselves.

Such 'influence activity' might be used by a normal manager, but it would include wider political activities such as seeking more power and authority within the organisation. Survival is clearly not the prime informal network activity for a normal manager, but a normal manager might include some general defence activity in their networks. Finally, normal managers both give and receive information. You as a no-decision manager will concentrate on receiving it.

Now that you have reviewed the activities you need to engage in for your networks, you need to get to work and set up seven separate and specialised informal networks.

Influential people network

One of your first tasks will be to identify the most influential people in your organisation and target them with all five of the informal network activities.

The 'spokesperson role', according to Mintzberg, should be used to 'satisfy the influential people who control the organisational unit'.

You need to adapt and expand this role when setting up your influential people network.

You both give and collect information from this network. You should give information freely – enough to 'satisfy the influential people' on any subject and about anyone. This is also your moment for self-promotion and for showing off your expertise. You should take this opportunity to collect information on what is happening around the boss and the boss's boss, what they think, what are their current projects and their thoughts on people in the organisation, including any useful gossip and rumours.

This network is important for you, both to monitor and to maintain the secrecy of your status as a no-decision manager. The influential people in the organisation must not know that you are a no-decision manager, but the network is a source to obtain more information on the company and the people in it. You can also look here for potential people to take decisions for you.

Headquarters network

Your headquarters network should include junior managers in headquarters who are not yet considered influential, but who can provide you with information on what is going on in the organisation and who you may need as allies sometime in the future. These junior managers sometimes have a significant influence on their bosses, so it is useful to have close relationships with them.

You should also use this network to monitor secrecy levels. People in headquarters must never learn that you are a no-decision manager. Finally, this network also gives you information to improve your knowledge of the company and the key people in it.

Colleague network

Most of your colleagues will know that you do not make decisions. So the main objective of the colleague network is to ensure that this information does not filter up to your boss or to others above you in the hierarchy.

It is at this level that you should continuously search for candidates to take decisions for you. Information can be collected here on all subjects. This informal network can also help you monitor the frustration levels of your team.

Employee network

You need to monitor what is happening to employees below you in the formal hierarchical structure. This is especially true if you are in top management. You will need to set up a separated specialised informal network with employees throughout the company, which will give you information on the wellbeing and motivation of employees, their frustration levels generated by working with you as a no-decision manager, and all relevant information and rumours that are circulating in the organisation.

Human Resources network

This is an important network for you and needs to include as many people as possible in the Human Resources department, at all levels and in all locations. As you know, Human Resources is a key resource for people-related information, and you need to tap into this source. You can give information out to Human Resources people, but give it selectively, only to senior managers depending on the relevance of the subject. You can use this network to monitor both secrecy and the frustration levels of subordinates.

You should use this network for self-promotion, establishing that you are a 'great' manager who knows the people, and to maintain secrecy. You might be able to find people in this network who will make decisions for you.

Technology network

The technology network is centred internally on the engineers and technicians within the organisation but also includes specialists from suppliers, clients or any independent organisations – be they universities, research organisations or other institutions. Here collecting information is key, and you should use it to stay up to date and be aware of new technology being studied and discussed in your industry.

Figure 18: Separated specialised informal networks

Specialised network	Activities in each network				
	Information	Monitoring	Influence	Survival	Delegation
1) Influential people network	Collect and give information	Level of secrecy of your status as no-decision manager	Show off your 'three greats' skills	Show off your 'three greats' skills and keep up the pretence that you are not a no-decision manager	Look for opportunities for diagonal delegation
2) Headquarters network	Collect information	Level of secrecy	Obtain allies for the future	Show off your 'three greats' skills and keep up the pretence that you are not a no-decision manager	
3) Colleague network	Collect information	Level of frustration		Make sure that your colleagues do not inform top management that you are a no-decision manager	Look for opportunities for sideways delegation
4) Employee network	Collect information	Level of frustration			
5) Human Resources network	Collect and give information	Level of secrecy and frustration	Show off your 'great understanding' skills, i.e. that you know the people in the company	Make sure that your colleagues do not inform top management that you are a no-decision manager	Look for opportunities for diagonal or sideways delegation
6) Technology network	Collect information				
7) Competition and industry network	Collect information				

Use Figure 18 as a checklist to monitor your progress in setting up your informal networks to ensure that you do not forget the activities that you need to cover with each one. With five separate activities and seven informal networks, it is sometimes difficult to remember which network does what.

Competition and industry network

You need to build a competition and industry network carefully over several years, mainly including people outside the company: suppliers, clients, previous colleagues, knowledgeable people in the industry, friends, experts – indeed anyone with knowhow and information. This is an information-collecting network.

Figure 18, Separated specialised informal networks, summarises the interaction of the different separated specialised informal networks showing the activities of each network: those of collecting information with restricted giving, monitoring for secrecy, and frustration, self-promotion, survival essentially by promoting core skills and maintaining secrecy and finally, the continuous search for candidates to make your decisions.

Blandish the bosses

Your boss is undoubtedly the most important person in the organisation for you as a no-decision manager. He or she is the ultimate decision-maker with the power to dismiss you. Your survival therefore depends principally on this person. The next most important person in the organisation is your boss's boss, and you need to cultivate a special and personal relationship, to make sure that both your boss and your boss's boss maintain a high opinion of you.

The special relationship with these two people in the organisation is known in no-decision management jargon as 'blandish the bosses'.

Your boss

All experienced no-decision managers are specialists: experts and exceptionally competent at managing their bosses. You must acquire this skill, because without it you'll find it impossible to survive in the long term.

Much has been written on 'How to manage your boss', and you must learn and use the whole range of techniques available.

Here are a few:

- Analyse what the boss wants. Then systematically give it to them, when and how they want it.
- Adapt to your boss's style and working habits.
- Analyse what is out of bounds. Do not go into this space.
- Deliver on expectations.
- Avoid surprises. If there are any surprises tell your boss openly and immediately and be the first to do so.
- Ensure you obtain wins for your boss. Make an analysis of their priorities, both official and unofficial. Help them personally. Take on your boss's priorities even unofficially.
- Make your boss look successful wherever possible.

In other words – keep your boss happy.

Blandishing the bosses is more than merely managing your boss effectively. There are more things to do.

Focused filtering

You must keep contact daily with your boss – preferably verbal, never written. Keep your boss informed of all activities in your department or organisation. Information relating to current, pending and upcoming decisions should be abundant. The objective is not providing information per se. You must put your boss in a position where they think they know what is going on, and so give their opinion on many subjects, ensuring that you can absorb the deemed decisions.

You should always pass on good news immediately. You should not communicate any bad news, any difficulties or any problems. You must carefully filter the news moving up to your boss, making sure you always put yourself in the best possible light. This process is called 'focused filtering' in the no-decision management jargon. Information is focused only on what you, the no-decision manager, want your boss to hear, especially if the information might potentially show you in a bad light.

> Case study 25 – Discovering focused filtering
> Theodore is a no-decision manager working in a key workshop in the manufacturing department of his company. One of his qualified and long-serving employees, Luca, has decided to leave the company. He informs Theodore.
>
> At the end of the discussion, Luca says to Theodore:
>
> 'As you know, I have known Elliot (who is Theodore's boss) for over 20 years. He hired me for my current position. As soon as we have finished talking, I would like to call him to let him know that I have resigned.'
>
> 'No,' says Theodore. 'Let me call Elliot first. I will let you know when I have spoken to him, and then you can call him yourself.'
>
> It was Luca's turn to be surprised. Here was his no-decision boss giving him a precise order and making a decision!
>
> *Comments on case study 25*
> Theodore realises the danger of Luca telephoning Elliot directly. By informing Elliot first, Theodore will control the information received by his boss, enabling him to explain that he is in no way the cause of Luca's resignation but that the fault lies elsewhere.
>
> When Luca eventually talks to Elliot, Elliot never asks the reason for his resignation – a clear sign that Theodore has adequately massaged the message in such a way that he cannot be blamed for Luca's decision to leave the company.

> There is nothing wrong in doing this. A normal manager might do the same once in a while. But for a no-decision manager this behaviour is almost a systematic reflex to control all information going up to the boss whenever he thinks he is in danger. Constant vigilance and information control are key elements for survival as a no-decision manager.

Special relationship

You need to develop a special relationship with your boss. For instance, you have to know how much information you can give before 'saturation' sets in. You must learn how to filter and feed information to your advantage, without being heavy-handed or excessive. You must be able to extract decisions and opinions from your boss surreptitiously, all the time employing the deviating upwards delegation technique, to get them to make decisions in your place. In essence, you must influence their behaviour by persuading them to accept your limitations as a no-decision subordinate without consciously recognising you as one.

Coping in a crisis

Although you should not generally tell your boss any bad news, the exception to this rule is that you must quickly communicate a crisis upwards. You need to make it a matter of principle for you to be the first to announce a crisis to your boss, not in a spirit of openness, but more to ensure that the information is passed on in such a way as to limit your responsibility. You also need to identify someone else to make the multiple and rapid decisions that will follow from the crisis.

You must learn to guide the discussion to persuade your boss to take over the crisis themself or to find another manager in your influential people network who you have already identified as being capable of making decisions in your place.

Manage the amount of information

You must be careful to manage the quantity of information you give to your boss and never exceed whatever limit your boss has. You need to know your boss well enough to know what the limit is for information overload. If ever you exceed it, problems will start.

They will most likely say something like:

> 'I don't need all this detailed information you are giving me. Just go ahead and decide for yourself. If you have an important decision to make, let me know but only after you have decided.'

Now you are in serious trouble. You will have to deviate delegation to someone else – anyone other than the boss – to get your decisions made for you. This is very inconvenient. Remember that the reason you give your boss information in the first place is to elicit an opinion so that you can convert it into a deemed decision.

If you break the boss's information overload barrier you will lose an important source of decision-making. You will have to settle for getting fewer decisions made, which will increase the frustration levels of your subordinates, which in turn increases the risk of the secret getting out that you are a no-decision manager. You can, of course, try to transfer some decisions to the other experienced managers in your team, or to your colleagues, but this is much harder than getting the boss to make them for you.

Your boss's boss

Blandish the bosses includes managing your boss's boss. You need to set up yet another special relationship. Here the seduction level is by nature less intense. You don't need daily contact and you don't need to attempt to deviate delegation that would bypass the formal hierarchy. Information, though, is still key. You need to get your boss's opinion on projects or subjects directly related to you and your boss, to facilitate discussions with your boss later.

Influence at this level is also important. You need to pass on a constant message at every meeting with the boss's boss: 'I am a great manager doing a great job,' giving detailed examples of the excellent work you're doing.

> **Case study 26 – Systematic blandishing of the bosses**
>
> Caleb is an experienced no-decision manager. He has an extensive internal network and has good contact with his boss's boss, Alexander. At one of his visits to headquarters, he meets Alexander in the corridor.
>
> 'How is the new product introduction going?' asks Alexander.
>
> 'Great,' replies Caleb. 'The three major customers I visited have all put in massive orders and are doing special promotions on the product.'
>
> 'Plus,' he adds, 'Sales are well over budget. My team is executing the plan exactly as I instructed.'
>
> *Comments on case study 26*
>
> The message is always the same: 'I am a great manager doing a great job.' And, 'I am doing my job well.'
>
> Normal managers will naturally try to impress their boss's boss. They will not, however, do it with as much persistence, consistency or force as a no-decision manager.

One tactic for blandishing your boss's boss is to discuss ongoing projects with them, then put forward your boss's opinion and sit back and wait for the reaction. If the reaction is favourable, you can launch an exercise of influence by laying out the merits of the project, forcefully pushing the advantages in a sales pitch for the project, showing just how 'great' you are.

If, however, the boss's boss reacts unfavourably to the project you should immediately agree that the project is faulty and show some distance from it. Then you should quickly relay this information back to your boss with this early warning that part of top management is not in agreement. Here you will gain some points from your boss, for showing how well informed you are.

Further, you will have been warned and now you must take the time to prepare a plan to come out ahead in the difference of opinion between your boss and the boss's boss regardless of whether the project is finally approved or not.

An important principle to remember here is that as a no-decision manager you must never venture an opinion on any subject to the boss or the boss's boss before verification. If the two bosses agree, you can voice your approval. If they don't agree, your best bet is to hang back and wait until they resolve it. Do not get involved in any arguments.

Handling of hierarchy

'Handling of hierarchy' is a special survival action directed at colleagues of your boss and key managers in headquarters, which involves setting up special relationships with all of these people. It has nothing to do with the concept used on the boss's boss of 'I am a great manager doing a great job'.

It's immaterial to these people whether you are a great manager, or even whether you are performing your job adequately or not. You are making a good impression for strategic reasons. You are looking for allies for the future, for mutual help and support if ever needed, and of course for potential candidates for deviated delegation. To do this you need an exchange of important information and some self-promotion on your 'three greats' where you show that you are an expert who may be able to help in the future. You can show off your great knowledge of the industry, technology and the competition and your understanding of the company and its people to gain credibility and build trust.

> **Case study 27 – Proficient handling of hierarchy**
> Annabelle is a no-decision manager in charge of sales in Germany and is based in Frankfurt.
>
> Her subordinate, Dylan the administrative manager, discovers by chance that the rent on their offices is much higher than

the rent paid by other tenants in the building. Dylan decides to cancel the lease and find new, cheaper offices closer to the centre of Frankfurt.

Approval from headquarters is required for the relocation. Annabelle of course has no opinion on the subject, so Dylan discusses the project with the three senior executives in head office who will be involved in the final decision. All three have no objections to the move, requesting simply that the formal approval process be followed.

Dylan then spends several weeks searching for new premises, negotiating the rent and preparing a rental agreement, and he submits the project directly to the chief financial officer of the group for approval.

Some time later, Annabelle announces to Dylan that the project has been rejected because the assistant controller, Paul, is not in agreement.

'Who cares what the assistant controller thinks!' exclaims Dylan in frustration. 'All senior management approve the project. I checked before we even started to look for new offices.'

'The assistant controller, Paul, does not agree to rent new offices in Frankfurt,' is Annabelle's meek reply. End of story.

A shocked Dylan makes discreet enquiries to find out what happened. For the three executives in head office this was a minor decision and they were completely indifferent to new offices for the sales team in Frankfurt. The chief financial officer of the group simply passed the project down to the assistant controller, Paul, for a review of the financial analysis. Paul called Annabelle directly and announced that he was not aware that the division needed new offices in Frankfurt and said he did not agree. Annabelle did not back Dylan but instead agreed with Paul to withdraw the project from formal approval.

Comments on case study 27
This situation can happen in any company without the involvement of a no-decision manager. Paul would legitimately not agree with the project and persuade his bosses not to approve it. Or, as in this case, he would be upset that he had not been informed and do whatever he could to ensure the project did not go ahead. Annabelle, even if she were a normal manager, could change her mind and agree with Paul to cancel the project.

However, most normal managers would defend their team, especially after work was completed on a recommendation, and argue their case before accepting defeat within the normal approval process.

Here, the normal approval process was abandoned in advance because Annabelle, as a no-decision manager, just wanted somebody else to make a decision. She did not care who, or what the decision was. Paul decides, so she follows. Plus she knows that Paul has convinced his bosses not to approve the new offices.

But the most important issue for Annabelle is that she sees an opportunity to make a long-term ally of Paul by agreeing with him that Dylan should have consulted him at the outset and by showing Paul that she considers his opinion to be critical. Annabelle is simply applying the handling of hierarchy to help ensure her own future security.

Dylan, of course, should have contacted Paul at the outset. That was his mistake. The rest is normal company politics, which he did not adequately manage.

Relationship rectangle

The usual hierarchy is made up of the no-decision manager's boss, his colleagues, the no-decision manager's boss's boss and his colleagues, plus the rest of the headquarters staff of the organisation. This is the 'relationship rectangle' within which the no-decision manager operates. All members of the rectangle must be managed to some degree, depending on their influence and place in the hierarchy:

1. Blandish the bosses involves two people: the boss and the boss's boss.
2. Handling of hierarchy involves the boss's colleagues and also their senior and key managers in headquarters.
3. The Influential people network involves just that: influential people, often found to be colleagues of the boss's boss.
4. The Headquarters network involves the junior managers in headquarters who, in theory, have little influence but who can sometimes be very important.

You need to select each candidate for influence and put them into one of the four groups above, adapted to the reporting structure of your organisation and to your own level in the organisation. The easiest way is to take the organisational chart of your company and pick the managers for each group. You are free to move the managers from one group to another as circumstances change. You may find that it can be difficult to select the managers for the two groups Handling of hierarchy and Influential people network.

Figure 19, Relationship rectangle, shows the organisation chart of a hypothetical company with the hierarchy of the no-decision manager: the boss and colleagues, the boss's boss and colleagues and headquarters. It shows the overlap of different groups, namely: the influential people network, blandish the bosses and handling of hierarchy groups within the no-decision manager's hierarchy.

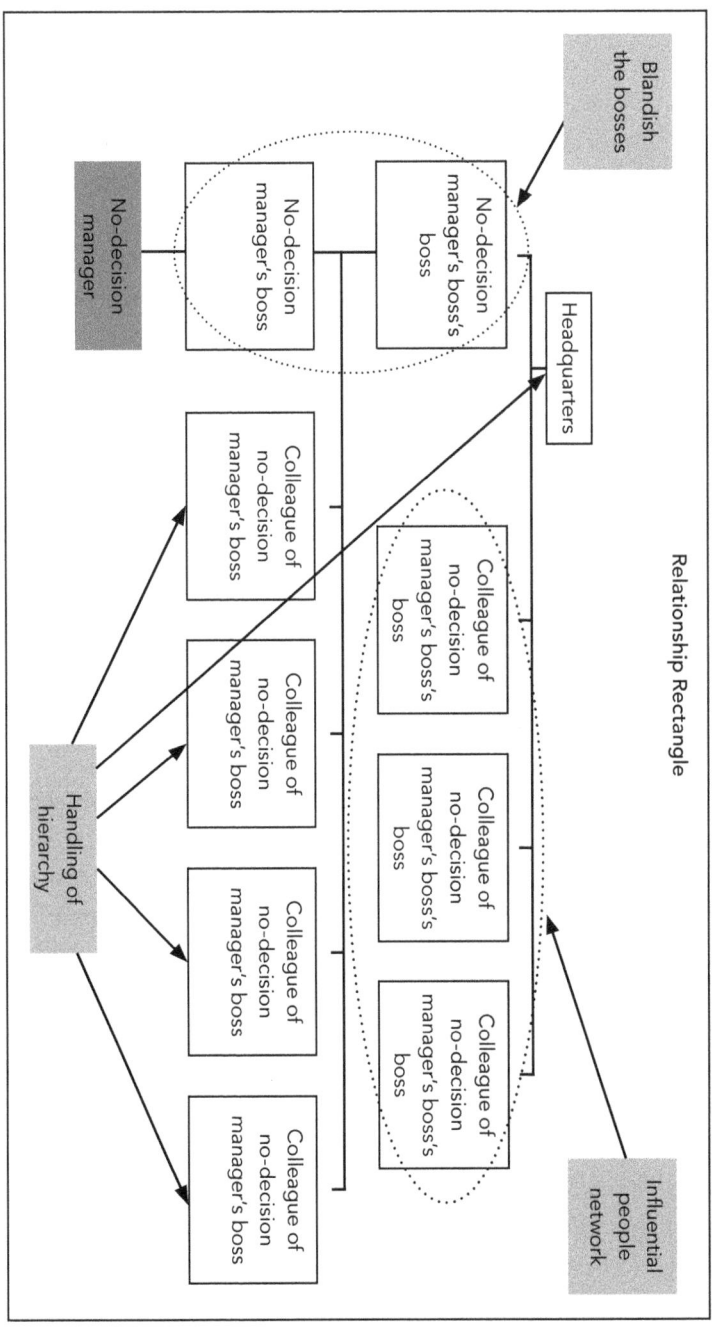

Figure 19 : Relationship Rectangle

Rumsfeld resolution

The 'Rumsfeld resolution' is simply the satisfactory outcome of a deviated upward delegation. Although former US Defence Secretary Donald Rumsfeld did not invent the concept, he made it famous through his quote: 'If in doubt move decisions up to the President.'

It is easy to get the boss to make the difficult decisions. The no-decision management movement has shown their appreciation for Donald Rumsfeld by naming this fundamental concept after him.

You, of course, must push the concept to its limit and try to make your boss decide the most simple, the trivial and the important decisions, but without overload, fatigue or refusal. Chapter 4 explains the process of deviated upward delegation and the other delegated decision types.

To be successful you need to make a detailed analysis of the decision-making preferences of your boss. These may differ depending on the type of decision at hand. Your boss's preferred style could be any one of directive, individualistic, analytic, fact-based, conceptual, behavioural, consensus seeking, rational, or intuitive – or some combination of several of these styles at the same time.

Your boss might have a consensus-seeking style for strategic decisions, a directive style for repetitive or routine decisions, a fact-based style for operational decisions, a conceptual style for innovative decisions, a rational style for programmed decisions, and to be intuitive with important decisions.

Then, you as the no-decision manager have to convince, manipulate, push and cajole your boss into deciding for you without any awareness of what you are actually doing, all the while adapting the process to his style and decision type.

You will find it impossible to have a long career as a no-decision manager without being successful at applying the Rumsfeld resolution. On a regular basis you will need to persuade your boss to take all the important decisions and as many of the others as possible. You must analyse his decision-making style carefully to avoid mistakes.

Case study 28 – Almost failing in the Rumsfeld resolution

Maya, an experienced no-decision manager, needs to hire someone to head up her accounting department. Florence from Human Resources contacts a recruitment agency to make the search, with instructions to present two candidates for the position. She decides to present two candidates from the agency and one internal candidate from the accounting department, namely Michael, who she has identified, following the company's procedures, as ready for promotion.

Maya convinces her boss to interview all three candidates, persuading him that the position is important and that she needs his opinion on all three. Maya's hope of course is to get her boss to decide on one candidate, a classic attempt at applying the Rumsfeld resolution.

Her boss, however, considers that all three candidates are excellent, and says to Maya:

'It's up to you. You decide. All three candidates are capable and would be valuable to accounting in the long term.'

A reasonable position by the boss, but terrifying for Maya as a no-decision manager. The decision is now hers to make. So what does she do? At first, nothing: permanent procrastination. Then she has endless meetings with Florence to discuss the merits of each candidate. This process takes several weeks and luckily for Maya eliminates one of the candidates, who accepts a position in another company.

The second external candidate is more patient, so Maya calls him in for another interview and then waits long enough for him to refuse to work in a company that takes so long to decide.

Eureka! There is only one candidate left: Michael, waiting for his promotion. Maya has successfully pushed the decision up to her boss. She calls him and says, 'I have decided to promote Michael!'

Comments on case study 28
Initially, Maya fails in her attempt at applying the Rumsfeld resolution because her boss does not choose one of the candidates. However, by self-elimination of candidates, permanent procrastination and holding an unnecessary second interview, she succeeds.

This behaviour could, of course, be similar to that of a normal manager who is hesitating between the different candidates and finds it difficult to decide. The convention in this company for the handling of this hiring process is that Maya's boss meets only the final candidate who she chooses for the position. But as a no-decision manager, she has managed to change the convention with the request to her boss to see all three candidates.

In this instance it is Florence in Human Resources who decides both to select a recruitment agency and to present Michael for promotion (deviated downward delegation), and also Maya convinces her boss to interview all three candidates (deviated upward delegation).

Organisations that no-decision managers should avoid
While the Shelter will provide the main support for you to continue as a no-decision manager, you must also consider other factors or survival will be short-lived. Two types of organisations never tolerate no-decision managers.

If you find yourself in one of these by mistake, you will be dismissed immediately. When interviewing, you need to ask the right questions to enable you to refuse a position in these two situations.

No-decision managers in great companies

No-decision managers do not join 'great companies'. Rosabeth Moss Kanter explains why in her *Harvard Business Review* article 'How Great Companies Think Differently' (2011):

> Great companies create frameworks that use societal value and human values as decision-making criteria.

Decision-making is everywhere in great companies. This is clearly not an environment that is friendly to no-decision managers. Further, no-decision managers do not have 'societal value'. Their only interest is in not making decisions. And they are not big on 'human values' either. For no-decision managers, such values do not exist in relation to their subordinates and employees lower in the hierarchy. 'Human values' are only relevant with their bosses and others higher up in the hierarchy.

The article concludes:

> Leaders in the great companies can tell a different story about the basis for their decisions. In so doing, they are able to produce new models for action that can restore confidence in business and will change the world in which we live.

Here we talk of 'decisions', 'actions' and 'change'– all words that are absent from the vocabulary of no-decision managers. It is easy to imagine how the tactics of 'active avoidance' would be abhorred in these companies. Delay decisions would be despised, deviation of delegation detested and 'outrageous behaviour' belittled. No-decision managers would not have time to set up their separated specialised informal networks, or show their expertise in the three greats, or be able to even start blandishing the bosses in these great companies before discovery and dismissal overtook them.

There might not even be time to figure out that the manager is a no-decision manager before dismissal. Their lack of clear leadership by itself would have identified them as unsuitable.

No-decision managers in organisations with decentralised decision-making

It is not only great companies that rapidly reject no-decision managers. In some organisations decisions are decentralised. These companies have a method of operating that encourages initiative, welcomes risk-taking and requires managers at all levels to decide on their own. These may not be 'great companies' but timely decision-making is a key characteristic of them. You will find it difficult to work in this type of environment. Instead of hiding out in excellence, your non-existent initiatives and complete lack of decision-making will quickly show up.

Further, in these organisations, your boss will not make decisions for you as a no-decision subordinate. Two of the pillars of the Shelter will quickly collapse: secrecy and survival; and you will be dismissed from the organisation.

> **Case study 29 – Deciding in decentralised companies**
> Edward from Case Study 20 has recently been promoted from a marketing position to his first managerial position as country sales and marketing director in Scotland. He needs to reorganise the sales force to adapt it to structural changes in the market. He sends his report to headquarters hoping that a decision will come down from them.
>
> But his misfortune comes from working in a decentralised decision-making company where management believes that each country manager should know the local market and customers better than headquarters, and so is in the best position to make decisions, even the important ones.
>
> His boss and headquarters put Edward under pressure to choose one scenario and put into place the new organisation. As a no-decision manager he is unable to make the decision and after a few weeks is fired.

Comments on case study 29

Edward is an inexperienced no-decision manager and makes many mistakes in deploying no-decision management tactics. He uses only permanent procrastination as a decision avoidance tactic. He does not have time to learn how to use the basic skills of deviated delegation and structured survival effectively.

But his greatest error, which cost him his job, was to accept a promotion in a company that he knew to be one where decisions are consistently pushed down the organisation and not taken at headquarters. Even if he had learned all the skills of no-decision management it would have been very difficult for him to survive in this organisation.

Bosses that no-decision managers should avoid

Two types of bosses will not tolerate no-decision managers: no-decision bosses and micro-managers. Accordingly, as a no-decision manager, you must choose your career path carefully. It is important when you are promoted or when you are searching for a new position in a new organisation to question your new potential boss on their management style and immediately reject the position if this boss is one of these two types.

If, however, one of these two types of manager is suddenly promoted to be your boss, be aware that your survival time is severely reduced regardless of anything you have learned as a no-decision manager. There is no way out – you will be fired unless you are able to move quickly to another part of your organisation.

No-decision boss

No-decision managers must never work for a no-decision boss. Two hierarchical levels of no-decision management bring any organisation to a complete standstill and quickly bring extreme frustration to subordinates. But above all, a double level of no-decision-making will be detected rapidly by the hierarchy, and the more senior no-decision manager will ensure that the blame for non-decisions will be put on the no-decision subordinate. The senior no-decision manager will then persuade their boss to fire their no-decision subordinate. It is always the no-decision manager lower in the hierarchy who faces the rapid end to their career.

> ### Case study 30 – A no-decision manager working for a no-decision boss
>
> Adam is a no-decision manager who has just been hired as head of a large marketing department. One of Adam's subordinates is Matthew, a no-decision product manager who has been in the marketing department for three years.
>
> Matthew has to prepare the annual budget for his product line. The budget he prepares is simply the sum of the propositions of his six product specialists. Adam in turn does the same, and he sends Matthew's budget up to his boss for approval. Adam's boss decides to cut Matthew's overall budget by 20%.
>
> As a true no-decision manager Matthew is unable to allocate the budget reductions to each of his product specialists. He just does nothing: permanent procrastination.
>
> But Matthew's six product specialists know that the overall budget has been lowered and they wait for him to allocate reductions to each of them. No decision comes down from Matthew, so the product specialists just go ahead and spend what they initially proposed, as though they were unaware of the budget cut. It is after all not up to them to volunteer that their budget be reduced.
>
> A few months into the year, Matthew's expenses explode compared to the approved budget. His boss, Adam, is not

able to order a reduction and because he is a true no-decision manager he must blame Matthew to protect himself.

A few months later, Adam's boss orders that Matthew be fired for not being able to control the expenses of his department.

Comments on case study 30

Adam, as a no-decision manager, is unable to help Matthew and give him a precise order to reduce expenses, which is fatal for Matthew. Adam is correct in blaming Matthew for not reducing expenses, but a normal manager in Adam's position would have been able to avoid the budget overrun.

Matthew is not even able to decide to reduce every product specialist's budget by 20%, which a normal manager who couldn't allocate specific reductions would probably do. He is relatively inexperienced as a no-decision manager and does not yet know of the deemed instruction concept and so considers even a 20% reduction to every product specialist to be a decision.

Micro-manager boss

No-decision managers must never work for a 'micro-manager' boss. This, as you probably know, is a boss who exercises excessive control over you and goes into minute detail on everything. He or she takes so much control that they make all the decisions – which in theory is a perfect situation for the no-decision manager. Unfortunately, because they go into so much detail they give you, the no-decision subordinate, numerous minor decisions to make quickly, which is quite impossible for you or any no-decision manager. By so doing, they quickly realise that you are a no-decision manager and will dismiss you.

To sum up, no-decision managers must not interview for positions in great companies or decentralised organisations. If they manage to get through the interviewing process for these types of jobs, discovery that they are no-decision managers will take just a few weeks and then they will be rapidly dismissed. No-decision managers must also check the management styles of their immediate bosses when interviewing and refuse positions where the boss is a no-decision manager or a micro-manager.

Information on no-decision managers

Decision dilemma

Despite your best efforts, because you are a manager, the inevitable will happen: your boss will force you as a no-decision manager to make an important and visible decision on your own. It is after all a manager's job to decide and make important decisions.

Most no-decision managers will not make the decision the first time they are asked. There is really no dilemma for them. It is not even a choice – it is a no-decision way of life. However, if the situation is repeated, the decision dilemma becomes a matter of staying on in the job or being fired.

The no-decision manager needs to ask themself the following question:

'Is it more difficult to make the decision and go through the inevitable stress, discomfort and terror of decision-making or to suffer the humiliation of the firing process, deal with unemployment, look for another job, go to interviews, and start another no-decision management career in a different organisation?'

Many no-decision managers cannot decide even at such an existential survival point. They just hope for the best, saying to themselves:

'Maybe my information sources are wrong and I will not be dismissed this time.'

It is at this moment, after they have repeatedly refused to make decisions more or less ordered directly by the boss, that many no-decision managers are found out and then fired. They have no more excuses or explanations to hide behind.

Some, however, may decide to decide.

Case study 31 – Reaching the survival point

Harper has to make a decision on financing. She is the no-decision financial controller for Hungary in a multinational company. Her analysis shows that her country needs additional short-term financing, which she fixes with the European Treasurer and which can be provided by any one of three banks in Hungary.

The European Treasurer asks Harper to choose one of the banks for the project and negotiate the terms of the financing. He is, however, not interested in the details of the project and says to Harper,

'Get it done by the end of February and let me know which bank you have chosen.'

Harper has nowhere to go. She cannot deviate delegation in any direction. It has been made her decision and hers alone. Many weeks pass. She receives the propositions from the banks and waits (permanent procrastination). By the end of April she still cannot choose which bank to appoint.

At the beginning of May, the European Treasurer tells Harper that there are insufficient funds to pay the salaries of the Hungarian branch at the end of the month.

Harper's choice now is clear. She can either choose a bank to provide financing or do nothing. If the salaries are not paid because of insufficient funds, Harper knows that she will be dismissed.

Desperate, she chooses a bank.

Comments on case study 31
But Harper chooses too late. By waiting until the last minute she

> allows the cash position of her country branch to deteriorate to such a dangerous level that the corporate finance director puts her under scrutiny. She does not last long. Some months later, she is discreetly asked to leave the company.
>
> Had Harper not made the decision she would have followed no-decision management to the end and she would have been fired anyway. She reaches her 'survival point' and is forced into making a decision, but the decision is difficult and she makes it too late, so she is fired.
>
> The 'survival point' is the only instance in which no-decision managers will make a decision. It is the only exception to the no-decision management rule. Harper's example shows that it does not always work.

No-decision managers do not always survive

Despite all these techniques for survival, whether structured or not, no-decision managers do not always survive. When they are inexperienced and unskilled, survival is precarious. When they are experienced and accomplished, survival rates are better, but they depend on correct and effective application of the four pillars of the Shelter: Survival, Skills, System and Secrecy. Secrecy and Survival are the key supports. Skills and System are secondary ones. If any one of the support pillars fails, the no-decision manager's personal Shelter collapses and the no-decision manager will be fired.

If the secret that they never take a decision becomes known to the boss, dismissal is usually swift and decisive. If survival has not been adequately developed, the no-decision manager will soon be considered inadequate and incompetent. The action to fire them may not be as swift or as violent, but it is as inevitable and certain.

If one of the secondary pillars: skills or system, fails, the personal Shelter will not immediately collapse. It will become fragile, shaky and lopsided but will stay upright on the three remaining pillars. The no-decision manager keeps his job, but will be under scrutiny. If the three required skills of great knowledge, great understanding and great analysis are not fully developed, any of these deficient skills will not on their own collapse the Shelter, nor will the relative inexperience in performing the tactics of the No-decision-making System, except for one tactic: deviating delegation. Incompetence in deviating delegation is dangerous especially with regard to upward and diagonal delegation. Without adequate skills in these areas, no-decision managers end up being confronted with many more decisions to make on their own, and are unable to find someone else to make them in their place, which seriously increases the risk of detection.

Summary – steps 24–31 to become a no-decision manager

Step 24 Set up the seven separated specialised informal networks with the five special no-decision management actions, and use Figure 18, Separated specialised informal networks, as a checklist.

Step 25 Systematically apply the five rules of blandish the bosses when dealing with your boss:

    a) Learn the basic techniques for managing your boss
    b) Learn the techniques of focused filtering
    c) Get into a special relationship – know your boss well enough to change their behaviour into making decisions for you
    d) Plan ahead for a crisis: be the first with the news and prepare who will make your decisions for you
    e) Manage the limit of information overload.

Step 26 Apply the two rules of blandish the bosses when dealing with your boss's boss

a) Get into special relationships
b) Manage influence and information.

Step 27 Handling of hierarchy – build relationships with colleagues of your boss and key managers in headquarters to show off your expertise in the three greats.

Step 28 Use the relationship rectangle (Figure 19) and your company's organisational chart to select the managers for each of the four groups: blandish the bosses, handling of hierarchy, influential people network and the headquarter network.

Step 29 Perfect the Rumsfeld resolution by making a detailed analysis of the different decision-making preferences of your boss.

Step 30 Avoid organisations that are 'great' companies or organisations that have decentralised decision-making.

Step 31 Avoid having no-decision managers and micro-managers as your boss.

Annex 1 summarises the steps required to become a no-decision manager.

7

How to Become an Enlightened Subordinate

'How to' advice for subordinates

Initial reactions to a no-decision boss

Your first encounter with a no-decision boss will be a pleasant one. They are generally friendly, approachable and invariably intelligent.

In discussing your new boss with a colleague you might say:

'My new boss seems friendly and knows the industry very well.'
'He seems to know what he wants in his new job.'
'He appears to be good-humoured and courteous.'
'My first impressions are good. She comes across as knowledgeable and approachable.'

Your positive feelings will continue up to the moment the first decision needs to be made by your boss and you are on the receiving end of the inevitable tactic the new no-decision boss will use to avoid making it. This will usually be permanent procrastination but it could be any of the other tactics available. Your reaction might now be:

'OK, so the new boss is slow in making decisions. Let's give him
the benefit of the doubt and wait.'

After the second or third decision that your no-decision boss should make but does not, your emotional journey with them starts. It goes through several phases.

Your first emotion is simple surprise. Surprise that no decisions are being made.

'He is the boss after all and is there to make decisions. Yet he is not
taking any.'
'That's four simple decisions that are waiting to be taken, and we
have reminded her. Why is she waiting?'

You will start talking with your colleagues and learn that you all think that decision-making seems to have come to an end. You wonder when the boss will make decisions. You wonder why he or she has not done so. You begin to wonder about the consequences for you and your department of the delay in making these decisions.

Your initial surprise will eventually shift towards insecurity, especially when your boss starts to use other more sophisticated decision avoidance tactics. You will at first assume that you are at fault and have not provided sufficient good-quality information to enable your new boss to make the decision.

You might start to ask:

'Is it my work that is not good enough?'
'Is it my fault that the boss cannot make these decisions?'

Or, for instance, if the no-decision boss uses 'ignoring' as a tactic, the questions might be:

'Why is she suddenly ignoring me?'
'How can I contact him to get a decision made?'

After a time you will discover that you are never able to produce enough valid information to get a decision made, and that the volume of information requested for even a simple decision is far in excess of what you consider necessary.

Frustration

Your insecurity will soon be replaced by frustration, and that frustration will have several degrees of intensity.

Mild frustration

Mild frustration is brought on initially by the extra work necessary to produce incremental information, then by judicial absence when you find that your new no-decision boss is never in the office, cannot be contacted and is rarely available for meetings. Your discussions with him or her will stay cordial and friendly, but nothing gets done, nothing moves forward and no decisions are made, even simple ones. This will cause you some exasperation, and then intense irritation and annoyance every time you are confronted with each new tactic used to avoid decision-making.

> **Case study 32 – An encounter with mild frustration**
> Sashi, a young software programmer, works for Harvey, her no-decision IT manager. She has finished preparing her new programme and is trying to persuade Harvey to authorise its diffusion into the company's system. Sashi's programme makes the weekly backup more automatic and reliable, and it saves employees time.
>
> All Harvey has to do is send out written instructions authorising the introduction of the new programme. But for Harvey this is not only a decision, but worse – it is a written one. He is never going to send the instructions.
>
> But Sashi doesn't know this yet because this is the first time she

> has worked for a no-decision manager. Harvey just waits, doing nothing.
>
> Sashi prepares a long report on the advantages of her new programme, with the usual to and fro imposed by Harvey in several requests for 'incremental information'. She waits in mild frustration for a decision that never comes.

Moderate frustration

By now, like Sashi, you will be spending time trying to persuade your new no-decision boss to make the pending decisions. You will try many different persuasive tactics: simple discussion, persuasion with insistence, seduction, mild coercion or maybe even a bout of anger, to see which one gets a decision.

> **Case study 32 continued – Discovering moderate frustration**
> Sashi is bewildered. In trying to force a decision from her no-decision boss, Harvey, she spends hours discussing her new programme with him trying to persuade him to sign the release. But all she manages to obtain from him is his repeated agreement that it is a good programme, well-adjusted to the needs of the backup process.
>
> Sashi's own team in turn becomes impatient and starts putting pressure on her to get the programme approved. To salvage some of her own self-esteem, she invites Harvey to attend a presentation on the new programme in the presence of her team. Harvey's comment at the end is simply, 'Good presentation. Well done.'
>
> But no decision follows.

At least Sashi has shown her team that she is not the person holding up the decision.

When your repeated efforts to try to force a decision fail, and with your boss gradually increasing the number of decision avoidance tactics, mild frustration will increase to moderate frustration. Now you will start to judge your boss's ability and behaviour, saying things like:

> 'He never decides, he is never in the office, he is never available, he never seems to do anything. He is lazy.'
> 'She has no courage to make even the most simple decisions.'
> 'He won't listen, he does what he wants, he is so rigid.'
> 'She must be incompetent – she cannot even make a simple decision.'

Case study 32 continued – Moving on to moderate frustration
Sashi is now deep into moderate frustration. She discusses the new system with her colleagues who complete the backup each week and who will benefit most from the programme when it is introduced.

They all agree that it is exactly what they need. Some of them talk to Harvey to recommend that he gives his agreement.

It is a now a simple decision for Harvey, but he still does not decide.

Severe frustration
Your journey from moderate to severe frustration will proceed inevitably with time. As the length of time you wait increases so will the intensity of your frustration.

Case study 32 continued – Overwhelmed by severe frustration
Sashi has all sorts of emotions going through her – annoyance, resentment, disappointment and more – with her no-decision boss and she moves into severe frustration. She really cannot understand what is going on. There is universal approval from

> her colleagues of her programme and yet Harvey will not give her the approval to go ahead.
>
> He is the boss after all – in a management position with extensive experience. He is paid to make this decision. It is his responsibility. Yet he does nothing.

Acute frustration

Now that you are experiencing severe frustration you have a choice whether to escalate it up to acute frustration. This is when you lose control and let your frustration and anger overwhelm you. You might for instance start shouting at your no-decision boss. You might walk out of a meeting. You might slam the door. You will most likely not go this far, but you will feel like doing something similar.

As Molly Ringle wrote in her book *Relatively Honest* (2011):

> And I got out of there without punching anyone, kicking anyone, or breaking down in tears. Some days the small victories are all you achieve.

This is a good description of acute frustration. However, there are no 'small victories' when dealing with a no-decision boss. It is impossible to stay in acute frustration for long, so after a time its intensity will diminish and you will go back to the state of severe frustration.

> **Case study 32 continued – Control of acute frustration**
> Sashi is polite and inexperienced enough not to go into acute frustration against Harvey.
>
> Through discussions with her colleagues, she starts to realise that this is not the only decision that Harvey isn't making. She hears of several other decisions that are on hold, where her colleagues are complaining of his lack of decision-making. Now she knows she is not alone.

But she does start thinking ahead:

'I cannot continue like this, I will have to look for another job.'

She wants to get away from her no-decision manager as quickly as possible.

Comments on case study 32
Sashi has not read Molly Ringle's book but she feels like punching and kicking even without knowing that example. Her frustration level is very high.

Fundamental frustration
After having spent some time in a state of severe frustration you will eventually realise that your no-decision boss will never make decisions. This knowledge, a sort of negative awakening, moves you into a state known in the no-decision movement as 'fundamental frustration' – a type of permanent, severe frustration. You have suddenly found a boss who never decides. You probably never knew that such a manager even existed. But now you have one as your boss.

Whoever said, 'To conquer frustration, one must remain intensely focused on the outcome, not the obstacles,' has clearly never worked for a no-decision boss.

The outcome when working for a no-decision manager is not the decision that needs to be made. The outcome is that no decision will ever be made. If subordinates concentrate on trying to get a decision made, it will just increase their frustration. The advice does not work. In fact, focusing on the obstacle does not work either.

Case study 33 – Bypassing fundamental frustration
Ellis is in charge of a production line and is in fundamental frustration with his boss Hunter, the no-decision factory manager.

Ellis needs approval to buy equipment to reduce costs on his line. The approval level for these investments stops at Hunter's level. Ellis cannot understand why his boss cannot make this simple decision. The manufacturing plant has a goal to reduce costs. The amount is within the budget. The analysis is complete. The investment has even been discussed with Hunter's boss. But Ellis knows that Hunter will never sign off on the investment.

He decides to bypass Hunter by calling Hunter's boss in headquarters to talk about the investment. Hunter's boss asks one of the factory controllers to investigate and resolve the issue between Hunter and Ellis.

It is true that Ellis concentrates on the outcome and bypasses the obstacle – his boss – by getting his decision made through headquarters. But in the end this changes nothing in respect of subsequent approvals and decisions. He cannot continue to call Hunter's boss whenever he needs Hunter to make a decision.

Comments on case study 33
Ellis is unable to accept the situation that his boss never makes decisions, so he bypasses him. He is doing two things. First, he is letting management know that Hunter is a no-decision manager. Second, he is resolving his immediate problem. But he cannot continue to bypass Hunter whenever he needs a decision.

He feels some relief that upper management is now aware that his boss is a no-decision manager. But he has not resolved his own basic problem. He is still experiencing fundamental frustration and decisions are still not being made.

Some subordinates believe in their management and in their organisation, arguing that such an incompetent manager, one who never makes decisions, must be discovered sooner or later and will at some stage be dismissed. They believe that they, the subordinates, have more value to their company than the no-decision boss and so they will survive in the longer term.

Figure 20: Herzberg's Motivation-Hygiene Theory for subordinates in fundamental frustration

Original theory taken from Frederick Hertzberg's article 'One More Time: How do You Motivate Employees? ', (*Harvard Business Review*, January 2003)

Leading to dissatisfaction	Leading to satisfaction
Company policy	Achievement
Supervision	Recognition
Relationship with the boss	Work itself
Work conditions	Responsibility
Salary	Advancement
Relationship with peers	Growth

Reprinted by permission of *Harvard Business review*. Copyright © 1968 by Harvard Business Publishing; all rights reserved

Theory adapted for subordinates in fundamental frustration, adapted from Frederick Hertzberg's article 'One More Time: How do You Motivate Employees?', (*Harvard Business Review*, January 2003)

Leading to dissatisfaction	Leading to satisfaction
Company policy – same as a normal manager	Achievement– restricted by lack of decisions
Supervision– none	Recognition– none
Relationship with the boss – poor	Work itself– cannot get everything done through lack of decisions of the boss
Work conditions– same as a normal manager	Responsibility– none
Salary– same as a normal manager	Advancement– halted
Relationship with peers– same as a normal manager	Growth– none

Reproduced and amended with permission of *Harvard Business Review*. Original Copyright © 1968 by Harvard Business Publishing; all rights reserved.

If you choose to sweat it out, you will most likely stay in fundamental frustration for an undetermined time. This is not without risk to your mental and emotional health, if the waiting period is long.

Frederick Herzberg's Motivation-Hygiene Theory (shown in Figure 20) illustrates how bad you will end up feeling if you stay in a state of fundamental frustration. The first table in Figure 20 shows the job factors that lead to satisfaction, and conversely dissatisfaction, for the average employee. The second table shows how the subordinates of no-decision managers experiencing fundamental frustration fare on these factors. All the factors leading to satisfaction that are listed in the figure deteriorate without exception. You get nothing done because of the lack of decisions. You have no recognition and no responsibility. Any advancement is halted and growth possibilities for you are now zero. Regarding the factors for dissatisfaction there are two changes. You have no supervision from your no-decision boss. This can be considered as an improvement for some subordinates who will be happy that they can do what they want without supervision. However, others will be frustrated that nobody is giving direction to their work, so they do not know what to do. Whichever category you fall into, your relationship with the boss is deteriorating.

But, if your objective is to become an enlightened subordinate you must do your best to reject fundamental frustration and move on to another way of dealing with your boss.

Explicit exit

'Explicit exit' is the most natural choice when you are an inexperienced subordinate who has never had a no-decision manager as your boss and have reached fundamental frustration.

Up until a few years ago, this choice was called 'determined desertion' by the no-decision movement: 'determined' because there is a firm resolution to get away from the no-decision boss. But the military connotation of 'desertion' was considered too aggressive and negative, so the Shelter voted for a more neutral name, explicit exit. In simple terms, this means leaving the no-decision boss in one way or another.

There are essentially three ways to execute explicit exit:

a) Resign from the organisation
b) Get a promotion
c) Arrange to be laid off or dismissed.

The easiest and quickest way is to just quit your job as soon as you can, when faced with a no-decision boss. The slowest way is to try to gain a promotion. If you didn't start doing that before your no-decision boss arrived, then this will take time and persistence.

> Case study 33 continued – Executing explicit exit
> Ellis is fed up with working with his no-decision boss Hunter, even though he has started to find ways to get around Hunter's lack of decision-making. Management now knows that Hunter is a no-decision manager. Ellis is the one who told them. But nothing has happened. Hunter is still the boss and he is still making no decisions.
>
> Ellis decides that he cannot continue working under these conditions so he prepares his CV and starts interviewing for jobs in another company. But before he completes the process, he is promoted as factory manager in Poland with a different boss. He achieves his immediate objective, to get far away from Hunter, his no-decision boss.
>
> Hunter is not so lucky. His no-decision status is acted on and he is dismissed.
>
> *Comments on case study 33*
> There is nothing unusual about this situation. Many people leave their organisations because they do not get on with their boss. Ellis, though, wants to leave because his boss does not make decisions.

The most complex way of executing explicit exit is to get yourself fired. Your new no-decision boss is not going take the decision to fire you, so you need to identify another manager more senior to do it – usually your no-decision boss's boss. Then you need to choose an offence or error so great and so visible that the no-decision boss will be ordered to terminate you. Not only is this complicated, but it could be dangerous for you in pursuing a future career in the same industry.

However, if your objective is to become an enlightened subordinate you have a decision to make. If you are genuinely suffering while working with your no-decision boss, then clearly explicit exit is the fastest and most effective way to end the suffering and get on with your career. But before you decide, ask yourself the question: what are you going to do if you have to work with another no-decision boss in another organisation in the future? Leave again? Leave every time you find yourself working for one?

My advice is: do not decide to leave just yet. Read on. See what alternatives you have in terms of working with your no-decision boss. Then, if you think that becoming an enlightened subordinate is interesting, forget about resigning for the moment and carry on working for your no-decision boss in one of the different 'enlightened' modes. If nothing else you will learn how to work with no-decision managers positively and not suffer from the experience. And anyway, you can always leave whenever you want. It is still your decision.

Reticent resignation

'Reticent resignation' is usually the choice after eliminating explicit exit and deciding to stay with a no-decision boss. If you choose this option you are ready to endure the lack of decision-making, in a sort of passive submission, resigned to your circumstances. You agree to put up with your no-decision boss and distance yourself from frustration.

You attitude becomes:

> 'It is, after all, up to the boss to make the decision, not the subordinate.'

And you become resigned to the no-decision environment.

'It is not my problem, and anyway, I cannot do anything to change it.'

You can, of course, see the damage your no-decision boss is doing to your department or organisation but you feel you are unable to influence the situation. You will reluctantly slip into reticent resignation, putting up with a lack of decision-making. It does not stop you complaining, but you complain only to your colleagues. You continue to exchange stories and experiences on the latest decision avoidance techniques, the impact on your respective teams and the damage being done to the departments. But you no longer complain to your boss.

Reticent resignation is still a negative choice, but you can stay in it over long periods of time, more easily than if you're in a state of fundamental frustration.

However, if your objective is to become an enlightened subordinate, do not stay in this negative emotion. Move on to a more positive one.

Relentless resignation

Employees further down the hierarchy in the organisation – that is, those not working directly with the no-decision manager – will be drawn into a similar form of resignation. The no-decision movement calls this 'relentless resignation', and it is less intense but also involves no hope of having any influence on the situation.

At some stage, these employees will realise that there is a no-decision manager somewhere further up the hierarchy. They will recognise that no important decisions are ever made – not because of their immediate boss but because of someone higher up the ladder. These employees may talk to their boss, who, depending on his or her emotional state, may or may not confirm that the boss is a no-decision manager. They will, however, eventually realise that there is nothing they can do to influence decision-making. Anger, they know, is a waste of energy so resignation eventually sets in for the long term. The choice of leaving the organisation is always available, but those who decide to stay will do so in this state of relentless resignation.

When the no-decision boss is in top management and responsible for many employees, after a few years his or her organisation will be working with most employees in a state of relentless resignation. This reduces performance levels, generates low morale and results in an overall negative attitude. It is often the cause of the decline and slow death of the organisation if the no-decision boss's hierarchy allows them to stay in place for many years. Employees will carry out their allotted hours of work each day with no challenge, no enthusiasm, and no initiative, having lost hope of any improvement in their organisation.

This situation is similar to having any toxic manager in a key position within an organisation; one, for instance, who constantly makes bad decisions or just an indecisive manager who is slow to decide.

Constant conflict

If you are someone who is combative, you will choose what is called in the jargon 'constant conflict'. Here you stay in a continuous state of confrontation with your no-decision boss. You decide to fight. You pressure your boss every time a decision should be made, usually in anger, holding long emotional discussions in an attempt to force a decision.

Having moved from fundamental frustration into constant conflict, you know quite well that your no-decision boss will never make a decision. However, you believe it is unfair that a senior manager should be left in place, allowed to get away with never making decisions. You believe that if you make your no-decision boss's life as miserable as possible, this will force them to either make a decision or resign to get away from the pressure. You will also find that the bouts of anger provide a form of relief from the strain and frustration of working for a no-decision boss.

Case study 34 – Working in constant conflict

Farida is a sales co-ordinator for her company's distributors in Ireland. She has been in the company for many years, while her boss Anna, the no-decision sales manager, has recently been promoted.

Farida moves quickly into fundamental frustration with Anna until she discovers that her remuneration is restricted by her boss. Farida's commission is based on gross margin. She proposes to increase the prices of her distributors in Ireland in line with those in England and Scotland. And with no decision from Anna, her frustration turns into anger.

For Farida it is a question of principle:

Principle 1, there is no reason not to align prices in Ireland with those in the UK.

Principle 2, Anna systematically refuses to make any marketing decisions.

Principle 3, Anna is the boss and yet does not make any decisions.

These differences in opinion continue for several months to such a level that Farida is provoked into constant conflict with Anna and they have bitter arguments every time they meet. Farida regularly and vehemently argues her case for price increases, but Anna never agrees with the increases.

During a regular business review with headquarters, Anna's boss discovers the important difference in margins between the distributors in Ireland and those in the UK for the same products. He immediately instructs Anna to increase prices in

> Ireland in line with those proposed by Farida.
>
> Anna implements the order from her boss and signs the letters authorising the price increases. Despite this victory, Farida stays in conflict with Anna. She cannot come to terms with the permanent lack of decision-making of her boss.
>
> *Comments on case study 34*
> Anna, even if she was a normal manager, would be quite entitled to refuse Farida's proposals for price increases. She is after all the boss, and it is her responsibility. There could be many other reasons for the conflict between the two.
>
> Anna, though, gives no real explanations for her refusals other than using classical no-decision tactics to delay decision-making until her boss decides for her. And the only reason Farida is angry with her boss is because she refuses to make decisions.

However, constant conflict is not a long-term solution for anyone, and if your objective is to become an enlightened subordinate, you must abandon this alternative as well.

Peaceful patience

A small minority of subordinates sometimes discover on their own that there is a positive way to work with no-decision bosses. It requires an active choice, involves three steps and, in the past before this book was written, was only possible if you had read a little Aristotle and Wordsworth, without necessarily having studied philosophy or English literature!

However, when it is explained to subordinates (which has never been done in writing before), a majority do eventually choose this mode of working with no-decision managers.

Your first step is to acknowledge that your new boss is never going to make a decision and simply to decide to live with this. Your pain experienced from working with him or her comes in the form of frustration, resignation or conflict – whatever state you have chosen.

The second step is to choose to become calm and uncomplaining, and accept and live through your negative emotions, i.e. become patient. Patience requires the calm acceptance of your negative emotion towards your no-decision boss. As Aristotle said: 'Patience is bitter but its fruit is sweet.'

But on its own, patience is not sufficient. You need a third step. This involves banning what Wolff-Michael Roth called 'uncomplaining endurance of pain, affliction and inconvenience' in his 2011 work *Passibility: at the Limits of the Constructive Metaphor.* Aristotle called this 'banning the bitterness'. Here you need to adopt a process of internal psychological introspection relying on the advice of the major 18th-century English Romantic poet William Wordsworth. It is now well known that Wordsworth wrote his poetry from the standpoint of 'emotion recollected in tranquillity'. You just need to adopt his strategy. You no longer live in your emotion. You transcend it and look back on your time spent in negative emotion from a perspective of 'tranquillity'.

You really don't need to have studied or even have read any Wordsworth. Just move into the state of tranquillity by adopting the 'Wordsworth Way':

Step one – acknowledge that your boss will never decide
Step two – be patient and combine this with
Step three – tranquillity (eliminating the bitterness from your patience).

In the jargon of the no-decision movement this state is called 'peaceful patience'. Peaceful patience is simply patience minus the frustration, resignation or conflict that comes with working for a no-decision boss. You understand that a decision will never be made. You have surrendered to this reality and have accepted, with no aggressiveness, that your boss will never make decisions. You stop the pressure for decision-making. You reach a place of peace and acceptance.

Case study 35 – Learning about peaceful patience

Esme and Toby are two subordinates of Maryan, a no-decision manager. Esme is in fundamental frustration with Maryan. Toby is in peaceful patience.

In a discussion one day about their boss, Toby says to Esme:

'Why are you always pestering Maryan? You know she never makes any decisions and yet you're always so upset.'

'It is so annoying that we never get anything done. She makes excuses all the time, gives us extra work to do, and then never decides,' replies Esme.

'Why don't you just accept that she never decides and do your work as best you can, without the decisions?' suggests Toby. 'That's what I do. She is the boss after all. Not making decisions is the way she runs her department even if we don't like it.'

It takes a little time for Esme to understand Toby's wise advice, but, eventually, she sees that there is an alternative to her unsatisfying fundamental frustration and eventually moves into peaceful patience with Maryan.

Comments on case study 35
The only thing that Esme changes is her attitude towards her boss. The work is the same. Maryan still does not decide. Still nothing gets done. Esme continues to work as before.

But now that she is in a state of peaceful patience she does not have to waste her time reminding Maryan that a decision is pending and that it needs to be made. Life is peaceful.

OK, so by adopting peaceful patience you have now achieved a more positive working relationship with your no-decision boss. You can choose to remain in this state, as many subordinates do. It is after all a pleasant emotion. Your boss may not take any decisions, but they never give you any orders, never set you any deadlines, never monitor or comment on the work you do or don't do, and are now permanently friendly towards you. There are no constraints. It is a state where you can enjoy the show and watch the no-decision tactics deployed on others with detachment. You don't need to take any initiatives, just work passively with your no-decision superior. You carry out your tasks as best as you can without any decisions being made.

On reaching this higher level you are on the way to becoming an enlightened subordinate but you are not there yet. You still have another step to take.

Aphonic acknowledgement

To become a truly enlightened subordinate you need to move into a state that the no-decision jargon labels 'aphonic acknowledgement'. You have three separate ways into this state.

Not only do you have to know a little Aristotle and some Wordsworth to get to here, now your essential reading includes Dickens.

Silent pact

In the passage in *Great Expectations* by Charles Dickens where Herbert is nursing Pip's burnt arm and hands after a fire on a boat, Pip narrates:

> Neither of us spoke of the boat, but we both thought of it. That was made apparent by our avoidance of the subject, and by our agreeing – without agreement – to make my recovery of the use of my hands, a question of so many hours, not of so many weeks.

Remember, silence always reigns between the no-decision boss and you the subordinate on the subject of no-decision management. It becomes your shared but never acknowledged secret.

Dickens captures the situation beautifully:

'Neither of us spoke…but we both thought of it.'

'It' in your case is the avoidance of decision-making, known to both of you but never discussed.

'…that was made apparent by our avoidance of the subject.'

So you must continue to avoid the subject of decision-making or the lack of it.

'…and by our agreeing – without agreement.'

You make a silent pact with your no-decision boss to go into aphonic acknowledgement and take decisions in place of the boss.

By entering into aphonic acknowledgement you implicitly agree to make the decisions normally made by your boss. In peaceful patience you do not take over the decision-making function. But aphonic acknowledgement transfers decision-making from the no-decision boss to you, the subordinate. You take the initiative.

Aphonic acknowledgement, then, is peaceful patience with an added feature: decisions are made by you, the subordinate. This is the level of at which you reach enlightenment when working with a no-decision manager.

> ### Case study 36 – Making a silent pact
> Ethan is the newly appointed IT department head, and arrives with a reputation as a no-decision manager. Myra is a subordinate in Ethan's department. She has already experienced working with no-decision managers, so she is looking out for an incident

that will provoke a silent pact with him, to enable her to move into aphonic acknowledgement.

The opportunity comes with the upgrade of the company's computer hardware. The budget was agreed before Ethan's promotion, but the ultimate decision on the make, model, size, timing and type of hardware configuration has been left to Ethan.

Myra makes out her report, sets up a meeting and prepares all the documents for Ethan to sign. She takes two minutes to explain the project, looks up at Ethan and gets his silent agreement – without any discussion.

Then Myra says: 'I'll sign everything.'

Myra signs the documents authorising the investment and sends out the orders. She takes the decision without any apparent reaction from her boss Ethan.

Comments on case study 36
Myra chooses an elegant way of moving into aphonic acknowledgement by being open with Ethan and telling him exactly what she is doing. She is an enlightened subordinate.

Deviated downward delegation
The second way to achieve aphonic acknowledgement does not use the Dickens model and is more brutal, but very simple. You just start making decisions that your boss would normally take. You don't tell your boss. You implement deviated downward delegation for the boss, or 'take it anyway' as a subordinate, as discussed in Chapter 4. There is no agreement here between the two of you. You decide to take your boss's decisions. That's all.

Case study 37 – Applying 'Take it anyway'

Olivia is a no-decision senior product manager in charge of a large team at headquarters. Eva is in a state of peaceful patience and has never made any of Olivia's decisions. She is a product manager who wants to revitalise her product line. A new product has been released by research and development, so Eva wants to phase out the old products and concentrate her efforts on the new one.

She completes her report to Olivia with her proposal to stop production of the old product immediately, and to start commercialisation of the new one within the next two months, with a special discount on the old products to reduce inventories and minimise any potential losses of excess components. She receives no reaction from Olivia on the report.

Eva knows that Olivia will not make the decision. She risks having to maintain the old and new product simultaneously for a long time. She co-ordinates with research and development and production to decide with them the most effective date to phase out the old product line, and then sends out a memo to the sales team to announce the decision.

Apart from giving her no-decision boss the initial report she does not consult or inform Olivia of what she is doing. She just takes the necessary decisions as though she has full authority, which she does not. These decisions are Olivia's to make, but Eva makes them for her.

Comments on case study 37

Instead of the silent pact approach, Eva goes ahead with the take it anyway approach. She decides herself what she thinks is best without informing Olivia, apart from her initial report.

> By making this decision Eva moves into aphonic acknowledgement and becomes an enlightened subordinate working for Olivia.
>
> A normal product manager working for a normal manager would wait for input and for the decision of their boss before announcing a product phase-out. Had Eva been working with a manager who makes decisions, she would have worked closely with her boss to organise and plan the product phase-out.

Outrageous behaviour

The third way to reach aphonic acknowledgement is to recognise your no-decision boss's 'outrageous behaviour' for what it is and understand the two messages that it is giving you.

You may not yet, as a subordinate, have encountered 'outrageous behaviour' from your no-decision boss. If you have not, go back to the section Outrageous behaviour in Chapter 4 and read what happens when no-decision bosses decide to do something outrageous. Your boss will suddenly do something out of character and ludicrous, which will seem to you to be quite stupid.

No-decision bosses do not act in a stupid manner to wind up subordinates emotionally. They have not had a moment of madness. They are in reality trying to send you, the subordinate, two messages:

1. Stop pestering me for a decision
2. Come and work with me positively.

'Stop pestering me for a decision' is straightforward. You or another subordinate have been pushing too hard for a decision from the no-decision boss and this 'outrageous behaviour' will come across as a rather violent release of this pressure to make a decision.

'Come and work with me positively' is more devious and

complicated to understand because your boss will never say it out loud. You, the subordinate, have to go through the intellectual exercise of wondering why your boss has suddenly had a moment of madness and then you must come to a conclusion that what they are asking is for you to come directly into aphonic acknowledgement and take their decisions for them.

If you, the subordinate, are currently in a state of fundamental frustration or reticent resignation, or even in constant conflict with your no-decision boss, this is the moment to make the jump into aphonic acknowledgement, having just experienced an act of 'outrageous behaviour' from your no-decision boss.

Imagine what it is like for the subordinates who have never had all this explained to them. They have no idea why their boss is behaving in such an outrageous manner. They have to convert this behaviour into a message. They then need to understand the message. But this is still not sufficient. They have to work out that working with a no-decision boss in a positive manner is even possible. They have to know that the state of aphonic acknowledgement exists. Then they must choose to accept it, while they are in a highly charged emotional state – either frustrated or angry with their no-decision boss.

In conclusion, there are three ways into aphonic acknowledgement for subordinates who work for a no-decision boss. Two ways are available through peaceful patience. The most elegant is with a silent pact and the most direct is through deviated downward delegation. The most complex is through 'outrageous behaviour'.

Figure 21, Working for a no-decision manager: the emotional journey, graphically shows the different states of working with a no-decision boss, and the three routes into aphonic acknowledgement.

Frederick Herzberg and his Motivation-Hygiene Theory shows you what an excellent choice aphonic acknowledgement really is. Three of the factors leading to satisfaction, according to Herzberg's theory, will improve significantly. Your ability to achieve will have no limits. You will have the freedom to work on whatever you want and take on the level of responsibility that you feel comfortable with. OK,

Figure 21: Working for a no-decision manager: the emotional journey

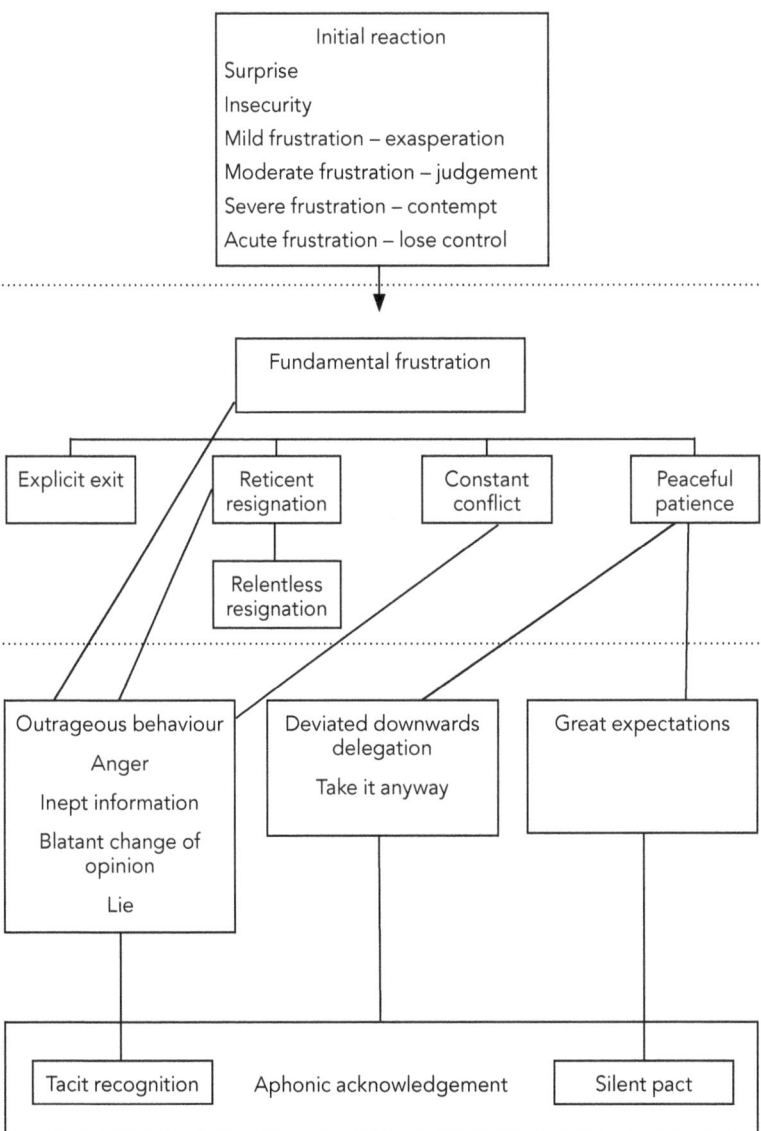

so you have no recognition and your advancement is halted, but this would be the case whenever you work with a no-decision boss anyway. Among the factors for dissatisfaction there are these two major changes. As always with no-decision bosses you will have no supervision; however, your relationship with them will improve significantly. See Figure 22, Herzberg's Motivation-Hygiene Theory for enlightened subordinates in aphonic acknowledgement.

Figure 22: Herzberg's Motivation-Hygiene Theory for enlightened subordinates in aphonic acknowledgement

Leading to dissatisfaction	Leading to satisfaction
Company policy – same as a normal manager	Achievement – freedom to achieve
Supervision – none, so satisfactory	Recognition – none
Relationship with the boss – excellent	Work itself – can do what they want
Work conditions – same as a normal manager	Responsibility – take whatever they want
Salary – same as a normal manager	Advancement – halted
Relationship with peers – same as a normal manager	Growth– limited but can learn from the boss

Adapted from Frederick Hertzberg's article 'One More Time: How do You Motivate Employees?' (*Harvard Business Review*, January 2003)

Reproduced and amended with permission of *Harvard Business Review*. Original Copyright © 1968 by Harvard Business Publishing; all rights reserved.

Compare for a moment Figure 20 Herzberg's Motivation-Hygiene Theory for subordinates in fundamental frustration with Figure 22. Applying Herzberg, there is clearly no case for staying in fundamental frustration compared to moving into aphonic acknowledgement. The latter state is better for you and is better for your no-decision boss.

By moving into aphonic acknowledgement you have now become an enlightened subordinate. You are in the highest possible positive state working with your no-decision boss,

but you are not finished yet. You need to decide which level of enlightenment is best for you.

Summary – Steps 1–6 to become an enlightened subordinate

Step 1 Relive the emotional journey through the different stages of frustration into fundamental frustration, understand how you get there, and then ultimately reject it.

Step 2 If you are thinking of explicit exit and of leaving, stop searching for another job for the moment. Carry on working with your no-decision boss.

Step 3 Reject both reticent resignation and constant conflict. You have two ways forward: either through peaceful patience or by waiting for your no-decision boss to display 'outrageous behaviour'.

Step 4 If you have chosen peaceful patience, choose a way forward into aphonic acknowledgement, even if it is pleasant enough to stay in peaceful patience with your no-decision boss in the long term. You have two ways in: either through a silent pact with your no-decision boss or through a policy of take it anyway.

Step 5 If you have chosen 'outrageous behaviour', pester your no-decision boss for decisions and wait for the moment of 'outrageous behaviour'. When it comes, understand the two messages: a) Stop pestering me for a decision and b) Come and work with me positively in aphonic acknowledgement.

Step 6 Make your move into aphonic acknowledgement. You now know the different ways to achieve this.

You are now an enlightened subordinate but you are not finished yet. You need to decide which level of enlightenment is best for you.

Annex 2 summarises the steps required to become an enlightened subordinate.

8

Choices for an Enlightened Subordinate

'How to' advice for subordinates

So you have discovered that an enlightened subordinate is one who has reached a state of peaceful patience but takes the decisions of the boss, and you have decided to try it out. Take a few simple decisions that would normally be made by your boss, and see what happens.

Nothing!

Exactly, nothing happens.

Your boss just doesn't react. You are an enlightened subordinate.

Now you need to start looking after yourself. There are four actions here that are optional, but strongly recommended, before finally choosing which of the three levels of enlightenment you prefer.

Take your freedom

Your first action is to take your freedom and enjoy the autonomy. As you already know, no-decision bosses never supervise their teams. They do not manage their subordinates. Your boss will simply leave you alone. You can do what you want. But how far should you go?

There are many different approaches to this. It is a personal decision. Some subordinates choose power, some choose fun and some just profit from a working environment without management control, with few constraints and no pressure. Some even choose not to do any work at all.

Do not be afraid. You can go a long way in decision-making while taking your freedom. You can disrupt systems for your own personal use, or even for the good of your company, as is shown in the three case studies 38 to 40.

Subordinates who choose power

> **Case study 38 – Taking power as your freedom**
> Carter is the no-decision regional manager. Leah is his Human Resources manager, who has worked for him for many years. She is in aphonic acknowledgement.
>
> Leah over the years has gradually taken on Carter's role as boss for the salary increase process.
>
> Annual salary increases are merit-based in the company, so individual increases are decided for each of Carter's direct reports, and Carter's approval is also required for the individual increases of all other subordinates in the region. Far too many decisions for Carter, the no-decision boss, to make.
>
> Leah has taken everything over. She not only decides on the increases of Carter's management team, including her own, but she also decides the increases for all the others. Substituting for Carter, she informs each individual manager of his or her annual merit increase in individual interviews with each of them. Carter has nothing to do and nothing to decide.
>
> Amazing as it seems, Carter deviates downward delegation by

allowing Leah to take his salary increase decisions for him and transforms a moment of motivation into one of discouragement for his management team.

In Human Resources, Leah wants power. And she takes it by fixing the annual salary increases of her colleagues and of their teams. She is now a powerful and feared manager in the company because people have to defer to her to be sure of a decent pay rise.

Comments on case study 38
The time of the annual salary increase is a multiple decision-making period and is usually a complicated time for no-decision managers. Leah simply eliminates these decision-making moments for Carter.

The company procedure of salary increases is distorted by Carter and Leah: Carter because he cannot decide, and Leah because she uses Carter's weakness to take control herself.

Had Carter been a responsible manager he would never have allowed Leah to take over the process, even with some level of monitoring and control. This change is a serious breach of company policy that has a significant impact on Carter's management.

It is a negative example resulting in negative consequences for the company and many of the managers, except for Leah, who obtains the power that she is seeking. It is absolutely not a recommended action for subordinates, but the example of Leah shows just how far subordinates can go in the pursuit of power while working with a no-decision manager.

Bypassing the no-decision manager

> **Case study 39 – Disrupting systems for the benefit of all**
>
> John is an experienced no-decision director. Charlotte, the finance manager, has recently been promoted into John's team by headquarters. She has worked with John in the past and knows him as an experienced no-decision manager.
>
> During the introduction of the new accounting system, she sees an opportunity to speed up the investment and expense approval process with John. Approving represents a decision for a no-decision manager, and John is no exception. The new system requires a 'click' from John's computer for the electronic authorisation of important expenses and investments.
>
> Charlotte announces to John:
>
> 'You are travelling a lot, so I will put my authorisation level up to yours in the new system so that I can approve expenses when you are away.'
>
> Travelling is not of course an excuse, as John can connect to the system at any time anywhere in the world. No reply from John.
>
> From here on Charlotte alone approves all the major expenses and investments.
>
> *Comments on case study 39*
> In any normal organisation, John would have had to agree in order for Charlotte to be able to modify the system and change the authorisation process. And in some organisations even John would not have the authority to make this change. But organisations with no-decision managers in senior positions are not normal or ordinary.

John, had he been a normal responsible manager, would never have allowed Charlotte to make the change. Nor would Charlotte ever have made this suggestion to a normal manager. As a finance manager, her suggestion is inappropriate. His failure to reply to her suggestion is disgraceful.

Charlotte, however, believes that she is improving the process by giving herself the authority to approve investments and expenses at her boss's level. She is not doing it for her own personal gain. She knows that leaving John to approve expenses would slow down or even halt the whole approval process, which would harm the company. She is sticking her neck out for the good of the company.

Subordinates who choose fun

Case study 40 – Let's have some fun
Sana is in charge of Human Resources and she is the first of Adam's team to arrive in a state of aphonic acknowledgement. She previously worked with an experienced no-decision boss, and when no-decision Ruby is promoted, Sana decides to take advantage of her freedom and chooses to have some fun.

Sana's fun is travelling, being out of the office, staying in hotels and eating out in restaurants, visiting the country and seeing places. She spends three weeks a month away from the office.

Luckily for Sana, her company has offices in most towns in the country so she takes her car and drives to wherever she wants, visits the office and talks to the people – all supposedly in her Human Resources role.

> None of her colleagues understand what she does during these visits, or why Ruby, her no-decision boss, allows her to flit around the country like a tourist.
>
> *Comments on case study 40*
> A manager like Sana has a significant level of freedom while working with a no-decision boss. Her behaviour would be impossible if she had a normal manager as her boss.

A normal manager would set goals for the department, fix objectives for subordinates and prioritise projects to be completed. Your no-decision manager does none of these things. They fix no direction. They leave it for the subordinates to decide what projects to complete, or else they just don't get completed at all.

A normal manager would motivate their team, praising work well done, criticising when it is done poorly and disciplining inappropriate behaviour. Praise, criticism and discipline will be absent from your no-decision manager's repertoire.

A normal manager would help subordinates to complete their work. Your no-decision manager never coaches you and will never help you.

With freedom you receive no support

As a subordinate working for a no-decision manager you are on your own. There will be no praise, no compliments, no thanks, no recognition, no encouragement, no criticism, no blame, not even a comment – no reaction at all to anything you do. This all appears very negative but it isn't. What it means is that you have a lot of freedom. You can do what you want.

You must never forget that no-decision managers never give support to subordinates on anything – not just decisions – and they never defend them. They consider that providing support and defence is equivalent to making decisions.

By taking on aphonic acknowledgement and becoming enlightened you reverse the roles. You, the subordinate, decide when to go and see your no-decision boss. You decide what to discuss with your no-decision boss. You fix your own objectives. You set your priorities. You can almost act as though you have no direct boss at all. The limitations will come from the rules and norms of your organisation and from your boss's boss. And of course this freedom comes with the autonomy to decide whatever you want in your department or your organisation.

Learn from your no-decision boss

Your second action on looking after yourself should be to learn from your no-decision boss. No-decision bosses have a lot that they can give you. Remember, though, that they do not help subordinates, so you will have to get the information yourself in an indirect way. At the worst you can observe and learn.

As already explained, no-decision managers are hiding in excellence. Their excellence will be found in the three greats, which they have mastered, and in survival in organisations, but more specifically survival in your organisation. They are available for observation and examination.

Three greats

The three greats are the easiest to learn from: great analysis, great knowledge of the industry, and great understanding of the organisation and the people. Discreet but direct questioning is the most efficient way to obtain this information from your no-decision boss. After all, while your boss is explaining the detail to you, no decisions need to be made. Open questions may elicit a lot of information. Ask your boss 'What do you think of…?' And if you can give some information back the exchange will be more productive.

Informal networks

Information on the separated specialised informal networks will be more difficult for you to obtain and will require close proximity to your boss to evaluate what networks have been set up, how they work and what information they provide. Some general questions might reveal information that can be discussed in detail.

For instance:

> Who are the influential people in the organisation?
> Who is the specialist in headquarters for a technical issue?
> Who should I talk to solve a particular problem?

Blandish the bosses

What your boss does in blandish the bosses is probably the most useful for you, but it is also the most difficult to observe, because you are rarely present during the exchanges between your boss and the boss's boss. And these will always be a closely held secret.

Even so, when you are present during a meeting, a presentation or corporate gathering, for instance, there are still occasions to learn. You can, by astute observation, concentrate on watching the behaviour and attitude of your boss and listening to the way they talk to the hierarchy. All interactions are important, from the non-verbal to the exchanges between them, noting the tone, the content and above all the way your no-decision boss replies to difficult questions.

These observations can then be compared to the exchanges between you and your boss. With you, your boss will be natural – showing their usual behaviour. With their boss, blandish the bosses will be the norm. Differences will indicate the contrived, calculated behaviour designed to manage the boss and might be useful.

Handling of hierarchy

Handling of hierarchy is also complicated to observe. You can, however, develop your own personal relationship with the people in headquarters and then question them on the behaviour of your no-decision boss. This will be possible with the informal internal networks that you set up yourself. But it requires constant concentrated deliberate questioning of members of your network on your no-decision boss's behaviour and contacts. Who has your boss been talking to? About what? For how long?

Finally, don't try to learn too much too quickly from your no-decision boss. Be selective based on your own needs, your strengths and weaknesses and then take your time. There is no rush.

Protect yourself

The third action is important for you. Protect yourself. You are about to go on a path of taking decisions that your boss should make, knowing quite well that if the decision turns out to be a bad one you will be attacked by your own boss and the blame will be on you alone. You will become more exposed, so you need to protect yourself.

Two things are important:

a) Information
b) Internal networks.

Information

For each decision you make in the place of your no-decision boss you have a choice: to inform or not to inform.

You know by now that no-decision bosses have no preference over whether they are informed or not. They know intimately what is going on in their organisation, so will know of the decision sooner or later. What is important for them is not *what* has been decided, but that *something* has been decided.

However, it is good practice to inform your no-decision boss of the decisions you have taken. This is not to get approval because naturally none will be given, but more out of courtesy and to maintain good relations.

> **Case study 41 – To inform or not to inform**
> Wallace is a young manager working as a store controller with Max, the no-decision director of a large retail store. He has recently discovered aphonic acknowledgement and is enjoying his freedom and independence.

He discovers that he can make decisions in areas outside his own official responsibility. He is recognised by colleagues and staff members as someone who takes decisions and is consulted more and more for decisions that they know will never come from their boss.

But he is still reluctant and uncomfortable making these decisions, so he goes to his no-decision boss with open questions, such as:

'What do you think of this?'
'What is your opinion on Marcel's proposal?'
'What should we do here?'

The hope is that he gets a decision (which of course he knows he will not) or at worst some information to help him decide on a subject of which he had little or no knowledge.

He of course gets nothing helpful from his boss, apart from platitudes like:

'See what they are doing in the other stores,' or
'Ask Jonathan what he thinks.'

But at least these questions inform his boss that he is on the point of making a decision on this subject.

Comments on case study 41

Wallace is consulted by his colleagues when they learn that he is willing to make some decisions regardless of whether he knows anything about that part of the business. As he is inexperienced in aphonic acknowledgement, he ventures to consult Max before deciding. A more experienced enlightened subordinate might not inform him at all.

Having decided to inform your no-decision boss of pending decisions, you must then decide whether to do it in writing or verbally. Written information gives you a limited form of protection whereas verbal information gives you none at all.

The lowest level of written protection would be an email from you with details of the decision after it has been taken. You will never get a reaction. But if the decision turns out to have been a bad one and your boss has done nothing to change it, which of course they will never do, part of the blame can eventually be given as evidence that your boss knew, did not react, so was in agreement.

The next level is an email to the boss with details of a decision before you take it.

> 'Just for your information on Monday next week I have an appointment to sign the contract with supplier X.'

Again you will not get a reaction. But this time if the decision turns out to be bad you can show that your boss had time to change it, which of course you know would never happen. But more blame can then be deflected on to your boss if and when necessary.

Your highest level of protection comes with the same email as above but with a copy to your boss's boss. Here no reaction from your boss's boss will usually indicate that the decision is acceptable. A reaction will prevent a bad decision. You should use this level of protection with all important decisions, where practicable.

It may not be possible to copy in the boss's boss in this way. Protocol or company culture may not allow it. If so, then another person in the hierarchy or a colleague of your boss can be copied in for limited protection, before the decision is made.

Freedom to take decisions in the place of your no-decision boss comes then at a cost. But many subordinates decide not to inform their no-decision bosses of decisions. First, they do not want to be informed. Second, they do not need to be informed. Third, their networks will inform them quickly of the decision and you accept the associated risks.

Informal networks

Just as the no-decision manager has built internal informal networks for survival, so you as a subordinate in aphonic acknowledgement should build a similar network for your own protection. Your informal networks should collect information for instance on whether there is support in the organisation for your decisions. They can also cultivate allies within the hierarchy around your boss's boss.

Remember that if your no-decision boss resorts to a lie in one of their bouts of 'outrageous behaviour', even if not directed at you personally, they become a liar manager. Their level of toxicity towards you doubles! You have a combined no-decision boss and a liar boss.

As discussed briefly in Chapter 5, liar managers as bosses need special treatment from subordinates. Important statements from the boss must be verified and this can be done through informal networks. Here you will need to expand your informal network to all levels of the company, their teams, colleagues and other departments. Repeated lying must be detected quickly for your own survival too.

Finally your network can also be used to monitor the status of your no-decision boss.

- Are they likely to be fired soon?
- Are they well installed as a no-decision manager?
- How long will it be before they are discovered?
- What will happen when they are discovered?

If you are not an internal network type person then you can try to learn from your no-decision boss on how to set them up and how to work them. But you must set them up. An inefficient internal network is better than none at all.

Measure the consequences

Your fourth personal action should be to start measuring the consequences of your decision to be in aphonic acknowledgement and be enlightened. We have already discussed the lack of support from your no-decision boss and this is an important one, but there are two others that you need to manage.

Career on hold

As a subordinate of a no-decision boss your career is on hold, especially when you are in aphonic acknowledgement. Your boss benefits the most from you taking their decisions and is not going to let you go. Promotions within the organisation will be actively resisted and transfers to other departments will not be allowed. In essence your career will not move forward while you are working for your no-decision boss. He or she may not take decisions but the energy put into keeping you in place will surprise you.

Many subordinates take a long time to realise that if they stay with a no-decision manager, any further advancement in their careers is suspended. The only way for subordinates to leave is by leaving the organisation through explicit exit. You have been warned.

In the short term this is of course not an issue. You are free. You can do what you want. You have valuable things to learn from your boss – always useful in any career. But you may not want to stay in your current position for the next 30 years. Do not forget your boss is in it for the long term and is not going anywhere, unless they are dismissed.

Now that you are aware of this, you need to manage the situation. The most logical thing to do is to fix a reasonable horizon working with your no-decision boss but prepare your endgame now. If you think you can persuade your boss's boss to promote you, then work on it. If you think you should leave, start the process of looking for a new job. If you are happy with your freedom, do nothing and just stay where you are.

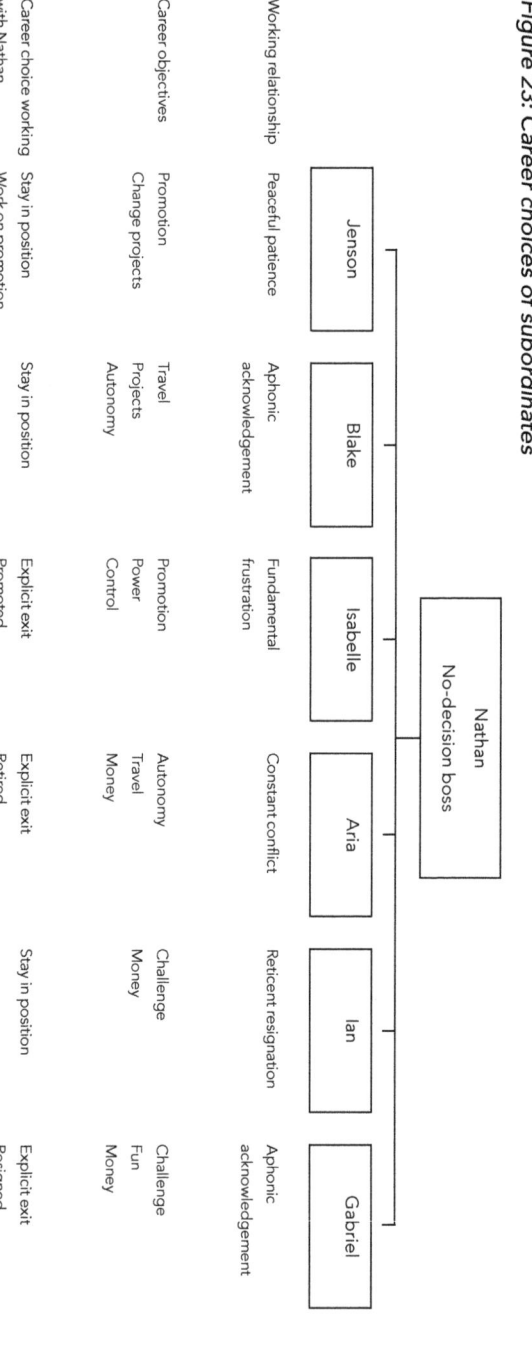

Figure 23: Career choices of subordinates

Case study 42 – The different ways to work with a no-decision boss

Figure 23, Career choices of subordinates, shows an imaginary but nevertheless typical team working with their no-decision boss. It gives a summary of their chosen working relationships, their career objectives and how they have chosen to work with their boss.

Nathan is a senior no-decision manager. He has six direct reports.

Jenson chooses to work with Nathan in peaceful patience after spending some time in fundamental frustration. He is ambitious but patient and decides to sit out the period with his no-decision boss and get on with his own job to modernise his department. His aim is to show top management his ability to improve his department in the hostile environment of no-decision management.

Blake recognises early that Nathan is a no-decision manager and moves directly into aphonic acknowledgement with him. His objective is to enjoy his freedom through extensive travelling but to manage large projects that give him visibility with headquarters to keep his options open in the event that Nathan is discovered.

Isabelle is ambitious but impatient, so she chooses a different strategy. She stays in fundamental frustration and immediately starts to work with Nathan's boss for a promotion within the company to get away from Nathan as quickly as possible via the option explicit exit through promotion.

Aria chooses to stay in the more violent form of constant conflict with Nathan, who provokes many instances of 'outrageous behaviour' that she basically ignores. She works strictly within the scope of her position. She never takes the decisions of Nathan nor tries to circumvent them. And to fuel the conflict, she submits all decisions for Nathan to take, knowing that he will never decide anything. Aria is close to retirement and so knows that she only has a few years before leaving, thus applying explicit exit through retirement.

Ian has just arrived and soon discovers that his new boss is a no-decision manager. He decides that it is too soon to search for another job and that he has to remain in place for a reasonable time, going into reticent resignation.

Gabriel recognises, with regret, that he is working with yet another no-decision boss. He moves, as does Blake, into aphonic acknowledgement through the take it anyway route. He recognises, however, that his career objectives are jeopardised. He enjoys his freedom having fun with Nathan for a while but eventually resigns.

Comments on case study 42
Out of Nathan's six subordinate managers two are in aphonic acknowledgement, one in peaceful patience, one in fundamental frustration, one in reticent resignation and one in constant conflict. Three out of six plan to leave one way or another.

So as a subordinate, take your time, profit from the chance of freedom and the learning opportunity but actively manage your career.

Never fired
Another consequence of working with a no-decision boss is that you suddenly acquire job security. You will never be fired by your no-decision boss. Firing someone is a decision. The only way to be

fired is if your no-decision boss gets an order to fire you, from their boss or from headquarters.

How far do you help your no-decision boss?

Now that you have looked after yourself, you need to decide whether to help your no-decision boss get decisions made by others, and if so how far you are willing to go.

Do you intervene for instance directly with your no-decision boss's boss?

Do you help to get decisions made with your boss's colleagues?

Or with others?

Do you intervene at all?

As always, it is up to you.

As a rule subordinates generally limit their help to diagonal deviated delegation, usually in headquarters. But you decide.

Case study 43 – How far to help in deviated delegation

Samuel is a senior manager working in research and development. He works for his no-decision boss Teddy. Samuel is an enlightened subordinate in aphonic acknowledgement and has an important investment to make for one of his key research and development projects. It has been included in the R&D budget but needs to be authorised by Teddy, who as a no-decision manager does not care whether the project goes ahead or not.

Samuel considers he has three possibilities to get the investment authorised:

a) Sign the approval himself
b) Persuade Teddy's boss to approve it
c) Persuade Harrison, the financial director, a colleague of Teddy, to approve it.

Samuel does not want to take the risk of signing himself. The project is too large and too visible for his signature to go unnoticed in the company, and there is a risk of it being cancelled if headquarters finds that the authorisation process has not been followed. But Samuel does not have a good enough relationship with Teddy's boss to persuade him to approve the project, in place of Teddy.

He decides to approach Harrison. He completes the investment approval documents with the necessary technical and financial analyses, and says to his boss Teddy,

'I have completed the investment approval documents for our key research and development project and will discuss them with Harrison in headquarters next week.'

With Harrison in headquarters Samuel starts the conversation as follows:

'I have talked to Teddy but I would like to discuss with you the best way to finance this key research and development project. I also want to make sure that you in headquarters are aware of the detail and are OK with the project before we go ahead.'

The discussion ends with Harrison concluding, 'I will call Teddy and tell him that we approve the project and make sure that it gets signed as quickly as possible.'

Comments on case study 43
Talking to the finance director is sufficient in this case for Samuel to get his project approved. He helps his boss Teddy to do this through deviated diagonal delegation.

Choose your level of enlightenment

You are now ready to decide on the level of enlightenment that you want to work in with your no-decision boss. As already defined, an enlightened subordinate is one who is in aphonic acknowledgement (i.e. in a state of peaceful patience but who agrees to make decisions in place of the boss).

You essentially need to decide on the range of decisions you are willing to make on behalf of your no-decision boss.

> Do you take them all?
> Or only some?
> If so which ones?
> How do you decide?

There are basically four levels:

1. Enlightened individual
2. Enlightened manager
3. Enlightened co-ordinator
4. Enlightened leader.

1. Enlightened individual

We have already discussed the individual level of enlightenment. Here you take the decisions your boss should take only to ensure the type of freedom that you have chosen for yourself.

If for instance your freedom is to travel, then you take the necessary decisions. If you are after power then you take the power decisions to give you influence. All this is very personal and selfish.

2. Enlightened manager

To be an enlightened manager, you limit the decisions you make to your own department and your own team. If for instance you are in charge of research and development you will take decisions on your own department's budget, prioritise your department's projects, sign the necessary expense authorisations for only for research and development expenses, etc. These are the decisions that would normally be undertaken by your boss for your department, but you make them. You do not at this level make decisions in marketing or production, for example, if you are in charge of research and development.

It is true that most enlightened subordinates stay at this level. Going further is often considered too dangerous.

3. Enlightened co-ordinator

The enlightened co-ordinator is a compromise between taking only your *own* decisions as an enlightened manager or taking *all* the decisions as an enlightened leader (see below). Here, in addition to taking the decisions of your own team, you take on the information role of your no-decision boss to help the boss's team, i.e. your colleagues, move forward. This involves informing colleagues of the decision you have made and inviting those in aphonic acknowledgement to share the decisions they have made with you, so you can inform the others. This is a fulfilling role that obtains recognition, respect and gratitude from your colleagues.

> **Case study 44 – Excelling in the co-ordinator role**
> Albert and Chloe are colleagues working for their no-decision boss Ruby. When Albert announces his retirement, Chloe says to him, 'We shall miss you when you leave. You are the only one in Ruby's team who brings us together. You give us important information from headquarters and others in the team. You make the situation more manageable with Ruby never deciding anything. And you give us a shoulder to cry on.'
>
> 'Yes,' says Albert, 'I do spend much of my time coming round to see you. You guys never seem to talk to each other; you all work in a vacuum on your own. Someone needs to make sure we all know what is going on.'

> **Comments on case study 44**
> The co-ordinator role is recognised by all. The no-decision boss is aware of it. The colleagues appreciate it.

In the management team shown in Figure 23, Career choices of subordinates, if Blake for instance took on the co-ordinator role he would work extensively with Jenson, Isabelle and Ian, giving them all the information that their boss would normally give them. Blake might go as far as to hold meetings with these three to discuss issues or problems and try to find solutions. He would reach out to Aria in constant conflict but would be careful not to be seen to be helping the boss because she is in conflict with him. He would ignore Gabriel, as he is into taking his freedom and not interested in the rest of the team.

4. Enlightened leader

An organisation whose official boss is a no-decision manager becomes leaderless and starts moving in an unknown direction. Decisions are being made in the organisation by those who have accepted deviated delegation and by team members in aphonic acknowledgement. However, many decisions that should be made are not.

As a quick reminder, a typical team working for a no-decision manager is depicted in Figure 3: Action-Centred Leadership TM After John Adair, representing a manager who neglects the circles. It is this team that you, an enlightened subordinate in aphonic acknowledgement, take over as the unofficial leader in place of your no-decision boss.

Of course, you have no official or formal authority. You do not have any legitimacy. You do not have the title and you do not have your boss's salary, but the position is there for the taking. What you do get though is the experience of being a leader with limited risk in difficult conditions, which will be useful in your future career.

The decision principle

To become the unofficial leader you need to adopt what the no-decision movement ironically calls the 'decision principle', which simply states that 'any decision is better than no decision at all'.

In practice this means that you, as the unofficial leader, do not try to move the organisation in your own direction – the one you would want to take if you were the official leader – but in whatever direction is the most convenient. Convenience here means:

a) accepting all decisions of your colleagues in aphonic acknowledgement and
b) turning the proposals of the managers for whom you are the unofficial leader into decisions, regardless of whether you agree with them or not.

In essence as the unofficial leader you accept whatever the managers, i.e. your colleagues, want to do.

Any direction is better than being at a standstill with no decision being made. You, for instance, inform your colleagues who are in fundamental frustration, reticent resignation and peaceful patience that you will now make all the decisions that their no-decision boss is not making. You will find that they will accept your new role without question, first, because decisions will at last be made, and second, because you will systematically agree with all their proposals and decide accordingly.

The concept of decision principle has been borrowed from a quote attributed to Theodore Roosevelt, which says:

> In any moment of decision, the best thing you can do is the right thing, the next best thing is the wrong thing and the worst thing you can do is nothing.*

*Innumerable sources attribute this quotation to Theodore Roosevelt. However, the Theodore Roosevelt Center at Dickinson State University (www.

theodorerooseveltcenter.org) considers there is no proof, saying 'This statement is often attributed to Theodore Roosevelt, but no known source can be found to verify the attribution.' However one source, Wikiquote (wikiquote.org), attributes the quote to John M. Kost on 25 July 1995 in S. 946, the Information Technology Management Reform Act of 1995 in a hearing before the Subcommittee on Oversight of Government Management and the District of Columbia of the Committee on Governmental Affairs in 1996.

No-decision managers like this quote. Not for the emphasis on 'wrong' and 'worst', which they reject, but for the 'nothing' part: 'the worst thing you can do is nothing'. No-decision managers do this all the time when they are in permanent procrastination. They wait for something to happen and do nothing during the wait. For them, this is not the worst thing they can do at all but, on the contrary, one of the best. It is for this reason that they have adopted the quote, and just ignore the word 'worst'.

But as the new unofficial leader working in no-decision management, you need to agree that doing nothing is not acceptable, whether it is the worst thing to do or not. There is no point in becoming the new leader, and then doing what no-decision managers do themselves: that is, nothing. You are now the leader so you need to make the decisions. The easiest way is in accordance with the decision principle.

So with your colleagues in aphonic acknowledgement working also as enlightened subordinates, you accept, encourage and agree with all the decisions they make, regardless of whether you are in favour of them or not.

Having announced that you are the leader of the group, you automatically become the co-ordinator. This involves informing colleagues of the decisions you have taken and inviting those in aphonic acknowledgement to share the decisions they have made with you, so you can inform the others.

You now need to share the decisions you have made with your no-decision boss. They are after all the boss, and if you inform them they are more likely to pass on the information they get from the boss's boss and headquarters. This you share as the new leader. Your boss as the official leader will always have access to more information than you do.

Beware of dangerous colleagues

As unofficial leader there are two types of colleague who are dangerous for you, so you need to adapt your behaviour towards them. The first are your colleagues in constant conflict with their and your no-decision boss. You cannot make the decisions for them. In fact they will not allow you to make them. They will only accept decisions from their no-decision boss. So here you must just accept that no decisions will be made in this area.

The second type of colleagues that pose a danger to you are those people in aphonic acknowledgement whose freedom is power. In the case of these colleagues you will need to negotiate your space around their power structures, depending on what they are. Let them take the decisions they want. Let them act as they want. But be aware that when they see you taking over as the unofficial leader they may want this position too.

The perfect team

If your boss's team has only you as an enlightened subordinate and there is nobody in constant conflict, you will be able to bring some order back into the team, which would look again like Figure 2, Action-Centred Leadership TM After John Adair.

The circles are back as circles. You can repair the broken team. The individuals are available for developing, and the tasks can be easily achieved. Harmony and order is restored and you have a functioning team.

However, there are the three preconditions for this idyllic state:

1. All subordinates of the no-decision manager are in a state of frustration or resignation

2. No subordinates are in constant conflict
3. You are the only subordinate in aphonic acknowledgement and willing to take on the leadership role.

Figure 2: Action-Centred Leadership™ After John Adair

[Venn diagram with three overlapping circles labeled:
- TASK — Achieving the task
- TEAM — Building and maintaining the team
- INDIVIDUAL — Developing the individual]

Reproduced with the permission of Adair International. Copyright © Adair International

This happens so rarely that it is more a textbook case study situation in an ideal world. It is unlikely that you will ever come across something this perfect.

Case study 45 – The unofficial leader Joel

Joel's no-decision boss Helen is a top manager in charge of Southern Europe. She has six managers reporting to her, one in peaceful patience, one in constant conflict, two in reticent resignation and two in aphonic acknowledgement – one of whom is Joel.

Joel decides to take over as unofficial leader in place of Helen, the no-decision boss. He decides not to announce this upfront to Helen, but she quickly realises what Joel is doing when he informs her of the decision he is making for her three managers in reticent resignation and peaceful patience.

The corporate culture does not allow Joel to set up formal or informal meetings with his new unofficial team so he adopts daily contact with each member, bringing them information on the decisions taken and news from Helen and headquarters.

Helen unfortunately does not reciprocate with information in exchange for Joel's new role, so he decides to go to headquarters in Birmingham regularly to get the information normally provided by the boss.

Comments on case study 45

Joel's role is quickly accepted by all members of Helen's team through the information that he brings from his contacts in headquarters. He fills a void of information that helps all the managers do their jobs more effectively and gains visibility in headquarters through his regular visits.

But the real improvement in team morale comes from Joel's decision-making for managers not in constant conflict or aphonic acknowledgement.

Accept partial leadership if need be

What happens more often is that you are able to take on only partial leadership and bring under your control the subordinates in frustration or resignation, but you have to work with other enlightened subordinates in aphonic acknowledgement who stay independent and take their freedom without you.

This situation is illustrated in Figure 24, Action-Centred Leadership TM After John Adair with an impaired team.

Figure 24: Action-Centred Leadership™ After John Adair with an impaired team

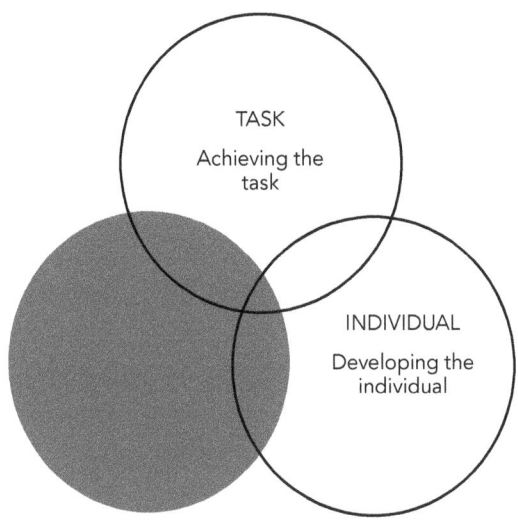

This diagram represents a no-decision boss and an unofficial leader with two team members in aphonic acknowledgement refusing to work in the team and refusing to acknowledge the leader. Here the circle representing the team is blotted out showing that it will be difficult to build and maintain with two members apart and not helping to achieve the task. The unofficial leader is likely to be less effective than an official one in developing the other individuals.

Reproduced with the permission of Adair International.
Copyright © Adair International

The enlightened subordinates are having a good time in their freedom mode. You can try to bring them into the team and sometimes they might come in, but you will find that they prefer to remain outside your leadership. Above all you must ensure that you do not take away any of the freedom they have built up. The overall team is broken but you can still develop a team with the remaining members, even though your ability to achieve all the tasks will be limited.

This situation for you as the unofficial leader is not as fulfilling as having total control as a legitimate leader, but it still gives you leadership experience. Whatever level of unofficial leadership you manage to obtain, this is the highest state of enlightenment that you can achieve while working for a no-decision boss. So take it while you can – even if only partly. It will never harm your career even if you mess it up. It is here that you can learn how far you can go as a leader.

Remember the dangers

But keep in mind the dangers. You must remember at all times that your no-decision boss never accepts accountability for your decisions if they turn out to be controversial. They will do everything in their power to push the blame for your decision back on to you, the unofficial leader. The wider the range of decisions you make the more exposed you become.

Remember also that if your decision is a success you will not get the credit. Your no-decision boss will accept accountability and responsibility and take all the credit. Your involvement will suddenly disappear. They will not inform their boss that the decision was made by you and that they were not involved in it at all.

This behaviour, of course, is not limited to no-decision bosses and is often used unfairly by more normal managers – ones who make decisions. Just remember, though, that it will be systematic for your no-decision boss. They are not after all going to tell their boss that you have become the unofficial leader of their team and that you have effectively taken it over!

You are now an enlightened subordinate working in harmony with your no-decision boss having taken all the decisions that are best for you personally. Congratulations!

Summary – steps 7–13 to become an enlightened subordinate

Step 7 Take your freedom and enjoy the autonomy and then choose the way you want to work in freedom.

Step 8 Learn from your no-decision boss and choose the subjects that are the best for you to learn:

From within the 'three greats'
Informal networks
Blandish the bosses
Handling of hierarchy.

Step 9 Protect yourself with information and informal networks.

Step 10 Know the consequences of working with your no-decision boss: your career is on hold but you will never be fired.

Step 11 Decide how far you help your no-decision boss to get decisions made for them by others.

Step 12 Choose your level of enlightenment:

Enlightened Individual
Enlightened manager
Enlightened co-ordinator
Enlightened leader.

If you choose the enlightened leader level then gradually take the necessary steps to become the unofficial leader of the team:

- Adopt the decision principle and agree with the decisions made by your fellow enlightened subordinates together

with the proposals of the other managers.
- Inform colleagues that you will now take all the decisions.
- Become the co-ordinator of your boss's team.
- Share the decisions you have made with your no-decision boss.
- Beware of the danger from colleagues in constant conflict and those whose freedom is power in aphonic acknowledgement.
- Take over the broken team, bring the individuals into it and try to persuade those in aphonic acknowledgement to accept your leadership.

You are now an enlightened subordinate working in harmony with your no-decision boss, having taken all the decisions that are best for you personally.

Annex 2 Summarises the steps required to become an enlightened subordinate.

9

How to Manage a Team of No-Decision Managers

Information on no-decision managers

Effect of no-decision managers on organisations

Action-Centred Leadership™ After John Adair representing a manager who neglects the circles, in Figure 3, and The Managerial Grid adapted for no-decision managers, in Figure 4, explained in Chapter 2, give the best visual illustration of the effect of no-decision managers on the people in organisations.

No-decision managers are harmful to the organisation

Further, management gurus who specialise in toxic managers agree that no-decision managers are harmful to organisations and their employees. One of these gurus, Robert Sutton, calls his toxic managers 'assholes' and in his book *The No Asshole Rule* from 2007 writes:

> The damage that assholes do to their organizations is seen in the costs of increased turnover, absenteeism, decreased commitment to work, and the distraction and impaired individual performance

documented in studies of psychological abuse, bullying and mobbing.

No-decision managers also bring these indirect and hidden costs into their organisations. While their behaviour cannot be considered 'psychological abuse, bullying or mobbing', it has the same effect on employees working in fundamental frustration and reticent resignation, and on the organisation or department of which they are in charge. The competent employees leave. Absenteeism increases. Tasks are carried out mechanically. And the frustration encourages unproductive chatter on how the boss never makes decisions and the effect it is having on their work.

Manfred F.R. Kets de Vries specialises in the more spectacular toxic managers, the top executives who have personality disorders. In his *Harvard Business Review* article 'Coaching the Toxic Leader: four pathologies that can hobble an executive and bring misery to the workplace – and what to do about them' (2014), he writes:

> But if the boss's psychological makeup is warped, business plans, ideas, interactions and even systems and structure of the organisation itself will reflect his or her pathologies.

Although Kets de Vries is not specifically describing no-decision managers, their 'psychological makeup' is undoubtedly 'warped', so his findings here also apply to no-decision managers. Ideas remain ideas and are never implemented. Interactions are essentially limited to passing information to the no-decision manager for their own use. When no-decision managers leave the decisions to their subordinates to make, it is the subordinates' preferences that are implemented into the systems and structures of the organisation, without any common strategy or direction and without control from their no-decision boss. And in conclusion, Kets de Vries's title, where he states that these executives 'bring misery to the workplace', reflects clearly what no-decision managers also bring to their subordinates.

Some toxic managers are successful

But it also turns out that some of these toxic managers bring success and high financial rewards to their companies even in the long term. This is surely part of the reason why organisations leave toxic managers in place, despite the hidden costs.

Another guru who specialises in toxic managers, Ray Williams, posted in his blog in January 2016, 'The Rise of Toxic Leadership and Toxic Workplaces' (raywilliams.ca):

> Many people easily forgive these toxic leaders and the harm they cause because they measure their success solely in financial terms or because they bring charismatic entertainment value to the organisation.

And it is here that no-decision managers deviate from the norm of the average or spectacular toxic manager.

1. They are never leaders.
2. No-decision managers, more or less by definition, never bring 'success in financial terms' to their organisations. It is quite the opposite; their non decision-making slowly brings the organisation to a stop and over the long term will probably kill it.
3. It is inconceivable that no-decision managers 'bring charismatic entertainment value to the organisation'. It is true they are affable, approachable and knowledgeable – some might even be charismatic – but they entertain nobody and they destroy rather than create value. They are in hiding, keeping a low profile to ensure their secret remains secret.

Kets de Vries in ' Coaching the Toxic Leader: four pathologies that can hobble an executive and bring misery to the workplace – and what to do about them' does admit, however, that 'some people are impossible to change'. This clearly applies to no-decision managers, although he does not really cite them, when he writes in this same article:

> in no small part because many companies support (and are even breeding grounds for) dysfunctional behaviour.

No-decision managers certainly do have a managerial form of dysfunctional behaviour, but there is still a mystery around why companies support them.

Why does top management accept no-decision managers in their organisations?

But no, it is not a total mystery. There are two reasons;

1. Ignorance
2. Pivotal Positioning.

As explained in Chapter 6, most bosses will not tolerate no-decision managers. As soon as they discover that one of their team is a true one, he or she will be dismissed.

1. Ignorance

Most of the time, management does not know that there is a no-decision manager in their organisation. This is the case when the no-decision strategies for survival, secrecy and excellence work effectively. Structured survival is being applied precisely; the bosses are being seduced and the hierarchy is handled correctly with the message that the no-decision manager is doing a good job. The boss is making the important decisions in place of their no-decision subordinates and the separated specialised informal networks are functioning at their best. Secrecy is maintained and the no-decision manager is able to control information rising up from the team to the hierarchy.

The three greats are sufficient to divert the attention away from the major weakness that the no-decision manager never makes a decision.

In essence they in hiding in the organisation and management is unaware of them.

Management should, however, know that it has no-decision managers in the organisation. It is part of their job. They are after all toxic managers and toxic managers harm organisations.

2. Pivotal positioning

But some no-decision managers do exist in organisations with the knowledge of top management. Not only are they tolerated, but some are promoted into senior management positions. This situation is obscurely and nonsensically called in the jargon 'pivotal positioning'.

So why are they tolerated? Despite the small sample of no-decision managers studied, the lack of information from the bosses, and the scant findings from observations in the presence of the no-decision manager, three reasons were found for why they remained long-term in their organisations even though management was aware of their no-decision status.

3. Too dear to dismiss

The first reason is supposedly an economic one, coming from a concept called 'Too dear to dismiss', with 'dear' as in costly or expensive. This situation exists in a few European countries, but not in the USA or the UK.

It arises when a no-decision manager is discovered by top management late in their career and is considered too expensive to be fired. Top management will compare the cost of the lay-off with the total salary left to be paid before retirement. When the cost of lay-off is greater than the combined salary left to pay, the no-decision manager will be left in place in pivotal positioning. Dismissal of managers in the USA or in the UK does not have such a high cost other than the risk of a tribunal so pivotal positioning is rare.

These no-decision managers will generally be in charge of a department that is performing just below average with experienced subordinates in peaceful patience or aphonic acknowledgement holding it together.

Case study 46 – Too dear to dismiss

Finn has been a no-decision manager in charge of his department for many years. He is close to retirement and realises that he is in pivotal positioning. His boss knows he is a no-decision manager – in fact everyone in the company knows that he is a no-decision boss – yet he has not been fired.

He realises that he can more or less do what he wants without risk of dismissal. He decides to cut down on his working hours. He then makes a test with one of the important meetings at headquarters. He doesn't turn up and he gives no reason. His second-in-command, Amelie, is left to handle the meeting. He receives no comment from his boss. Amelie, though, is not too happy at being suddenly alone in front of headquarters staff in an important meeting.

At the next meeting Finn calls in sick. Again there is no reaction from anyone except Amelie. And gradually he manages to miss most meetings. He attends a few, just enough to show he is still there acting as the boss. He takes it easy until he retires.

Amelie meanwhile goes into in aphonic acknowledgement and starts to make decisions in his place, which secures his position even more. Many of his team, though, continue working in fundamental frustration, unhappy and unmotivated because of his lack of decision-making.

Comments on case study 46

Without being officially informed, Finn has guessed that he is now safe in his position until retirement, providing his behaviour remains stable and he does not provoke his hierarchy too much.

Normal managers might of course have similar tactics without being no-decision managers, doing just the minimum amount of work to avoid being fired, especially if they think they are also in the category 'too dear to dismiss'.

a) Personal preferences of a boss

This is the second reason for placing a no-decision manager into pivotal positioning.

> **Case study 47 – A Personal Preference**
>
> Lucas has a passion for mechanical engineering that he executes through his no-decision manager. He enjoys taking detailed engineering decisions, whether it is replacing a broken part or designing better ones. However, as a senior manager he can no longer make these low-level decisions.
>
> Theo is a no-decision research and development manager who has been working with Lucas for many years. Their arrangement is simple. Theo, as a no-decision manager, never makes any decisions. He merely implements the decisions of his boss. Lucas and Theo have a one-hour meeting every Friday. Theo prepares a weekly analysis of what is happening in his department. Lucas makes the necessary decisions from this analysis and Theo implements them every Monday.
>
> Theo is an 'invisible' no-decision manager. No one in the organisation except his boss knows that he is a no-decision manager. He makes decisions only on Monday, never at any other time.
>
> By maintaining Theo as his no-decision manager, Lucas is able to keep alive his passion for detailed mechanical engineering.
>
> Everyone assumes that Theo decides himself. No one knows he is just implementing the decisions of Lucas.

> **Comments on case study 47**
> Theo is able to go through his whole career using the one no-decision tactic, the Rumsfeld resolution, where his boss Lucas willingly makes all his decisions.

b) Successful structured survival

The third reason can occur when a no-decision manager takes advantage of a peculiarity in the organisation or in management and adapts their structured survival to put themself into pivotal positioning.

> **Case study 48 – Adapting structured survival**
> Arthur joins his quoted multinational straight out of university into a marketing position as a junior product manager in one of the subsidiaries in Europe. Over time he is promoted through the ranks to no-decision European Marketing Director.
>
> Right from the start of his career Arthur builds a special internal network of people in headquarters, with a specific goal to survive in the long term. This informal network includes anyone he can meet, from people at his own level to high-level directors. Any occasion is a good one to talk to someone and build a relationship. Over time he gets to know many influential managers and directors in the company, who gradually come to think of him as an excellent manager.
>
> One day one of Arthur's bosses learns that Arthur is a no-decision manager. This boss wants to fire him immediately but is stopped by Arthur's network in headquarters. Arthur lives through a difficult period of several months with this boss, who considers Arthur incompetent and treats him as such. Arthur knows his network is keeping him in his position and he does everything he can to survive. His boss gets a promotion and he survives.

Comments on case study 48
Arthur's network gives him long-term job security, effectively putting him into pivotal positioning. Local management is prevented from dismissing him.

Again, any normal manager can set up a similar network to Arthur's. It is not necessarily specific to no-decision managers. However, it is a tactic that can be used by them in certain circumstances, as shown by Arthur, to secure employment in the long term. But this tactic is not necessarily one that can be repeated by other no-decision managers in other organisations.

It does show, however, that with a careful analysis of the organisation and management, specific strategies for survival can maintain no-decision managers in place for many years.

Summary of pivotal positioning
So what general conclusions can be made about pivotal positioning?

It clearly exists in organisations. No-decision managers are allowed to stay in senior management with the knowledge of top management.

Pivotal positioning persists with the personal approval of a powerful boss. The no-decision manager's future depends entirely on the boss remaining in place. A change of boss will lead to the rapid departure of the no-decision manager. Having no-decision managers is never the general policy of an organisation. It is always an exception. In pivotal positioning such managers no longer hide in excellence, but survive in excellence.

And yet the ravages of no decisions on a department or organisation are significant. Employees and managers stay frustrated and unmotivated. There is a high level of staff turnover, with many of the best employees and managers leaving. And the department or organisation remains at a standstill from lack of decision-making.

'How to' advice for bosses of no-decision managers

How to identify a no-decision manager

The first thing you have to do if you want to build a team of no-decision managers is to find them in your organisation. The first place to look is in your own team. You will find it difficult to detect experienced no-decision managers who report to you. This is actually the most difficult step of all, because one of their main objectives is to hide their no-decision status from you.

The secret is to examine your subordinates who seem to be perfect. These are the ones who give you the following impressions:

> 'They anticipate everything I need'
> 'They adapt to my management style'
> 'They give me extensive, pertinent information as to what is going on in their department'
> 'They have a detailed knowledge of the industry and the competition'
> 'They know in detail the company's products and systems better than anyone'
> 'They understand their teams and their managers' subordinates'
> 'They are well appreciated by my own team and even my own boss.'

Normal managers of course also have these characteristics, so you must not jump to conclusions too quickly. You need to eliminate the normal managers from this group. What is important to note, though, is that all experienced no-decision managers have these characteristics. Any subordinates who do not have a majority of them will not be experienced no-decision managers. And it is better to manage a team of experienced no-decision managers than it is to manage a team of inexperienced ones. The experienced ones are the most difficult to find.

What you don't know yet (unless you have read Chapter 2 to

Chapter 6) is that these experienced no-decision managers are just doing their no-decision jobs.

- **Blandish the bosses** You will find that they give you pertinent, up-to-date and seemingly accurate information, regularly and frequently. Your own needs, requests and peculiarities are promptly adjusted, adapted and presented in the exact manner that you want. They are applying the tactic blandish the bosses.
- **Separated specialised informal networks** You will discover that your subordinates are incredibly well informed on what is going on not only in their own departments but also in the company as a whole. Unknown to you this information comes from their separated specialised informal networks.
- **Handling of hierarchy** You will discover the excellent relationships they have with your team, your colleagues and the people in headquarters, again without knowing that this is a strategy called handling of hierarchy in the no-decision management movement. So whenever you ask around to find out what people think of these managers, you will always get a good opinion back, unaware that you are being effectively managed without your knowledge.
- **Three greats** You will recognise the three greats even if you do not know the no-decision connotations: great knowledge of the business, great knowledge of the company and people and great analysis of alternatives for action.
- **Secrecy** And then without your knowledge your no-decision subordinates will apply their secrecy code and information up to you will be filtered so that you remain unaware that they are no-decision managers.

All these activities give you the impression that that these are competent, effective managers. They are after all hiding in excellence even if you are not yet aware of it.

Annoying habits

But then, over time, the initial impression of your 'perfect subordinate' will begin to wear off. This is when you need to become particularly attentive.

You will start to notice the annoying habit of deviated upward delegation. You will slowly discover that information is too plentiful. You know in too much detail what is going on in the no-decision manager's department. This will be accompanied by repeated questions like 'What would you decide?' or 'What is your opinion?' in various different forms.

Then over time criticisms from subordinates and information on lack of decision-making will start to filter through to you. You will start to notice the subordinate's department does not get things done quickly. A slow-growing nagging doubt will appear – a sort of steadily strengthening suspicion that all is not as it should be. It won't be one significant incident that unmasks your no-decision subordinate but many smaller, apparently inconsequential ones. Look out for this feeling. If you experience it you are probably on the right track to finding a no-decision manager in your team.

They are usually discovered by the accumulation of small incidents over time, where each incident on its own is not significant enough for management to take action. They seem to be good managers 'but' there are complaints and incidents. In the jargon of no-decision management this is often called the 'Build up of the Buts'.

Small incidents and minor complaints

Your first 'Buts' will be information that the subordinates are unhappy and frustrated with their no-decision manager as a boss. Small incidents and minor complaints will be reported, usually through Human Resources, yet the no-decision manager will have an adequate explanation when questioned.

Case study 49 – Accumulating minor complaints

Anna is a senior manager who has one of her team members, Joseph, working in a different country to her. Anna thinks Joseph is an excellent manager.

Every month Anna spends a day in Joseph's country. She has a two-hour review with Joseph personally and spends time with his subordinate managers, two of whom are Elisa and Riley.

Conversation with Human Resources

In a conversation with Human Resources Anna asks, 'How is Joseph's team working together?'

The Human Resources manager replies, 'I know Joseph has regular meetings with his team. I have had no specific feedback except that Elisa seems very down at the moment. Then Riley lost his temper with Joseph the other day, which is very unusual for him.'

When Anna asks Joseph about Elisa and Riley, his reply is:

'It is true Elisa seems a little frustrated at the moment, but I think she has some difficulties with her team. Riley on the other hand is not in agreement with the process we set up for the allocation of funds to the research and development department and he became upset last week when we discussed the allocation for his team.'

Budget presentation

At a budget presentation Amy, one of Joseph's team, makes the comment, 'We need a decision on the new product introduction. I am in favour of the process we agreed during the budget.'

'Yes,' replies Joseph quickly. 'One of the suppliers is late. I have a meeting with him next week.'

Discussion in the corridor

Riley meets Anna in the corridor during one of her visits and asks, 'Have you decided yet on the investment for the new equipment at the plant?'

Anna replies, 'That decision is up to Joseph. We have not discussed it yet.'

'OK,' says Riley, 'I will talk to Joseph about it again.'

Formal report from Human Resources

In a formal report from Human Resources on management practices, Anna sees that three of Joseph's managers have made comments on delays in decision-making.

'Yes,' says Joseph, 'These decisions were on the difficult manufacturing project where we were hesitating on the level of investment. You remember it related to the number and quality of robots to put in the new line.'

Comments on case study 49
Anna starts to notice that her excellent opinion of Joseph as a key manager is not matching up with the regular comments that are coming through three different sources:

a) Human Resources
b) Direct meetings with Joseph's team
c) And on the few occasions that she has a direct contact with Joseph's managers.

> Joseph seems to have good answers to these problems, but she notices that they are not problems brought up by Joseph to her directly, despite the detail that he gives her on what is going on in his department.
>
> She begins to recognise some inconsistencies that she has not been aware of up until now. But she still does not realise that Joseph is a no-decision manager.

Nothing gets decided

While all this is going on you will start to recognise that this manager's department or business never moves forward. Nothing seems to happen. It never seems to evolve. Nothing ever seems to get done. The department or business lags behind compared to others.

You will start questioning the department's performance, thinking:

'Why is everything so slow?'

'Why do decisions never get made?'

'She seems so competent but I can't see any progress.'

But when questioned – and this is very important to note – the no-decision manager you are trying to detect will always give you an adequate explanation. You will be reassured, but soon you'll start asking yourself questions about them again. Don't ignore these feelings. Your intuition, that all is not as it should be, is probably correct.

Spending time with your boss and headquarters

At some point you will discover that this particular manager spends much time with your boss and with people in headquarters or other senior or influential managers who have no apparent direct relationship with this manager. You'll think to yourself:

> 'He is always talking directly to my boss'
> 'She spends a massive amount of time with headquarters'

Again, on questioning the manager you will be given an adequate and probably very plausible explanation. But still your questions remain. Why is this manager spending so much time with the hierarchy?

Accumulation and consistency

Take stock and consider whether the manager concerned is associated with all five of these warning signs:

a) Too much information
b) Repeated requests for your opinion or advice
c) Reported incidents of lack of decision-making
d) Unexplained slow progress in the department involved
e) Too much time being spent directly with headquarters and your boss.

If you have evidence, however flimsy, on all of these five points on any of the managers in your team, you have probably found a no-decision manager. All you need now is to ask Human Resources to question the direct subordinates of this manager, discreetly but in detail. They will give you the final confirmation that you do have a no-decision manager in your team.

Remember now that your objective is to manage a team of no-decision managers so do not follow your instinct to fire them immediately.

DO NOT FIRE YOUR NO-DECISION MANAGER.

What you need to do now is put them in pivotal positioning.

Aphonic acknowledgement

If you want to manage no-decision managers effectively you need to understand aphonic acknowledgement and recognise those subordinates who have chosen it.

You will therefore need to go back to Chapter 8 and read the section on aphonic acknowledgement. You might also find it useful to learn the different levels of enlightenment that subordinates choose. See Chapter 8 in the section 'Choose your level of enlightenment'.

Reorganise the subordinates

Your next step is to have a meeting with the subordinates of your no-decision manager to tell them about aphonic acknowledgement and to invite them to adopt this stance. Those who refuse should be fired immediately and their seconds-in-command promoted in their place.

You now have a no-decision manager with a whole team of subordinates in aphonic acknowledgement. This is excellent but not yet perfect. This team will function even if it has no leader with members no longer in frustration and resignation. What will be difficult to control, though, is the direction of the team and its adherence to the corporate strategies. The managers in aphonic acknowledgement will take their decisions according to the type of freedom they have selected, so the team is likely to go off in the wrong direction. You need to add another element.

You now need to adapt the work of another management guru, Dr Meredith Belbin, to no-decision management teams. He developed his 'Team Role' theory where he revealed nine different behaviours of managers when working in an effective team. He learned that well-performing teams have different types of individuals who take on different roles in the team. For instance some members of the team need to be creative, others technical specialists, others focus on achieving the objective of the team. Each of the roles is complementary and allows members to work efficiently together.

Figure 25: Action-Centred Leadership™ After John Adair, with adapted Belbin Team Roles

A no-decision boss with team members in aphonic acknowledgement with the three key Belbin team roles

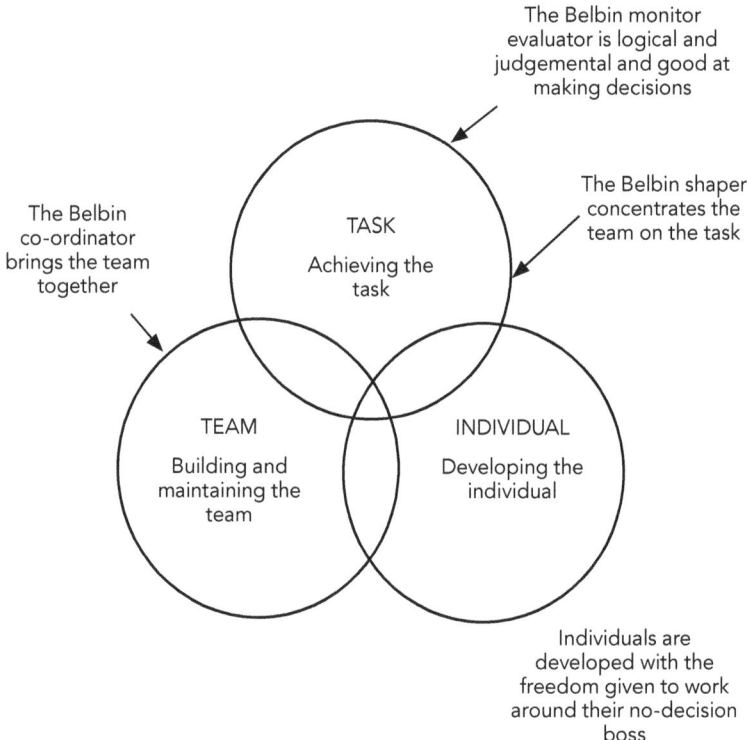

Reproduced with the permission of Adair International and Belbin Associates
Copyright © Adair International and Belbin Associates

When working with no-decision managers as the leader of the team, you do not need to learn and apply the whole of Belbin's model. You only need to fill your subordinate team with managers with three Belbin behaviour types, those who take decisions. There are three:

1. Shaper
2. Co-ordinator
3. Monitor Evaluator

The shaper is focused on the task and will get the team to work together.

A co-ordinator does just that. They give out the work that needs to be completed and are action orientated.

The monitor evaluator is logical and judgemental and good at making decisions.

Your new team will now become more like Figure 25, Action-Centred Leadership TM After John Adair, with adapted Belbin Team Roles, and represents a no-decision boss with team members in aphonic acknowledgement and the three key Belbin team roles.

Your no-decision manager's subordinates in aphonic acknowledgement are working as individuals, but with your direction they will perform some of the tasks together. The team, though, is broken and you need these three Belbin team roles to get them back working together.

You now need to analyse the subordinates you have chosen in aphonic acknowledgement to see whether you have at least one of each of these three Belbin team roles. If you don't you will have to find them quickly and promote at least one of each type of person into the no-decision manager's team.

You do not need the other Belbin team types in the team with your no-decision boss, as putting other team types in the team will not necessarily produce results in this situation.

a) The completer finisher with this name would be expected to help complete the task and should be included in the team; however, he or she is too interested in precision and detail and is likely to hold up decision-making, so is not necessary in the team
b) The resource investigator is not needed. Opportunities and contacts are surplus to no-decision management requirements.

c) Nor do you need the plant. Creativity and someone who solves problems is not essential.
d) Your no-decision boss is the expert because of their mastery of the three greats, so another specialist is unnecessary.
e) The implementer is also unnecessary. This is because implementing the decisions of others is one of the key qualities of your no-decision manager (see Chapter 4).
f) A team worker is a helper who gets team members to work together without confrontation. This person is diplomatic, a good listener and is excellent at conflict, prevention and resolution. They will bring the broken team back together. He or she can be added to the three essential members of the team.

The shaper and the co-ordinator will bring the team together and start working on common tasks as defined by you. The team is precarious, though, and there is no official leader although a co-ordinator or shaper will probably step up and take the unofficial role as leader, taking the place left free by the no-decision boss of the team. The organisation chart of this same team is shown in Figure 26, Organisation chart of the perfect team to manage a no-decision boss.

All you need to do now is present your strategies and objectives to the team. The 'aphonic acknowledgers' will do the rest.

You now have one no-decision manager in your team in pivotal positioning with subordinates willing to work with you. You are in a position to multiply their number so that 100% of your direct subordinates are no-decision managers if you can find enough of them in your organisation.

That's it! Managing a full team of no-decision managers is amazingly simple. And yet today most of them are dismissed as soon as they are discovered.

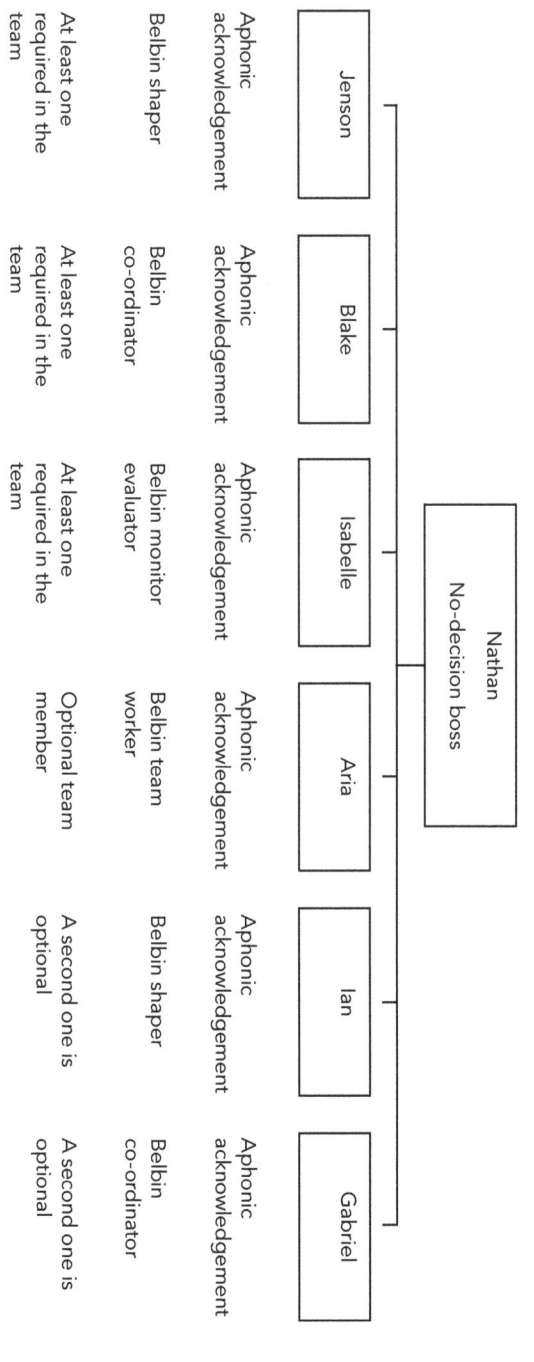

Figure 26: Organisation chart of the perfect team to manage a no-decision boss

Reproduced with the permission of Belbin Associates. Copyright © Belbin Associates

There are ten detailed steps to learn but they boil down to three essential actions: find the no-decision managers in your organisation, tell their subordinates about aphonic acknowledgement and read a little Belbin. With this you have a functioning team made up of no-decision managers.

Summary – steps 1–10 to manage a team of no-decision managers

Step 1 Find the no-decision managers in your team.

Step 2 When you have found them, DO NOT FIRE THEM!

Step 3 Put them in pivotal positioning.

Step 4 Learn to recognise the state of aphonic acknowledgement and the enlightened subordinate.

Step 5 Meet with the subordinates of the no-decision manager to invite them to take up the state of aphonic acknowledgement.

Step 6 Fire those who refuse to go into aphonic acknowledgement and promote their seconds-in-command.

Step 7 Analyse the subordinates you have chosen in aphonic acknowledgement to see whether there are any team workers, co-ordinators or completer finishers according to Belbin's team roles. (Figure 25, Action-Centred Leadership™ After John Adair, with adapted Belbin Team Roles).

Step 8 If you do not have at least one of each of the three key roles, find them quickly and promote them into the no-decision manager's team.

Step 9 Present your strategies and objectives to the team. The aphonic acknowledgers will do the rest (Figure 26, Organisation chart of the perfect team to manage a no-decision boss).

Step 10 Gradually multiply the number of no-decision subordinates directly reporting to you, until your whole team is made up of no-decision managers.

Annex 3 summarises the steps to manage a team of no-decision managers.

10

Comprehending No-Decision Management

Information on no-decision managers

Perpetual paradox

As you can now see, no-decision managers live comfortably in a perpetual paradox throughout their careers and force subordinates to put up with it whether they like it or not.

No-decision managers are unable to make decisions…	yet they can rapidly decide on tactics to avoid them.
They have clear and precise opinions…	but cannot act on them.
They are competent in their analysis of any situation, so have all the elements to make a decision…	but choose not to decide.
They have strong opinions…	but change them all the time.
They constantly change their minds…	until they adopt the boss's opinion as theirs and then never change their minds again.
They cannot decide themselves…	but can implement the decisions of others.

They allow subordinates to take their decisions for them…	but never take the responsibility for them.
They are knowledgeable about the industry, the company and the people so know the consequences of any decision better than anyone…	but in the end they never decide.
They appear friendly and approachable…	yet leave their subordinates adrift in negative emotion, encouraging frustration and anger
They are the friendly equals of their subordinates…	but are subservient to their bosses, ready to agree with whatever they say.
They are experts in the three greats: great analysis, great knowledge and great understanding…	yet they are often considered incompetent.
They make subordinates work in frustration and resignation…	while the bosses of no-decision managers think they have a great manager.
No-decision managers are despised by subordinates…	but respected by colleagues, suppliers, clients and people in headquarters for their competence, knowledge, and accessibility.
They are friendly…	but deceitful, devious and sometimes downright dishonest.
They allow enlightened subordinates in a relationship of aphonic acknowledgement to have their freedom…	but force them to give up their career progression.
Subordinates can learn from no-decision managers…	but no-decision managers never teach or help subordinates.
It takes courage and ingenuity to systematically avoid decisions…	but subordinates think no-decision managers are weak.

These contradictions make it complicated for subordinates to work with no-decision managers, yet their bosses find it easy because they never see the paradox.

New management concepts

As indicated in Chapter 1, both no-decision managers and their enlightened subordinates have invented new concepts in management and organisational behaviour. There are six that have been created by no-decision managers and one created by enlightened subordinates:

Created by no-decision managers:

1. Deemed decision
2. Deemed instruction
3. Decision dilemma and survival point
4. Deviated delegation
5. Outrageous behaviour
6. Hiding in excellence.

Created by enlightened subordinates:

1. Decision principle (created by enlightened subordinates).

Deemed decision

The first new concept is the deemed decision, discussed in Chapter 4. For simple and trivial decisions no-decision managers actively search for their boss's opinion. As soon as it is given it becomes a deemed decision made by the boss and then simply implemented by the no-decision manager.

For a normal manager it is obviously much easier to make a decision if you know, in advance, that your boss agrees with it beforehand. So in theory, when a normal manager asks their boss what they think of a future decision, and then decides only after their boss approves, there is no difference between a normal manager and a no-decision manager. In both instances the same decision is made, whether the manager is a normal one or a no-decision one.

No-decision managers, however, as you know, think differently to normal managers. No-decision managers take this tendency way further than a normal manager would. No-decision managers ask for the boss's opinions for trivial decisions, which a normal manager does not. They never take any decision if the boss shows any resistance. In their minds, no-decision managers are not making a decision, they are implementing a decision 'deemed' to be made by their boss. The difference you might say is slim, but difference there is, and normal managers do not resort to the table in Figure 11, The deemed decision, as do no-decision managers.

Deemed instruction

A second concept developed by no-decision managers is the deemed instruction, explained in Chapter 4. No-decision managers convert guidelines received from headquarters directly into instructions or orders to act. It is deemed by them to be an instruction to follow.

For a normal manager it is, again, easier to follow instructions from headquarters than it is to do something different. And many normal managers will follow these instructions in the same way as no-decision managers do, regardless of whether the instructions are realistic or not. No-decision managers, however, systematically follow guidelines or instructions from headquarters at all times, unless specifically requested otherwise by their bosses. They are just implementing decisions of others. Normal managers are not necessarily systematic when following these guidelines.

Decision dilemma and survival point

The third new concept is the decision dilemma and its related survival point explained in Chapter 6. It arises when the boss forces no-decision managers to make decisions on their own. Their dilemma is: should they make the decision or refuse? Most of the time no-decision managers will not make the decision, but too many refusals will lead to dismissal. The survival point comes when the no-decision manager estimates that this ultimate refusal to decide will lead to an immediate dismissal. Some no-decision managers have been known, as a last resort, to make a decision instead of being fired.

Normal managers do not have to worry about decision dilemmas or survival points in the ordinary course of their careers. They generally do not put themselves in a position where they refuse to make decisions over and over again, to the point where their boss will dismiss them.

Deviated delegation

The fourth new concept is deviated delegation, whether it be sideways, diagonal or upward. This simply means finding someone else to make the decision, as discussed in Chapter 4:

> 'Deviated delegation is the invisible acceptance of any decision taken by anyone in the organisation that should have been made by the no-decision manager.'

Normal managers are not in a permanent search for someone to take their decisions for them. They may, however, deviate delegation to subordinates in some form or another and follow some of the bad habits of no-decision managers. They may, for instance, never follow up on what subordinates do when they delegate a decision. Some may take the credit for decisions made by their subordinates. In fact, some may treat subordinates as badly as do no-decision managers, but their aim is not to try to force subordinates to decide in their place. Normal managers generally never resort to sideways, diagonal or upward delegation.

Outrageous behaviour

The fifth new concept is 'outrageous behaviour', as explained in Chapters 4 and 7. It is behaviour of a no-decision manager that is out of character, unexpected, sudden, a surprise to all and which is a signal to subordinates to come out of their negative emotional state and work serenely with their no-decision boss.

This is completely foreign to normal managers. If they want to say something to their subordinates they generally just talk to them, instead of sending obscure messages through bizarre behaviours.

Hiding in excellence

The last new management concept invented by no-decision managers is the hiding concept used for survival in their organisations in the long term, and explained in Chapter 5. No-decision managers hide in excellence. This involves acquiring and reaching excellence in three core skills, the three greats: great analysis, great knowledge and great understanding; and then using these skills to hide their lack of decision-making.

There is nothing wrong with normal managers having these three core skills in the same way as no-decision managers do. Moreover, normal managers often strive for excellence in these skills as well. Normal managers, though, do not use these skills to hide the fact that they aren't making any decisions. Not having these skills as a normal manager is a disadvantage, but not a serious risk of survival, as is the case with no-decision managers.

Decision principle

The decision principle is used by enlightened subordinates who have decided to become unofficial leaders of their no-decision boss's team, as explained in Chapter 8. The decision principle states that 'any decision is better than no decision at all'. This is a concept invented by enlightened subordinates who have decided to make decisions in place of their bosses, so that the organisation or department where they work continues to function.

'Any' in this context means accepting decisions of colleagues in aphonic acknowledgement and turning the proposals of the managers for whom they are the unofficial leader into decisions, regardless of whether they agree with them or not.

This is clearly a new management concept exclusive to dealing with no-decision managers. Normal managers do not, of course, have to make decisions in place of their bosses, so have no need to take up the decision principle.

New management activities

Two new management activities have been developed by the no-decision movement:

a) Formal and fortuitous filtering and
b) Focused filtering

Formal and fortuitous filtering

Formal and fortuitous filtering is simply 'telling on the boss', and is used by subordinates in any organisation when they are not happy with their bosses. It rarely happens in the case of normal managers. But in no-decision management telling on the boss is not rare at all. Subordinates do it all the time as their frustration against the lack of decision-making increases.

As explained in Chapter 5, fortuitous filtering is making a verbal complaint about the boss and formal filtering a written one. This name was invented by the no-decision-making movement because no-decision managers must monitor 'filtering' as part of their strategy to survive. It has been introduced as a specific managerial activity, to be learned within great understanding.

There is some debate as to whether this is a new management concept or just a new activity reserved for no-decision managers. In any event it is new. It is not recognised in management literature today.

Focused filtering

Formal and fortuitous filtering must not be confused with focused filtering. Focused filtering is the technique used by no-decision managers to filter out bad news being sent up to their bosses and to ensure that they are only given good news. It is described in Chapter 6 as part of surviving as a no-decision manager.

It is not a new management concept but a management technique, known to all. All managers, normal or otherwise, want to put a favourable slant on information going up into the hierarchy, to make them appear to be competent and effective managers. Some will go to great lengths, as do no-decision managers, to make sure that bad news or negative information never reaches the boss.

No-decision managers, however, have enhanced, improved and formalised this technique and given it a name. They actively manage information flow up into the hierarchy, especially to the boss.

Disclosure of decision avoidance tactics

Some business authors, either with the help of the Shelter, unknown to them, or in total contravention of the no-decision management secrecy rules, have published some of the tactics and behaviours used by no-decision managers.

One of the earliest was Robert M. Bramson, who in his book *Coping with Difficult People* (1981) hinted at the existence of a complete No-decision-making System but without giving details any of its components. He was also the first to explain the consequences of both 'outrageous behaviour' and permanent procrastination.

Then after a gap of almost 15 years George T. Fuller in his book *The Workplace Survival Guide* (1995) explained that his indecisive manager never took any responsibility for the actions of his subordinates or his team, or of anybody for that matter. His manager concentrated on self-protection, a behaviour systematically adopted by no-decision managers.

After another gap, this time of 10 years, the release of additional tactics accelerated. Gini Graham in her book *A Survival Guide for Working with Bad Bosses* (2005) revealed the Rumsfeld resolution through her invention of a new type of boss: the 'No-Boss Boss'. She did not, of course, call this tactic the Rumsfeld resolution, as her 'No-Boss Boss' is not a no-decision manager – just one who has difficulty in making decisions. Her boss searches for someone in the organisation to take decisions for them – a tactic borrowed from the no-decision movement.

This was followed up by Lynn Taylor, who invented a new type of boss – the 'TOT Ignoring Boss'– in her book *Tame Your Terrible Office Tyrant* (2009) to reveal the tactic of ignoring subordinates often used by no-decision managers to avoid decision-making. The manager called 'the avoider' by Marsha Evans and Elizabeth Gaynor in their book *Surviving and Thriving When Your Boss is a Jerk!* (2014) also uses the tactic of ignoring subordinates to avoid decision-making.

And then more recently, Amy Cooper Hakim and Muriel Solomon in their book *Working with Difficult People* (2016) revealed the tactic whereby subordinates take decisions for their boss, without using the actual terminology of deviated downward delegation and Rumsfeld resolution. Here though, this boss is called an 'overcommitter' and is not a no-decision manager, but does allow subordinates to decide in their place.

'How to' advice for no-decision managers

You are now nearly at the end of your quest to become a no-decision manager. You have a few more things to learn, and a few more steps to take before the final one: to renounce decision-making for ever and become a perfect no-decision manager.

Recognise the different emotions of your subordinates

You need to go back to Chapter 7 and learn to recognise the different emotional states that subordinates will choose to adopt in order to work with you, as a no-decision manager. Natural no-decision managers learn about these different states on their own as their careers advance. You, as a nascent no-decision manager, need to recognise each of these individually to be able to adapt your different decision avoidance tactics correctly.

There is, for instance, absolutely no point in directing a bout of 'outrageous behaviour' at a subordinate who is in peaceful patience or already in aphonic acknowledgement. Why make subordinates who are working positively with you angry? It will just make your life more difficult and possibly shock them out of their favourable attitude towards you.

You might for instance classify subordinates into two groups. Those who are hostile towards you: in fundamental frustration, reticent resignation and constant conflict, where you can apply your decision avoidance tactics against them. And those who work positively with you: in peaceful patience and aphonic acknowledgement, where decision avoidance tactics are of no use. But you must be able to identify and separate those in peaceful patience from those in aphonic acknowledgement, because they need different management attention from you as their boss.

Peaceful patience

You can easily recognise subordinates in a state of peaceful patience. You will notice that the frustration has gone and aggressiveness has vanished. But above all they will no longer push you for a decision. You can set up a more courteous relationship with them. But remember not to have any open communication with them about their move into peaceful patience. It is their choice and theirs alone.

With your subordinates exhibiting peaceful patience, one particular managerial role will disappear: that of applying decision avoidance tactics. And you can also eliminate the monitoring of the frustration levels in these subordinates, because their frustration has passed.

Aphonic acknowledgement

It is so much easier to have your subordinates in aphonic acknowledgement make your decisions for you than it is to convince someone in headquarters or your boss to make them. Your level of work on deviated downward delegation will reduce dramatically. You merely wait for the decisions to be made. Not that you care too much what the decision is, just that your subordinate is taking it for you.

However, monitoring must increase with your new aphonic acknowledgement subordinates. You need to monitor what decisions are being taken by your subordinates, to be ready either to take the credit for the good ones or to be ready to blame them for the bad ones. This, as you already know, is important for your survival. And, as with your subordinates in peaceful patience, here too your managerial role of decision avoidance disappears.

Achieving perfection as a no-decision manager

Avoiding detection

You should now go back to Chapter 9 and read the section 'How to identify a no-decision manager'. You have by now learned the standard no-decision strategies to avoid detection. However, this section gives you an insight from the boss's point of view into how no-decision managers are discovered by their bosses. It clearly highlights two important issues that you must be aware of but which are not specifically emphasised by the Shelter in structured survival.

Bosses use weaknesses in structured survival to detect you as a no-decision boss. This news is very important. There are five points of weakness. Three of them you have control over:

a) Too much information to the boss
b) Repeated requests for your opinion or advice from the boss
c) Too much time spent directly with headquarters and your boss's boss.

Do not ever overstep the mark in these three activities and give your boss a reason to doubt you. Do not give them too much information. It is better, for instance, to give your boss less information and forgo, say, a deemed decision than it is to get them frustrated by information overload. Do not ask for too many opinions. Consider spending less time at headquarters, or for instance camouflaging time spent there in legitimate meetings.

In the other two points of weakness, however, you have no control:

a) Reported incidents where decisions are not made
b) Unexplained slow progress in the department involved.

These two are a direct consequence of no-decision-making so are impossible to counter. But now that you know, be aware that you will ultimately be detected as a no-decision manager through them. Having more subordinates in aphonic acknowledgement would help, even though you have no direct influence in putting them there.

The second important point to note is that once the doubts have started to surface, your boss will use Human Resources to confirm whether or not you are a real no-decision manager. Human Resources clearly know that you are one, and they have been a great help to you in avoiding detection, so there is not much that you can do. Perhaps set up an early warning system with key Human Resource individuals. Now that you know, be aware.

Pivotal positioning

Chapter 9 also explains pivotal positioning. To attain perfection as a no-decision manager you need to be in pivotal positioning. It is the ultimate reward and status. The advantages for you are immense:

1. Work on structured survival can be reduced significantly.
2. Blandish the bosses can be eliminated.
3. Handling of hierarchy around headquarters and colleagues of your boss can be cut down to normal levels. Your boss will now willingly make your decisions for you.
4. You will no longer need to manage frustration levels of subordinates. This will now be done by Human Resources.
5. You can completely stop all activities relating to secrecy.

The amended Mintzberg model shows the reduction of the workload well. From the original ten roles of a manager, no-decision managers in pivotal positioning have only five that remain. See Figure 27, The no-decision manager's roles in pivotal positioning, which shows the reduced number of roles a no-decision manager has once they are in pivotal positioning.

The figurehead role remains, and as the nominal boss of the department or organisation you can continue to perform the ceremonial duties of the function. In the same way you remain the spokesperson of your department and maintain the outside contacts. You continue with the liaison role, especially acting as the go-between for your boss and your team. You can reduce monitoring and decision avoidance to a minimum. Some subordinates may continue to ask for decisions but many of the more sophisticated tactics can be abandoned and replaced with deviated delegation most of the time.

Figure 27: The no-decision manager's roles in pivotal positioning

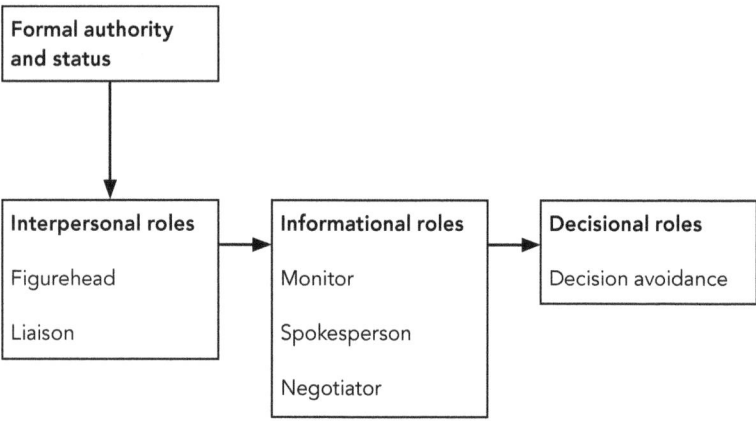

Adapted from Henry Mintzberg's article 'The Manager's Job: Folklore and Fact', (*Harvard Business Review,* July-August 1975) for no-decision management.

Reproduced and amended by permission of *Harvard Business Review*. Original Copyright © 1975 by Harvard Business Publishing; all rights reserved.

Figure 28: The Managerial Grid in pivotal positioning

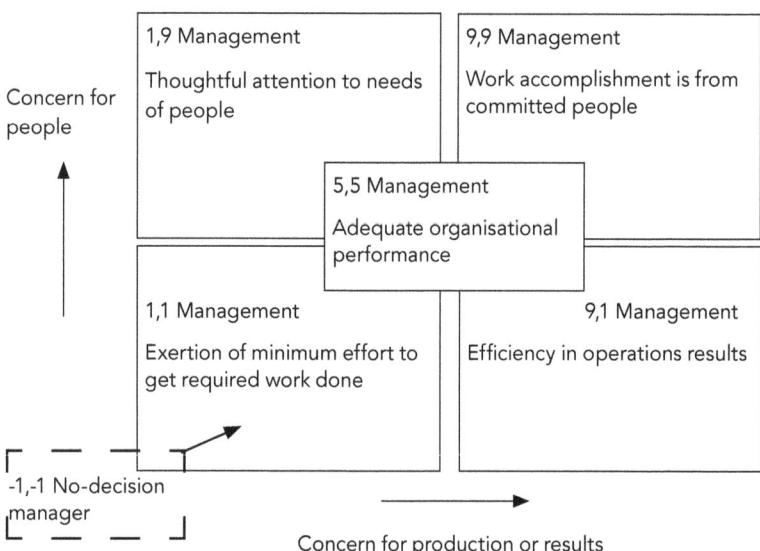

294

A no-decision manager in pivotal positioning can start to move into the zone 1,1 Management called the Impoverished Manager, not because of any change in behaviour, but because others will take decisions and have concerns for the people.

Borrowed from the article 'Breakthrough in Organisation Development' by R. R. Blake, J. S. Mouton, L. B. Barnes and L. E. Greiner (*Harvard Business Review*, November 1964) and adapted to include the no-decision manager.

Reproduced and amended by permission of Harvard Business Review. Original Copyright © 1964 by Harvard Business Publishing: all rights reserved.

Another advantage of going into pivotal positioning is that your subordinates become less frustrated and your boss willingly takes decisions for you.

This is illustrated in Figure 28, The Management Grid in pivotal positioning, where you as the no-decision manager move at least partly back into the square.

Unfortunately you have no say in the matter. Only your boss can put you in pivotal positioning. And he or she has to know that you are a no-decision manager before deciding to give you this privilege. If you tell, which you must not, you risk dismissal.

There is, however, one major drawback if you are in pivotal positioning, if ever you get there. It only lasts as long as your boss lasts in position as your boss. The minute your boss moves on, you automatically lose your protection. Because you are in pivotal positioning everyone knows you are a no-decision manager. Your new boss will know too, so you risk rapid dismissal.

Final steps to becoming a no-decision manager

Just before you take the last steps on your way to becoming a no-decision manager you might be feeling some apprehension. To reassure you, let's go back to Hertzberg and see what he has to say about the factors leading to job satisfaction and dissatisfaction.

Figure 29, Hertzberg's Motivation-Hygiene Theory applied to a perfect no-decision manager, shows how you will feel after your decision to be a fully fledged no-decision manager compared to how you feel today as a normal manager. Hertzberg says that there will be no change at all except for one significant improvement, in one factor of dissatisfaction: the relationship with your boss. It will move from normal to excellent as a no-decision manager, through your actions in blandish the bosses (Chapter 8). They will think you have become the perfect subordinate.

Figure 29: Herzberg's Motivation-Hygiene Theory applied to a perfect no-decision manager

Leading to dissatisfaction	Leading to satisfaction
Company policy – same as a normal manager	Achievement – same as a normal manager
Supervision– same as a normal manager	Recognition – same as a normal manager
Relationship with the boss EXCELLENT through blandish the bosses	Work itself – same as a normal manager
Work conditions – same as a normal manager	Responsibility – same as a normal manager
Salary – same as a normal manager	Advancement – same as a normal manager
Relationship with peers – same as a normal manager	Growth – same as a normal manager

Theory as applied to a perfect no-decision manager, adapted from Frederick Hertzberg's article 'One More Time: How do You Motivate Employees?' (*Harvard Business Review*, January 2003).

Reproduced and amended by permission of *Harvard Business Review*. Original Copyright © 1968 by Harvard Business Publishing; all rights reserved.

With this, Hertzberg shows that it is better to be a no-decision manager than a normal one! Here is the proof that you have nothing to worry about.

Decide on a motto

You will remember that one of the secrecy rules of the Shelter is that nothing about no-decision management can be put into writing.

No-decision managers have copied a method invented by liar

managers to identify fellow no-decision managers. It is tolerated by the movement, but not officially accepted, and is now an exception to 'the nothing in writing rule'. It is their unique but bizarre way of recognising another no-decision manager, and has become their unofficial motto.

On the back of their business cards no-decision managers have printed a quote from the late Tommy Cooper, a well-known British comedian:

> I used to be indecisive but now I am not sure.

This is the only public written evidence of the existence of no-decision managers and has become their unique way of recognising one another.

In recent years, however, the younger generation of no-decision managers have taken to former US President Barack Obama, not because he is a no-decision manager (quite the opposite), but because he has publicly admitted his dislike for making decisions while ironically being in the position in the world that requires the most important decisions to be made. He is quoted to have said:

> I'm trying to pare down decisions. I don't want to make decisions about what I'm eating or wearing because I have too many decisions to make. (*Vanity Fair* 2012 article by Michael Lewis)

The story goes, according to *Vanity Fair* and Michael Lewis, that while in office Barack Obama only wore grey or blue suits. He made two decisions upfront: blue and grey, and never needed to make a new decision each day. He reduced 365 decisions per year down to two made in 2012 and transformed decision-making into a routine task.

Late in 2012, a young but experienced no-decision manager, who will remain nameless, adapted Obama's quote to no-decision management and put it on the back of his business card, replacing Tommy Cooper's slogan.

He printed:

> I'm trying to stamp out decisions. I don't want to make decisions about anything – whether it's about what I'm eating or wearing, because one decision is too many to make.

It is clear that Obama's comments about decision-making arose because he was so busy making important decisions that he did not have time for the trivial ones such as deciding what to eat or what to wear. No-decision managers of course understood this, but they relished the former president of the United States of America openly announcing a decision-reduction programme. It was a big day for the no-decision management movement.

Today more and more of the younger no-decision managers have adopted this more modern misquote as their motto on the back of their business cards.

You now should decide which of these two mottos to print on the back of your new no-decision business card. Throw out your old cards and order the new set with the motto of your choice.

Your last decision

You have a significant advantage over natural, instinctive no-decision managers because you have been able to learn everything about no-decision management before actually making your last decision, which is the irony of all ironies, to decide to abandon decision-making.

SO GO AHEAD: ABANDON DECISION-MAKING FOR EVER.
You are now a no-decision manager. There is no going back.
Good Luck!

Summary – the final steps 32–39 to become a no-decision manager

Step 32 Go back to Chapter 7 and learn to recognise the different states that subordinates get into while working with you as a no-decision manager. Classify them into three groups, namely those who are:

a) Negative towards you
b) In peaceful patience
c) In aphonic acknowledgement.

You must learn to recognise these different states, to allow you to direct your different decision avoidance tactics just to those subordinates who are negative towards you.

Step 33 Learn to rapidly recognise subordinates who are in a state of peaceful patience. Remember to be courteous to them and to stop using decision avoidance tactics against them. You no longer need to monitor their frustration levels either.

Step 34 Learn to recognise subordinates in a state of aphonic acknowledgement. Be ready to take credit for their good decisions and to blame them for the bad ones.

Step 35 Go back to Chapter 9 and learn how no-decision managers are discovered by their bosses.

Step 36 Try to get into pivotal positioning as soon as possible to become the perfect no-decision manager.

Step 37 Decide on your motto.

Step 38 Print your motto on the back of your business card.

Step 39 ABANDON DECISION-MAKING FOR EVER. There is no going back!

Annex 1 The No-Decision Manager Manual summarises the 39 steps required to become a no-decision manager.

Annex 2 The Enlightened Subordinate Manual summarises the 13 steps required to become an enlightened subordinate of a no-decision boss.

Annex 3 Manual on how to Manage a Team of No-Decision Managers summarises the 10 steps required to manage a team of no-decision managers.

Annex 1

The No-Decision Manager Manual. The 39 steps required to become a no-decision manager

Step 1 Find a no-decision manager.

Step 2 Declare your allegiance to the no-decision movement.

Step 3 Request membership of the Shelter.

Step 4 Take the oath of secrecy and become a member.

You are now officially a no-decision manager BUT do not stop taking decisions just yet – wait until you know a little more

Step 5 Memorise the definition of a no-decision manager:

> a person who supposedly manages a team and pretends to control, direct or administer a business, an organisation, a government administration or a public or private institution or any part, and who refuses to arrive at an opinion or conclusion about a matter under consideration or who refuses to make a decision regarding a question or issue, on which there is doubt or dispute especially after considering several alternatives.

Step 6 Learn the three rules of the Shelter:

1. Nothing is ever put in writing
2. Meetings of the organisation are limited to a maximum of two no-decision managers at any one time
3. Publications on no-decision management are not permitted.

Step 7 Learn the four pillars of the Shelter: Secrecy, Survival, Skills and System.

Step 8 Memorise Figure 8, The no-decision manager's roles. Learn the three new roles and the four amended ones specially adapted:

New Roles

  1. Decision avoidance
  2. Secrecy
  3. Survival.

Amended Roles

  1. Figurehead
  2. Liaison
  3. Monitor
  4. Spokesperson.

Step 9 Discover, learn and above all practise the two instinct-based behaviours of permanent procrastination and imposing incremental information until they become second nature.

Step 10 Read, understand, reflect, experiment and remember the five active avoidance tactics.

Step 11 Read, understand, reflect, experiment and remember the four different delay decisions.

Step 12 Memorise the definition of deviated delegation:

> Deviated delegation is the invisible acceptance of a decision taken by anyone in the organisation that should have been made by the

no-decision manager, who silently refuses any accountability for the outcome of the decision unless the decision is approved by management.

Step 13 Learn the three rules of deviation downward delegation:

1. Wait for the subordinate to take the initiative
2. Renounce responsibility for the decision
3. Monitor nothing, never help.

Step 14 Learn deviation upward delegation and the two new concepts: the deemed decision (by using Figure 11, The deemed decision, as a memory aid) and the deemed instruction.

Step 15 Learn deviation diagonal delegation, especially if you work in a company with a matrix organisation with 'dotted line' responsibilities or in an organisation with a prolific headquarters.

Step 16 Be aware that deviation sideways delegation is an option, even if not always practical.

Step 17 Make sure you use implementing decisions as a decision avoidance tactic and then become an expert in implementing the decisions of others, precisely and to the letter regardless of the consequences.

Step 18 Choose the 'outrageous behaviour' that you feel comfortable with and apply it in a calculated, deliberate way – carefully timed to maximise the surprise and emotion of your subordinates. Do not lose control.

Step 19 Learn and implement 'great analysis' – developing alternatives, analysing alternatives and evaluation of alternatives – whenever you have to compile a report for a decision.

Step 20 Acquire 'great knowledge' of your business, the competition and any relevant technology.

Step 21 Develop a 'great understanding' of your organisation, your department and the people in them, above all to detect as early as possible any complaints of decision avoidance that may filter up through the hierarchy and ultimately reach your boss.

Step 22 Develop the behaviour of 'clear but changing opinions' so that it becomes natural, and learn the four steps for this behaviour:

a) Have an opinion – it doesn't matter what
b) Change it whenever you want
c) When you know what your boss thinks, make your opinion the same
d) Watch out for when your boss changes their mind and then change yours again.

Step 23 Learn the attitude of being 'friendly but uncaring' and memorise the definition:

Although friendly, no-decision managers neglect subordinates, are disinterested at best, never provide encouragement and never give any support when needed.

You can classify yourself as a great no-decision manager after having mastered these 23 steps. However, the most important lesson is still to come: how to survive as a no-decision manager.

Step 24 Set up the seven separated specialised informal networks with the five special no-decision management actions, and use Figure 18, Separated specialised informal networks, as a checklist.

Step 25 Systematically apply the five rules of blandish the bosses when dealing with your boss:

a) Learn the basic techniques for managing your boss
b) Learn the techniques of focused filtering
c) Get into a special relationship – know your boss well enough to change their behaviour into making decisions for you
d) Plan ahead for a crisis: be the first with the news and prepare who will make your decisions for you
e) Manage the limit of information overload.

Step 26 Apply the two rules of blandish the bosses when dealing with your boss's boss:

a) Get into special relationships
b) Manage influence and information.

Step 27 Handling of hierarchy – build relationships with colleagues of your boss and key managers in headquarters to show off your expertise in the three greats.

Step 28 Use the relationship rectangle (Figure 19) and your company's organisational chart to select the managers for each of the four groups: blandish the bosses, handling of hierarchy, influential people network and the headquarter network.

Step 29 Perfect the Rumsfeld resolution by making a detailed analysis of the different decision-making preferences of your boss.

Step 30 Avoid organisations that are 'great' companies or organisations that have decentralised decision-making.

Step 31 Avoid having no-decision managers and micro-managers as your boss.

Step 32 Go back to Chapter 7 and learn to recognise the different states that subordinates get into while working with you as a no-decision manager. Classify them into three groups, namely those who are:

a) Negative towards you
b) In peaceful patience
c) In aphonic acknowledgement.

You must learn to recognise these different states, to allow you to direct your different decision avoidance tactics just to those subordinates who are negative towards you.

Step 33 Learn to rapidly recognise subordinates who are in a state of peaceful patience. Remember to be courteous to them and to stop using decision avoidance tactics against them. You no longer need to monitor their frustration levels either.

Step 34 Learn to recognise subordinates in a state of aphonic acknowledgement. Be ready to take credit for their good decisions and to blame them for the bad ones.

Step 35 Go back to Chapter 9 and learn how no-decision managers are discovered by their bosses.

Step 36 Try to get into pivotal positioning as soon as possible to become the perfect no-decision manager.

Step 37 Decide on your motto.

Step 38 Print your motto on the back of your business card.

Step 39 ABANDON DECISION-MAKING FOR EVER. There is no going back!

Annex 2

The Enlightened Subordinate Manual. The 13 steps required to become an enlightened subordinate of a no-decision boss

Step 1 Relive the emotional journey through the different stages of frustration into fundamental frustration, understand how you get there, and then ultimately reject it.

Step 2 If you are thinking of explicit exit and of leaving, stop searching for another job for the moment. Carry on working with your no-decision boss.

Step 3 Reject both reticent resignation and constant conflict. You have two ways forward: either through peaceful patience or by waiting for your no-decision boss to display 'outrageous behaviour'.

Step 4 If you have chosen peaceful patience, choose a way forward into aphonic acknowledgement, even if it is pleasant enough to stay in peaceful patience with your no-decision boss in the long term. You have two ways in: either through a silent pact with your no-decision boss or through a policy of take it anyway.

Step 5 If you have chosen 'outrageous behaviour', pester your no-decision boss for decisions and wait for the moment of 'outrageous behaviour'. When it comes, understand the two messages: a) Stop pestering me for a decision and b) Come and work with me positively in aphonic acknowledgement.

Step 6 Make your move into aphonic acknowledgement. You now know the different ways to achieve this.

You are now an enlightened subordinate but you are not finished yet. You need to decide which level of enlightenment is best for you.

Step 7 Take your freedom and enjoy the autonomy and then choose the way you want to work in freedom.

Step 8 Learn from your no-decision boss and choose the subjects that are the best for you to learn:

> From within the 'three greats'
> Informal networks
> Blandish the bosses
> Handling of hierarchy.

Step 9 Protect yourself with information and informal networks.

Step 10 Know the consequences of working with your no-decision boss: your career is on hold but you will never be fired.

Step 11 Decide how far you help your no-decision boss to get decisions made for them by others.

Step 12 Choose your level of enlightenment:

> Enlightened individual
> Enlightened manager
> Enlightened co-ordinator
> Enlightened leader.

If you choose the enlightened leader level then gradually take the necessary steps to become the unofficial leader of the team:

- Adopt the decision principle and agree with the decisions made by your fellow enlightened subordinates together with the proposals of the other managers
- Inform colleagues that you will now take all the decisions
- Become the co-ordinator of your boss's team
- Share the decisions you have made with your no-decision boss
- Beware of the danger from colleagues in constant conflict and those whose freedom is power in aphonic acknowledgement
- Take over the broken team, bring the individuals into it and try to persuade those in aphonic acknowledgement to accept your leadership.

You are now an enlightened subordinate working in harmony with your no-decision boss, having taken all the decisions that are best for you personally.

Annex 3

Manual on how to Manage a Team of No-Decision Managers. The 10 steps required to manage a team of no-decision managers

Step 1 Find the no-decision managers in your team.

Step 2 When you have found them, DO NOT FIRE THEM!

Step 3 Put them in pivotal positioning.

Step 4 Learn to recognise the state of aphonic acknowledgement and the enlightened subordinate.

Step 5 Meet with the subordinates of the no-decision manager to invite them to take up the state of aphonic acknowledgement.

Step 6 Fire those who refuse to go into aphonic acknowledgement and promote their seconds-in-command.

Step 7 Analyse the subordinates you have chosen in aphonic acknowledgement to see whether there are any team workers, co-ordinators or completer finishers according to Belbin's team roles. (Figure 25, Action-Centred Leadership™ After John Adair, with adapted Belbin Team Roles).

Step 8 If you do not have at least one of each of the three key roles, find them quickly and promote them into the no-decision manager's team.

Step 9 Present your strategies and objectives to the team. The aphonic acknowledgers will do the rest (Figure 26, Organisation chart of the perfect team to manage a no-decision boss).

Step 10 Gradually multiply the number of no-decision subordinates directly reporting to you, until your whole team is made up of no-decision managers.

Annex 4
No-decision management glossary of terms

Term or Expression	Definition	Comments
Announce an action	Type of delay decision tactic within the no-decision making system.	Term invented by the no-decision movement.
Aphonic acknowledgement	The ultimate positive working relationship of a subordinate with his no-decision boss. The subordinate is often called an enlightened subordinate.	Too obscure to be anything but an expression invented by the no-decision movement.
Artificial agreements	Type of active avoidance tactic within the no-decision-making system. Used by the no-decision management movement simply as an untrue statement.	Term borrowed from A.C. Kapur in his book *Principles of Political Science* (1950) where he discusses the political party system and meaning changed.
Blandish the bosses	A special personal relationship between the no-decision manager and his boss (and boss's boss) to maintain the boss's opinion of the no-decision manager at its highest level at all times.	Silly term already used as in 'sucking up to the boss' but meaning modified by the no-decision movement.
Build-up of the 'buts'	Discovery of a no-decision manager in an organisation through the accumulation of small incidents over time.	Term invented by the no-decision movement.

Communist commendation	A term used by incompetent managers when they give identical salary increases to each one of their subordinates regardless of their performance or salary level.	Nothing to do with the no-decision management movement or with the Chinese, Russian or any other communist political party.
Comprehensive chronic procrastination	An action stolen from the no-decision movement and used by procrastination managers to delay actions, tasks and decisions.	Not a term invented by procrastination managers and not part of the no-decision movement.
Constant conflict	Subordinates choose to stay in a continuous state of confrontation with their no-decision boss.	Widely used expression not specific to the no-decision movement, but with a new meaning in the no-decision management context.
Consultant (use of)	Type of delay decision tactic within the no-decision-making system.	Normally hired to obtain results but just another delay tactic for the no-decision movement.
Decision dilemma	The moment the boss of a no-decision manager forces him into making an important decision on his own. The no-decision manager must decide whether to take the decision to avoid being fired.	Widely used expression used in the context of which decision to make, but used in the no-decision movement exclusively in the context of whether a decision should be made or not.
Decision principle	A principle used by the enlightened leader: 'Any decision is better than no decision at all.'	No relation to current thoughts on decision theory and absolutely nothing to do with the 'Ellsberg paradox'. Just a term invented by the no-decision movement.
Delay decision	Decisions designed to delay the moment of deciding.	An expression often used with 'delay' as a verb as in 'to delay a decision'. 'Delay' here is an adjective invented by the no-decision movement.

Deemed decision	Information from the boss is deemed to be a decision taken by them which no-decision managers can then implement.	Term borrowed from the Queensland Government in Australia when a decision is deemed to have been taken if no reply has been received, usually within 30 days.
Determined desertion	Act of leaving the no-decision boss as quickly as possible.	Legal term used in marriage and military law but recently discarded by the no-decision movement and replaced by explicit exit.
Deviate delegation	No-decision managers search their organisation for anyone who will make their decision for them.	Term which the no-decision movement claims they invented.
Deviated diagonal delegation	Tactic within the no-decision-making system. Act of persuading people in the hierarchy, usually in headquarters, to take a decision in place of the no-decision manager.	Term probably invented by the Supreme Court of Canada to describe the transfer of regulatory power to another level of government. Also found in Australian Public Policy discussions, but borrowed by the no-decision movement.
Deviated downward delegation	Tactic within the no-decision-making system. Subordinate decides to take decisions in place of their no-decision boss.	Usual term to describe delegation from a superior to subordinate but meaning changed by the no-decision movement.
Deviated sideways delegation	Tactic within the no-decision-making system. A colleague of a no-decision manager takes a decision in his place.	Sometimes called deviated lateral delegation but with a slightly modified meaning when used by the no-decision movement.

Deviated upward delegation	Tactic within the no-decision-making system. Attempt of the no-decision manager to get his boss to take a decision in his place.	Upward delegation is often used to describe cunning subordinates who get their boss to perform their work, but with a new orientation invented by the no-decision movement
Enlightened co-ordinator	A choice available for enlightened subordinates. Takes decisions of the no-decision boss for his own department only, and also helps his colleagues with an information role.	Term invented by the no-decision movement.
Enlightened individual	A choice available for enlightened subordinates. Takes decisions of the no-decision boss to help achieve personal freedom.	Term invented by the no-decision movement.
Enlightened leader	A choice available for enlightened subordinates. Takes over as unofficial leader from the no-decision boss.	Term invented by the no-decision movement.
Enlightened manager	A choice available for enlightened subordinates. Takes decisions of the no-decision boss for his own department only.	Term invented by the no-decision movement.
Enlightened subordinate	Another name for subordinates in aphonic acknowledgement.	Too obscure to be anything but an expression invented by the no-decision movement.
Explicit exit	Act of leaving the no-decision boss as quickly as possible.	Widely used expression not specific to the no-decision movement, but they give it a new meaning.
Five S's	The four pillars of the no-decision movement's Shelter.	Ludicrous name invented by the no-decision movement which unintentionally detracts attention away from the seriousness of the subject.

Focused filtering	No-decision manager making sure the boss gets only good news and news filtered by him.	Term often used in decontamination of gas-based fuels, but used by the no-decision movement well before this term was invented by the gas industry.
Formal filtering	Complaints from subordinates in writing which filter up to the boss of the no-decision manager.	A term used in mathematics, borrowed by the no-decision movement and original meaning changed.
Fortuitous filtering	Verbal complaints from subordinates which filter up to the boss of the no-decision manager.	Term used in the filtering of sunlight and in ophthalmology, borrowed by the no-decision movement and original meaning changed.
Fundamental frustration	A continuous state of frustration of subordinates on discovery that their boss will never make a decision.	Widely used expression in many different fields: teaching, travel, politics and others, borrowed by the no-decision movement and the meaning changed.
Handling of hierarchy	An activity to find and develop future allies in the organisation for mutual support when needed.	A term widely used in many fields but with another meaning when used by the no-decision movement.
Hiding in excellence	No-decision managers become experts in the three greats to hide their weakness of never making decisions.	Term claimed to have been invented by the no-decision movement.
Ignoring	Type of active avoidance tactic within the no-decision making system.	
Imposing incremental information	One of the two instinct-based behaviours of a true no-decision manager.	Pure invention of the no-decision movement but possibly originating from an accounting term 'incremental information'.

Incremental information improved	Type of delay decision tactic within the no-decision-making system.	Term invented by the no-decision movement, possibly originating from accounting term 'incremental information' and not to be confused with, but similar to, imposing incremental information.
Inconsequential information	Same as ineffective information.	Now a well-known term used to explain the origins of Twitter in 2006, but used for many years by the no-decision movement before this date.
Indispensable information	The normal level of information that any ordinary manager would need to make a decision.	Widely used expression not specific to the no-decision movement.
Ineffective information	Information which has no direct relevance to the decision under study. Sometimes called 'inutile information'.	Widely used expression not specific to the no-decision movement.
Inept information	An absurd request for information by a no-decision manager which is not related to the decision under study.	A term borrowed by the no-decision management movement from 'Information Sources in Engineering', by Roderick A. Macleod and Jim Corlett, in which they discuss information overload.
Information overload barrier	Too much information given to the boss so they no longer help in decision-making.	Term invented by the no-decision movement.
Insignificant information	Information that is interesting for the decision making process but unnecessary to make the decision.	Widely used expression not specific to the no-decision movement.

Inutile information	Information which has no direct relevance to the decision under study. Sometimes called ineffective information.	Widely used expression not specific to the no-decision movement.
Judicious abrupt absence	A type of judicious absence (see below).	
Judicious absence	Type of active avoidance tactic within the no-decision-making system.	Term borrowed from Charles Reade, possibly even invented by him in 1870, and used in the same sense, but now also a legal term to describe the absence of trial judges.
Liar manager	Manager that lies all the time.	Known type of manager, but few exist.
Meaningless meetings	Type of active avoidance tactic within the no-decision making system.	Often used term, no change in meaning when used by the no-decision movement.
Normal manager	Manager that takes decisions.	Many behaviours of no-decision managers are also used by normal managers, i.e. managers that make decisions in their normal business life.
Outrageous behaviour	Tactic within the no-decision making system.	No change in the meaning by the no-decision movement, but no-decision managers have several hidden meanings and messages when this behaviour is used.
Peaceful patience	Subordinates choose a state of patience on discovery that their boss will never make a decision.	Often used in the context of meditation or art, but with a new meaning when used by the no-decision movement.

Permanent procrastination	One of the two instinct-based behaviours of a true no-decision manager.	Term invented by the no-decision movement, now also the name of a blog and widely used on the internet to describe people who generally put tasks off which can be completed immediately. Has a different meaning when used by the no-decision movement.
Pivotal positioning	Acceptance of no-decision managers in organisations.	Not to be confused with an engineering term to describe double axis positioning used in patents for specialised hinges or joy sticks.
Relationship rectangle	Relationships with people in the hierarchy of the no-decision manager: the boss, the boss's boss, their colleagues and headquarters.	Term invented by the no-decision movement for relationships with the hierarchy.
Relentless resignation	Emotion felt by subordinates working for a no-decision manager.	Sometimes used in the press as an adjective as in 'relentless resignation gossip' or 'relentless resignation rumour' but used by the no-decision movement as a noun with a completely different meaning.
Reticent resignation	Emotion felt by employees working for a no-decision manager in top management.	A term probably first used in a biblical context to describe Joseph's feelings when he was in Pharaoh's prison and now borrowed by the no-decision movement.
Rumsfeld resolution	The moment a boss takes a decision in place of his no-decision subordinate.	A term invented by the no-decision movement, supposedly originating from Donald Rumsfeld's now famous quote. (see also Annex 1 for origins of the quote).

Selective shamelessness	No-decision managers are shameless with their subordinates but never put themselves into such a position with their bosses.	Term invented by the no-decision movement.
Silent pact		No change in the meaning or use by the no-decision movement.
Structured survival	A six-point survival plan for no-decision managers.	A term often used in the context of battered women in abusive relationships; this meaning is not in any way connected to the meaning used by the no-decision movement.
Survival point	The moment when a boss forces a decision on a no-decision manager. 'If I don't take this decision now, I will be fired.'	Economic term often used when an organisation is close to bankruptcy, but borrowed by the no-decision movement and the meaning changed.
Tacit recognition		No change in the meaning or use by the no-decision movement.
Task force	Type of delay decision tactic within the no-decision-making system.	Normally used by managers to obtain results, but just another delay tactic for the no-decision movement.
The Shelter	Name of the structure invented by the no-decision movement to help no-decision managers.	Not to be confused with the well-known British charity which helps homeless children.
Three 'i's	Short version of the second instinct-based behaviour of true no-decision managers.	A pompous name for yet another alliteration type action: imposing incremental information.
Too dear to fire	Expression used for no-decision managers in pivotal positioning who are close to retirement.	Term invented by the no-decision movement. Clearly a variation of the expression 'too big to fail'.

Unofficial leader	Subordinate who decides to take over the leadership of their boss's team.	Not a term invented by the no-decision movement, but used specifically for a subordinate who takes over from his no-decision boss.
Wordsworth way	A way for subordinates to move into peaceful patience.	Not to be confused with the name of a street in Measham, a small village near Burton on Trent in England.

Annex 5
Bibliography

Anonymous, Article, *Strategies to Deal with Indecisive Bosses*, www.employmentcrossing.com.

Blenko, Marcia W., Mankins, Michael C. and Rogers, Paul (2013), *The five steps to better decisions*, Bain and Company.

Bose, D. Chandra (2004), *Principles of Management and Administration*, Prentice Hall India.

Bramson, Robert M. (1981), *Coping with Difficult People*, Random House.

Cooper Hakim, Amy and Solomon, Muriel (2016), *Working With Difficult People*, Penguin Random House.

Damasio, Antonio (2005), *Descartes' Error: Emotion, Reason, and the Human Brain*, Penguin Books (first published in 1994 by G. P. Putnam's Sons, USA).

Dixon Wallace, E. (2002), *Twenty Studies that Revolutionised Child Psychology*, Prentice Hall Direct.

Drucker, Peter (2012), *Management*, Routledge.

Evans, Marsha, Gaynor, Elizabeth and Colt, George (2014), *Surviving and Thriving When Your Boss is a Jerk*, Kindle Amazon.

Fuller, George T. (1995), *The Workplace Survival Guide*, Prentice Hall Direct.

Graham Scott, Gini (2005), *A Survival Guide for Working with Bad Bosses*, Amacom York.

James, William (1890), *The Principles of Psychology Volume 1*, H. Holt.

Kets de Vries, Manfred F.R. (2014), *Four Pathologies that can hobble an executive and bring misery to the workplace – and what to do about them*, Harvard Business Review.

Kotter, John R. (1990), *A force for Change: How Leadership Differs from Management*, New York: Free Press.

Krzyzewski, Mike and Phillips, Donald T. (2000), *Leading with the Heart: Coach K's Successful Strategies for Basketball, Business, and Life*, Time Warner.

Kumar, Arun and Rachna, Sharma (2000), *Principles of Business Management*, Atlantic Publishers and Distributors.

Levav, Jonathan, *Danziger, Shai and Pesso Avniam, Liora (2011), Extraneous factors in judicial decisions*, Stanford and Ben-Gurion University.

Leibing, Mike (2009), *Working with the Enemy*, Kogan Page Limited.

Mintzberg, Henry (1975), *The Manager's Job: Folklore and Fact*, Harvard Business Review (July-August 1975).

Morris, Bob (2011), Rosabeth Moss Kanter: *An Interview by Bob Morris*, bobmorris.biz.

Moss Kanter, Rosabeth (2011), *How Great Companies Think Differently*, Harvard Business Review.

Northouse, Peter G. (2004), *Leadership Theory and Practice*, Sage Publications.

Piaget, Jean (1952), *The Origins of Intelligence in Children*, Translated by Margaret Cook, International Universities Press.

Rajendra, Rajiv (2014), *Lead 3D: The Future of Leadership is Here*, Random Business.

Reade, Charles (1870), *Put Yourself in His Place*, De Wolfe, Fiske & Co.

Ringle, Molly (2011), *Relatively Honest*, Central Avenue Publishing.

Roth, Wolff-Michael (2011) *Possibility: at the Limits of the Constructive Metaphor*, Springer.

Sutton, Robert I. (2007), *The No Asshole Rule*, Piatkus Books.

Taylor, Lynn (2009), *Tame Your Terrible Office Tyrant*, John Wiley and Sons.

Tierney, John (2011) *Do You Suffer From Decision Fatigue?* New York Times.

Williams, Ray (2016), *The Rise of Toxic Leadership and Toxic Workplaces*, raywilliams.ca.

Annex 6
Additional reading

More detailed information in books with references to managers who cannot make decisions

Coping with Difficult People by Robert M. Bramson (1981), Random House

> Managers who cannot make decisions are called 'Indecisive Stallers' in Chapter 8.
>
> 'Stallers are almost always pleasant and supportive' and when discussing a decision, subordinate can come away from the Staller thinking he or she is in agreement to decide. The motivation of Stallers, however, is different from those of no-decision managers. Stallers do not make decisions because they are afraid that their decision will hurt someone, whereas no-decision managers do not care whether they hurt someone or not. In addition, according to Bramson, Stallers have such a high need for a quality decision that they cannot decide. No-decision managers are not interested in the quality of decisions, but simply that the decision should either disappear or be made by someone else.
>
> Stallers will wait long enough so that the decision will sometimes go away or become irrelevant, i.e. they do nothing: a form of permanent procrastination, common to no-decision managers. However unlike no-decision managers, in the end Stallers will make a decision, especially when helped by their subordinates.
>
> 'Outrageous behaviour' is called 'overload'. Stallers can get

overload and become angry when the pressure from subordinates gets too much. This is a form of 'outrageous behaviour' used by no-decision managers, but in their anger Stallers will often make an unfair or unreasonable decision which will never happen with a true no-decision manager.

Tame Your Terrible Office Tyrant by Lynn Taylor (2009), John Wiley and Sons Inc

> Managers who cannot make decisions are called 'Fickle Terrible Office Tyrant' or the 'TOT Fickleness Boss', Chapter 14.
>
> The TOT Fickleness Boss is not so much a no-decision manager, but a manger who decides, then changes his mind and decides something else, before implementing the first decision. He is also a boss who cannot decide which decision to make when there are too many options open, but in the end with the help of subordinates will make a decision and stick to it.
>
> There is also the TOT Ignoring Boss who is always absent and does not reply to emails with the result that no-decisions are made, but will eventually make a decision. He uses similar tactics as a no-decision manager but is not one.

Surviving and Thriving When Your Boss is a Jerk by Marsha Evans and Elizabeth Gaynor (2014), Amazon Kindle

> The manager who cannot make decisions is called 'The Avoider'. The Avoider uses one of the tactics of the no-decision manager: that of ignoring the subordinate totally: no greeting and no eye contact. He gives the impression to the subordinate that he or she does not exist. The Avoider is not able to make decision because of anxiety.

Working With Difficult People by Amy Cooper Hakim and Muriel Solomon (2016), Penguin Random House

> Managers who cannot make decisions are called 'Put-Offs' and Stallers. Indecision is also considered with bosses that systematically over commit – the 'Overcommitters' – and ones that keeps changing their mind. These managers however will eventually make a decision when helped by their subordinates. The one piece of advice for subordinates, when dealing with overcommitters, is for them to make the decision for their boss. (They are explaining deviated downward delegation.)

Other books with references to managers who cannot make decisions

Dealing with Difficult People in the Working Environment by Henry Roberts (2015), Amazon Kindle

> The manager who cannot make decisions is called 'The Procrastinator', Level 2 Personalities.

Surviving the Toxic Workplace by Linda Duree (February 2010), McGraw-Hill Education

Articles with references to managers who cannot make decisions

https://hbr.org Managing 3 Types of Bad Bosses (2014) by Vineet Neyar, Harvard Business Review

> The manager who cannot make decisions is called the 'indecisive boss', who is a manager that will eventually make a decision. Vineet Neyer gives advice on how the subordinate can help the indecisive boss to make a decision.

https://hbr.org *Coaching the Toxic Leader* (2014) by Kets de Vries, Harvard Business Review

https://www.themuse.com *4 Tips for dealing with an Indecisive Boss* by Chris Thetford, themuse

> The manager who cannot make decisions is called the 'indecisive boss', and does include a boss who will never make a decision. Chris Thetford advises that the subordinate is 'not powerless' and in some instances can take the decision himself. He is explaining deviated downward delegation.

www.punchedclocks.com *5 Brilliant Ways to Manage a Bad Manager* (2015) by Sarah Landrum, Punched Clocks

> The manager who cannot make decisions is called 'the indecisive manager', but is a manager who will eventually make a decision. Sarah Landrum gives advice on how the subordinate can help the indecisive boss to make a decision that is different to Vineet Neyer's advice above.

https://scottboulton.wordpress.com *The Indecisive Leader: Making a Decision without Making a Decision* (2014) by Scott Boulton, The Armchair HR Manager

> The manager who cannot make decisions is called 'the indecisive leader'. Scott Boulton explains the effects of indecisiveness on an organisation or department and argues that no decision is in fact a decision and gives advice to indecisive managers.

https://blog.runrun.it *Decision Making Skills to Indecisive Managers*

> Managers who cannot make decisions are called 'indecisive managers' and the article gives advice to these managers on how to make a decision.

https://www.fastcompany.com *Two Ways to Handle a Hopelessly Indecisive Boss* (2016) by Amy Cooper Hakim and Muriel Solomon, Fast Company

> An article adapted from the book *Working With Difficult People* by Amy Cooper Hakim and Muriel Solomon.

www.forbes.com *Seven Ways to Conquer Indecision* (2012) by Steven Berglas, Forbes

> This is an article more about decisive bosses who have become indecisive, giving them advice how to become decisive again.

www.ebosswatch.com *Coping with a Toxic Boss* (2011) by Linda Duree

> The 'Big Picture Boss' uses similar tactics to those used by the no-decision manager to delay decisions.

Annex 7
To make a decision or to take a decision?

There is complete confusion in the process of decision-making when it comes to the definition of the two related phrases 'to make a decision' and 'to take a decision', which I have used abundantly in this book.

Approximately half of dictionaries, I consulted, do not have a definition for either, with comments such as the following:

> Sorry, no results for 'make a decision' in the English Dictionary.
> 'Take a decision' no word definition found.
> No exact matches found for 'make a decision'.
> 'Take a decision' phrase not found in the Dictionary.

The dictionaries that recognise the phrase 'to make a decision' provide three quite different definitions. Some proclaim that 'to make a decision' is only the actual moment of deciding but for others it also includes the process leading up to the act of deciding. And then to confuse the issue a few state that 'to make a decision' relates only to informal, personal or minor decisions.

For those that recognise the phrase 'to take a decision' they again give three quite different definitions. Some dictionaries say 'to take a decision' is only the act of deciding, not the process leading up to the decision. Others say it is both the act of deciding and what happens after the decision is made, but not before. And then to throw in another bout of confusion, some dictionaries proclaim 'to take a decision' is used only in formal, official, serious or important decisions.

But it gets worse. Many dictionaries proclaim that 'to take a decision' does not exist in USA English. It is an expression that has never managed to cross the Atlantic Ocean and is used only in UK

English. The Americans make. The British generally make, but sometimes take.

Then to add to this confusion, there is the ludicrous and absurd. It is always out there on the internet, in what is now called 'fake news'. The most absurd one I found, proclaims that 'to make a decision' relates to the 'gold command' decisions (whatever that means) made by top management, whereas 'to take a decision' relates to 'the spot supervision or low level management decisions'. Just nonsense!

Only the Oxford English Dictionary and two others take a simple approach and state that 'to make a decision' is exactly the same as 'to take a decision,' which in turn is the same as 'to decide.' This is the meaning of these phrases in my book.

Note: I have chosen not to name the nine English language dictionaries I consulted, except for the one I have used as my reference, the Oxford English Dictionary

Lightning Source UK Ltd.
Milton Keynes UK
UKHW010858180721
387318UK00001B/35